Diagonal Lengths

Diagonal Lengths

Rethinking Our World

Mickey Puri

Printed by CreateSpace
7290 B Investment Drive
North Charleston, SC 29418

Online Shop: www.createspace.com/3502061

Blog: www.DiagonalLengths.com

ISBN 978 1456368692

British Library Cataloguing in Publication Data.
A catalogue record for this book is available from the British Library.

Cover design by Michael Rackliff

Preface

Over the years it's dawned on me that society arrived at its current state through various twists and turns, some accidental, others due to the special interests of key stakeholders. Each time the direction was influenced by self-interests of powerful stakeholders, with no reason to expect the most optimal arrangement to have arisen. In short, there's every reason to expect the current arrangement of society to be far from ideal. Indeed there are numerous glaring major wrongs in modern society, however a tacit understanding appears to exist, especially amongst the decision makers that "that's the way it is..." with most willing to go along and pretend everything is fine - an unspoken group decision to go along with the status quo.

Increasingly it has felt like I'm on a set of "The Emperors New Clothes" with many seeming to tacitly accept the situation and for expedience content to continue with the status quo and go about their daily business.

The various wrongs are able to continue due to social and mental inertia, not being spotted or relegated as fringe causes.

Imagine a child born to a mother in prison. The child knows no other reality and will be found laughing, playing and singing along with the adults in the prison, unable to recognize the true nature of the prison walls. We too are somewhat like that child in the way we view society around us and in our acceptance of these various wrongs as the norm or as unchangeable given's.

As an optimist with the strong belief that no human organization or structure is cast in concrete, I feel like Archimedes that one can move the world with the right leverage and social support. I felt it's time to get off life's roller coaster and try and collate and document some of these in one location. It's my hope that you will engage with some of these and debate will set off a few tiny snowballs rolling, slowly gathering momentum.

To simply be yet another soul going through this endless cycle of life and death, and upon viewing the countless social edifices hanging precariously like stalactite's, to avert ones gaze and carry on partying no longer felt an option. I felt a calling to examine our social and organizational perceived wisdoms and poke them with the cold finger of logic to determine if put together now with a absolute absence of bias would a jury of twelve wise men and women still come up with the same answer, and if they differed then what might their answer be.

Am keen to use the book as a way of thinking outside the box, to examine what new approaches and combinations of our social infrastructure might look like and hopefully spawn discussion. Debate of this sort would almost certainly be political suicide for established politicians who would risk being classed as naive and out of touch, and therefore is a kind of no-man's land for them. By exposing the thinking in my book and letting some of these ideas become stalking horses for discussion and debate, hopefully one or two braver politicians might to their surprise, find enough support in the general public to be tempted to hitch a ride.

Rather than simply point at problems and bemoan their existence, I've tried to take a proactive stance and suggest novel and practical ways of dealing with them.

Pardon the cliché, but my hope is to get people to join me in thinking outside the box and realise there's a whole new world there to be had if we could only free ourselves from our historical legacies and intellectual straitjackets creating the illusion that our social frameworks are cast in concrete.

The somewhat cryptic title arose from observing behaviour at the swimming pool at a hotel I used to stay at regularly. Despite being a small pool, barely eight or nine strokes end to end, even though people were often alone in the pool, me included, they used to swim lengths parallel to the sides. One day it struck me a far better approach when on your own would be to swim along the diagonal adding three or four strokes to each length. In that sense, Diagonal Lengths represents a willingness to take a different slant on our social environment.

Some may regard the commentary as naive or childlike, however it's worth considering that had the child not spoken up, the emperor might still be without clothes. Others may regard it a utopian miracle wish list, however in their clever real-politick they miss the point that our social structures are entirely virtual constructs dreamt up by us rather than being immutable laws of nature. Therefore they are capable of being changed - even overnight - provided we can find that elusive Archimedian lever to mobilise and get sufficient people on side. To that extent I'm throwing down a gauntlet clutching a route map for future generations of politicians.

To avoid being distracted or blown off course and compromise on originality, I decided not to discuss any of the contents with anyone including friends and family, and therefore in the absence of feedback of any sort, it's a complete unknown as to how the book might be received.

Thank you for picking up and reading this book, and engaging in this project of social change. I'm not a professional author, and if my prose lacks polish then I apologise and hope the content and ideas prove captivating enough for you to continue.

Whilst reading the book, if you find things that strike a chord and resonate, I would urge you to translate that into action such as writing to your local media and Member of Parliament and mention your support and view. Hopefully that will give them too the courage to question and challenge the status quo of current structures. If you'd like to engage in dialogue on some of the topics raised in the book then please do visit my feedback and blog site on www.DiagonalLengths.com.

Perhaps at some point in the future this book may prove to have been like the flapping of the wings of a distant butterfly leading to future change, and if even one or two of the threads in the book inspires a few to question and lead to change as a consequence, then I will have succeeded.

In a time of universal deceit, telling the truth becomes a revolutionary act.
~ George Orwell

Individual Dedications

John Lennon for encouraging us to imagine the possibilities of a world without country and religious divisions.

Tarun Tejpal of Tehelka.com for his bravery and efforts to expose official corruption in India.

Satyendra Dubey, a rare Indian whistle blower, who lost his life in suspicious circumstances shortly after exposing corruption in India's highways programme.

Sir Bob Geldof and Bono for promoting free trade as a way out of poverty.

The president of the European Union in recognition of the role the EU has to play.

Barak Obama for his hope and message of change and voice of reason.

The Economist magazine for its incisive reporting and not being afraid to have an opinion.

Mary Wollstonecraft for her foresight and advocacy of women's equality.

Emily Davies for her contribution to the Suffrage movement and for women's rights to university access.

Lady Constance Georgina Bulwer-Lytton for her courage and contribution to the Suffrage movement.

George Washington for his prescience in warning us of the danger of political factions.

Martin Luther King, Jr. for his dream and dignity.

Liu Xiaobo for his courage in standing up for free speech in China and organizing Charter 08.

Aung San Suu Kyi for her steadfast commitment to achieving democracy in Burma.

Nelson Mandela, for his dignity and generosity in victory and the willingness to forgive and accept former political opponents.

Sir Edward Clay, British High Commissioner to Kenya, for his courage in speaking the truth and exposing corruption in Kenya.

Dara Shikoh, eldest son of Emperor Shah Jahan and victim of religious fundamentalism, for his belief there was no need for spiritual traditions to live in isolation from each other and for translating the Hindu Upanishads into Persian (Sirr-i-Akbar) in his search for common ground between Hinduism and Islam.

Mikhail Gorbachev for his pivotal role in overseeing a peaceful end to the cold war and the statesmanship to allow Eastern Europe to make their own decisions.

Margaret Thatcher for being a trailblazer in shrinking government's role in the economy through privatization, and setting an example copied by other countries.

Emperor Ashoka, a ruler in the Maurya Empire in India circa 256BC, one of the great moral reformers in the history of civilization and a pioneer of human rights.

Mustafa Kemal Ataturk, the founder of the Turkish Republic for his broad reforms and modernization of Turkey, creating a new political and legal system, making government and education secular and giving equal rights to women.

Mahatma Gandhi for showing the world that non-violence is more effective than armed struggle.

President Nicolas Sarkozy for his stance against the wearing of the burqa in France.

Mikhail Khodorkovsky, potentially a future Russian Mandela, for placing his desire for a strong independent civil society and political diversity in Russia above personal financial gain. His incarceration, a litmus test for Russian political freedom.

Stephen Schneider for alerting the world to the threat of climate change through his pioneering work on climate models and commitment to informed public debate.

Group Dedications

To the countless human rights martyrs around the world who have lost their lives at the hands of governments who by their actions have proven themselves illegitimate and unfit to govern.

To the silent millions around the world whose lives have been impoverished and futures silently stunted due to a lack of action and imagination of the worlds political elite, and the tacit acceptance by those who ought to have know better.

Personal Dedications

To my parents for not cluttering up my mind with religious dogma, and affording me the opportunity at a young age to study and travel in different countries around the world.

To my family, a special thanks for putting up with my being cloistered in my room working on "the book", I hope that now when they finally get a chance to read it, it lives up to their expectations.

Contents

# Section 4: Spiritual	**209**

Section 1

Politics and Organization

1. Countries

"Patriotism is your conviction that this country is superior to all others because you were born in it."

George Bernard Shaw

1.1   Introduction

So what are countries all about? It may have had historical relevance, however I find the country idea a confusing concept in our joined up global world, and am no longer certain whether countries still have a role.

Many may think it unpatriotic to even contemplate the question, however patriotism is just a birthplace lottery with the same individual being patriotic to whichever country they happened to be born in, and convinced that that happens to be the best country in the world.

I'm comfortable with the concept of a large tribe existing as a nation, but countries have tribes of all sorts mingling and living together. What magical change happens when you cross the border from one country to another – that necessitated a new country to come into being.

I think it's a question of history and a country could only expand to a size that could be defended by its rulers, and therefore size was a function of the time taken to request assistance and for that assistance to arrive. Were that time too high then the territory may well have been lost by the time central reinforcements arrived.

Initially with no modern communications, and travel between countries taking weeks, people in separate areas developed differently, with different religions, language, festivals, customs etc

During their development phase, had they all had the kind of instant access to others around the world that we have, then would they have developed along separate paths? I doubt it. So our difference is a function of separate and isolated development. What happens now that we have close communication – should we expect to see a gradual convergence of cultures and peoples?

The answer to that is clearly yes, with English emerging as a global language, a suit as a global business dress, even our food tastes have merged. So where will this convergence end? And as it continues what role does the Country concept play, and patriotic emotion aside, does it still make sense?

1.2   What is Distinctive about a Country?

So what's distinctive about countries, I mean what are the defining characteristics about a country, which sets it apart from others? Lets examine each candidate:

Language

There are many countries whose inhabitants speak multiple languages, and so language cannot be a determinant. Some countries such as France have a language that's more concentrated than elsewhere, but even in France many people speak English, German and other languages. In addition there are countries such as India with multiple languages being spoken each with its own grammar and script, and so language by itself is not a sufficient factor to warrant the existence of a country.

Apart from this there are countries, which spoke the same language, but then ended up splitting into two e.g. Korea and Vietnam, illustrating that language itself is not a sufficient factor to warrant a separate country.

Religion

Whilst it's true that people in a country are more likely to follow the majority religion, however it doesn't seem Religion by itself is a sufficient factor for defining a state. You only have to look at the Middle East where most countries have Islam as their religion, yet they exist as separate countries and have chosen not to merge.

In addition there are many secular countries and so Religion seems not to be a determining factor for a separate country.

Race / Tribe

Were a country to consist solely of a single type of people then that might make sense for requiring an organized entity such as a country. However most countries have people of all backgrounds and tribes, therefore race or tribe are not sufficient for defining our existing countries. E.g. the United States has people of all backgrounds mixing as citizens. Similarly India contains people of different backgrounds to the extent of having separate languages and scripts and yet it is now a country. Many African countries too consist of three or four major tribes joined up in a country.

That said Tribe is probably the most logical reason for having a country, and may be the motive behind the rather nasty ethnic cleansing witnessed in Europe and Africa where countries have tried to revert to a majority tribe as its defining characteristic.

Although Tribe could be a valid reason, in practice almost all countries consist of multiple tribes and that removes tribe as a rationale for a countries existence.

Value Systems / Culture

It's certainly true that many countries have different value systems and cultures, however I suspect that's a cause rather than an effect, and value systems can migrate as information, people and ideas move across borders.

1.3   So What's in a Name?

As another take on what's unique and distinctive about countries, lets have a look at the rationale for states joining or splitting, to see if that offers any clues.

India, Pakistan and Bangladesh

Prior to their independence in 1947, India and Pakistan were a single country with people eating the same food, watching the same movies and having the same culture. Sadly their politicians at the time of independence were unable to rise to the occasion and settle their differences, with the result that at Independence the country was split into two. One could argue Pakistan was to exist for the muslim minority, however prior to the formation of Bangladesh, India had the second largest muslim population in the world. I suspect the real reason for forming was irreconcilable political egos.

However curiously once the countries had "come into existence" they took on a mantle of their own, and people who had been neighbours – suddenly started treating each other as foreigners.

Even if one accepts the religion argument, the fact that Pakistan later split into the present Pakistan and Bangladesh despite both being Muslim states demonstrates the tenuous rationale for a country's existence.

The Former Yugoslavia

Another example of the fluidity of countries is the former Yugoslavia, which was formed after World War I with the coming together of the Serbs, Croats and Slovenes. Although Yugoslavia unravelled after the fall of communism in the 1990s and broke up into separate countries over a period of ten years, it demonstrates how for over fifty years this particular country existed and for those years its inhabitants called themselves Yugoslavians.

This demonstrates there's nothing magical or unique about the country concept and what territory or peoples are in or out, it's just a matter of the political reality at the time.

1.4   The Country Conundrum

As I cannot see any specific overriding reason for the existence of a country, let's look at it from another perspective and try and see how countries formed.

Initially, when humans were just developing, there were no countries, and our ancestors' moving out from Africa needed no visas, so a country is not a natural concept as such and was initially developed by powerful rulers to protect their territories and define the extent of their tax base.

Borders in the past were flexible, with regions moving between countries. An example being Sudetenland, which was in Germany till 1806, then became part of Czechoslovakia after the First World War. Similarly India consisted of various small states being ruled independently which later merged under particular rulers and ultimately under the English. The Roman Empire too had expanded to include large tracts of Northern Africa at one stage.

Therefore the specific reason for a country's existence comes down to its political momentum, with factors such as language, tribe, and religion being diversionary.

Thus our current set of countries with their borders is only where the Political process has brought them to date and there's nothing inherently magical or to be revered about any particular set of borders.

Each country is a product of its own and its neighbours' history, and is in effect a historical or legacy entity, existing in its current state only because that's where the process has brought it.

A country can be viewed as a group of people whose ancestors had decided at some stage in the past to come together for mutual benefit. From that perspective, the state or government is merely there as a bureaucracy to provide management and administrative services to the members of the group, and is not above or greater than the individuals in the country.

Therefore in reality a country can be seen as a conveniently sized administrative unit.

> *To the free man, the country is the collection of individuals who*
> *compose it, not something over and above them. He is proud of*
> *a common heritage and loyal to common traditions. But he regards*
> *government as a means, an instrumentality, neither a grantor of*

favours and gifts, nor a master or god to be blindly worshipped and served.

Milton Friedman

1.5   Country as an Administrative Unit

Once one views a country as a bureaucratic administrative unit, suddenly views such as patriotism, flag, national anthem etc. all seem jingoistic and hollow. Border lines too become dotted in the sense that if it makes economic and practical sense to move borders then so be it, it's nothing to get worked up over!

As a perspective, the land will still be there, long after those getting worked up over the actual border between countries, will have returned to the soil, and so if a country border exists then that's only because it's practical and of benefit to the inhabitants and not anything to get misty eyed over.

To an extent, belonging to a particular country is a bit like belonging to a club, and with that viewpoint changes, mergers, and transfers (from one club to another) really are just a matter of utility and should not be seen as deep emotional decisions to be agonized over.

The single phrase I have most discomfort with is the concept of "Motherland" or "Fatherland" – both terms are misleading in the extreme. Neither of our parents is a land unless you happen to be a tree!

1.6   The Distinction between Country and Tribe

Regarding one's country as a bureaucratic administrative unit, may seem worrying to some, who might feel they're losing an identity. However a distinction needs to be drawn between Tribe and Country. A Tribe is a set of people and regardless of where you draw the dotted lines for the country's administration, people still retain their tribal identity[1].

This was illustrated recently when someone who's a native of England explained he understood England, Wales and Scotland, but had difficulty coming to terms with what Britain was about.

As long as you have your tribal identity, then I think one can and should be a bit more relaxed about the wider bureaucratic identity that comes from being part of a country.

---

1   Which no one can take away

1.7 Why and for whom does a country exist?

Once you accept that definition of a country, then what is its purpose in a modern world? There should only be one legitimate purpose for a country to exist: for the efficient administration of its geographical territory and people – i.e. to serve its peoples interest and ensure that each individual is able to maximise their potential. It's worth noting that it's the people's interest and not that of the bureaucrats who operate the machinery of government.

Too often people confuse the country for the organs of the country and forget that all those organs are there to serve the people and to help them develop and grow. As Lincoln said about Government at his famous speech in 1863 at Gettysburg it is "for the people".

We'll examine this in further detail in the following chapter as it leads to some counterintuitive corollaries.

> *The only justifiable purpose of political institutions is to ensure the unhindered development of the individual.*"
>
> *Albert Einstein*

2. "For the People" leads to surprising corollaries

2.1   What does "For the People" really mean and lead to?

It means it's "For the People" and not for the Country or its organs. Too often people overlook this completely and talk of doing things for the Country – completely forgetting that the country is really just an imaginary construct and only exists because of what *it* can do for the people. Therefore the country is there to facilitate and do what's best for each and every one of its inhabitants.

"For the People" may seem a simple and self-evident statement however it leads to some surprising policy implications.

2.2   Devolution is a Basic Right of every Group of Citizens

What if a group of people living in a particular region feel that they would be better off if they had their own country and managed themselves. Then as it's the Country's duty to do what's best for this group of its inhabitants and if this group truly believes that self management is in their best interest, then a direct consequence of the Country's charter is to actively help this group to devolve and set up their own country. In short, *any* people should be free to devolve and set up their own country and the main country should actively encourage and assist them – if that is what the sub-group truly wish.

This seems counter intuitive, that a country should promote devolution if that's what regions want but that is what being true to the principle of "for the people" leads to as opposed to maintaining sacred bureaucratic cows.

As a country is ultimately a collection of individuals who have come together historically for self management and administration, it would be undemocratic for one group of individuals to assert that they had the right to manage and administer a sub group just because the predecessors of that sub group had given them the right – unless the current members of the subgroup agree.

There are of course some caveats there, if the original country has invested hugely in an area, which then wants to break away, then fine they can still break away but they may need to make some reparations to the others to payback for their earlier investment. Similarly if some vital resource is discovered in a region, the region cannot simply opt for devolution as a ruse to maximise their share of that resource – after devolution the original / parent country would need to be compensated with its share of that resource[2].

If it helps, a way of looking at this is that in some cultures people live in large extended families with the children either all living in the same house or next door to each other e.g. in separate flats in the same building. Extended families are fine as long as they're all happy with the arrangement, but often one of them will want to be a bit more independent and move away and they need to be allowed to do so – without forcing them to stay in the extended family if they're finding it stifling. Although the scale is different, it's pretty much the same situation as a region or sub-group in a country wishing to become independent if they're finding being part of the whole stifling their development.

2.3   Removal of Ego from Policy

Countries often develop egos where they want to have various entities or assets as a source of national pride or power. Once you realise that it's for the people (and not national ego) the real test of policy is whether or not it improves the lot of the ordinary citizen and not the country's ego.

This should directly lead to many things done at national level to be "out of scope" for a country and better done at an international level by groupings of countries. Politicians need to bear this in mind and relate things back to how it helps the common person as opposed to "it's in the country's interest" – the country is a bureaucracy and its only legitimate interest is looking after the people's interest.

2.4   Merge Countries if and where it makes sense for their inhabitants

Just as devolution is a basic right, equally justifiable is the concept of any two

---

2   These would need to be balanced off against the new state's share of its parent's resources, which are now being given up, with the formation of the new country entity.

countries merging if each of their sets of citizens becomes better off as a consequence. In this instance each Government is doing what is in the best interests of each of its respective sets of peoples.

An example of this was the successful coming together of East and West Germany. If it makes sense and both sets of people are better off in the new merged country then it's absolutely fine and people should not fall prey to emotional claptrap of keeping a particular flag, anthem, or currency going.

One of the resistances to doing this would be the myriad of politicians and civil services who would justifiably fear for their jobs e.g. the new merged entity would only need one prime minister!

Examples of where this may work could include the two halves of Cyprus, North and South Korea, and India, Pakistan and Bangladesh.

If we look at India and Pakistan for example, both countries have fought wars and diverted precious resources into military conflict with each other. If they merged that would remove at a stroke the need to fight each other and a huge peace dividend would be enjoyed by both sets of peoples, as well as creating a much larger market for their industries. I believe that if correctly explained, the common person might accept it, however political careers and egos would probably stand in the way, in fact at the time prior to partition, Mahatma Gandhi had suggested to Nehru that he allow Jinnah (who was leading the emerging Pakistani faction) to become the Prime Minister of an undivided India, however this proved a step too far for Nehru's ambition.

2.5   The Legality of Governments and Sovereignty

Once we accept that the only task of a government is the management of the state "for the people", this leads to the question that if the administration is acting in a manner that is not in the best interest of its peoples, then how is it to be viewed?

If an Administration is not fulfilling its prime task, then clearly it is failing its people and at minimum it is incompetent and needs to be changed. If however it resists removal – which it may by using its controls of the levers of state to remain in power and enjoy its fruits – then it in effect is an illegal government and needs to be recognized as such internationally.

However countries are meant to be "Sovereign" which gives them the rights to manage their own affairs within their territory. Sovereignty is overrated and I feel is misused by illegal governments as a shield to hide behind.

Many years back it was common for the police to view domestic incidents between a husband and wife as something private and internal and one that they, the police, should not be interfering with. Thus the law almost stopped at the front door of the house beyond which the husband had the right to pretty much do as he saw fit. That attitude has changed hugely and the police now get involved in domestic disputes. Sovereignty appears to me to be an analogous situation – allowing an administration to misbehave and hide from the international community behind a cloak of Sovereignty.

What we need is a set of internationally agreed minimum standards that all Governments must sign up to, which takes priority over Sovereignty. Failure to adhere to these standards should make the government an illegal one which has forfeited the right to rule and becomes a candidate for regime change or for joint management with the international community.

There is a duty of care that is ascribed to governments, but this needs to be articulated more clearly and in a measureable way, and with an agreed escalation procedure and timescales. Failure to do this is a crooks charter, if a group of crooked politicians can win or rig an election, then they can take over the country and in effect have the right to make and live by their own rules – literally having gained a license to print money.

An example is Zimbabwe, which was once a well run and prosperous nation, but has been brought to economic and social ruin through mismanagement, with the world community standing by impotently on the sidelines wringing its hands, chanting the mantra of sovereignty.

Sovereignty allows countries to ignore the problems in other countries, in the self-righteous belief that as they are a different country, therefore it's up to their government to resolve and sort things out. However if the people running the administration are crooked then it's disingenuous to expect "the country" to sort it out by itself. In this respect, I think Sovereignty a bad and dangerous concept unless countries have simultaneously signed up to and agreed a minimum standard of externally enforceable governance.

It is up to Government to make laws, however if the government is corrupt, and makes bad laws to suit itself, then who is there to police the Government. You might say that if the administration misbehaves, they'll be voted out. Fine, but if they're corrupt and fix the elections, then what are the poor electorate to do? In fact an administration doesn't even have to fix an election, they can simply ignore it, and sovereignty means they get away with their crime. For instance in Mynamar, Aung San Suu Kii has stayed in detention since winning the elections eighteen years ago in 1990. Shame on world leaders for allowing and accepting such a situation.

Until the world has agreed a common minimum governance standard and an agreed plan and schedule of actions to enforce it, I think Sovereignty needs to be shelved as a concept.

2.6   Colonialism

European countries colonised various parts of the world and these were generally seen as exploitative relationships and bad for the indigenous populations.

Once whilst in Tanzania, I travelled by road from Dar es Salaam to Bagomoya. Mostly the road consisted of a dirt track, however halfway the road changed to tarmac for a couple of miles and then reverted to dirt track. On enquiry, I was told the tarmac was the old road and that local people had broken and taken parts of it for use as hard core for houses. In effect after independence the country's infrastructure went backwards in the context of this road.

Another example is Zimbabwe, where the Mugabe regime presided over a continuous rundown of the economy and its productive capacity. A look at Zimbabwe's GDP helps underline this. Figure 2 shows how the Zimbabwe's GDP had risen strongly up till the 1980s, but after independence in 1980 it steadily declined by three quarters over twenty five years.

1960	1970	1980	1990	1997	2000	2005
281.11	361.26	913.65	831.42	691.68	587.17	262.71

Figure 2:   Zimbabwe GDP per Capita $'s

Although I believe that people native to a country are probably best placed to understand its issues and administer in a manner that's sensitive to the local culture, as the examples above illustrate, it's by no means a given that native administration is always best.

Therefore I don't believe colonialism per se was bad – if the alternative were corrupt and self-serving or misguided native politicians. At the end of the day, I wouldn't mind if politicians were pink with yellow polka dots (like the popular television character Mr Blobby) provided they did a good job and the common person in the street was better off – that being the only real test.

2.7   Auto-Colonialism

Colonialism was seen as bad because it was said that they did not have the locals' interest at heart and were exploiting the country. However when an administration of native people behaves the same as the colonials, then somehow it appears less of an injustice and not that compelling. I've therefore coined the phrase Auto-Colonialism where the natives of a country have colonised their country and are running it for their own benefits and not in the best interests of the people, as the effects are the same as colonialism except it's being done by a subsection of the native people themselves. It's somewhat similar to a cancer where a portion of the body turns upon itself, with Sovereignty giving Auto-Colonialism its cover and surgical immunity.

An example of Auto-Colonialism at its worst was in South Africa where a black Government disputed the causes of Aids whilst many thousands of South African's died from the disease. However had the same been done by the earlier White Government, then the world would have stood up and denounced this as yet one more evil of Apartheid and turned upon it. Sadly when the abuse is being done by your own kind, then like the earlier domestic disputes, the international police of public opinion is content to respect country borders and leave it to the people to sort themselves out.

2.8   Who's best placed to run a country?

Because of the dangers of Auto-Colonialism, I don't automatically think self-rule is necessarily right or best in the short term. Long term I'm convinced that it is, however there's a great danger that in the route to that point, one of the regimes will be corrupted and turn cancerous and become an Auto-Colonial regime. This I feel is the tragedy of many parts of Africa.

As it creates the atmosphere for wrong-headed concepts such as Sovereignty to flourish, I think the Country concept has serious shortcomings. For example, if one state within the US suddenly had a bad administration then the Federal Government would intervene, however if the US had been a set of 51 separate countries, then each would have shrugged their shoulders and said "it's up to them to sort it out for themselves". In this sense, I'm against the country concept as it curtails our concern for others at our borders[3] and despite being an artificial concept, it stops our humanity at our borders.

Until a government can meet a minimum standard of governance, I think it desirable that the international community get involved in governance by helping strengthen and run key democratic institutions, in effect co-governing the country. Remembering that the key job of government is "for the people" this should not cause any cries of colonialism etc as it's directly making things "better" for people by stopping the risks of illegal regimes forming and auto-colonialism. As the country matures and its democratic institutes strengthen and its electorate benefits from education to the extent that they can stop any auto-colonials hijacking the regime, then the role of the international community in co-governing should be steadily run down.

---

3   This is not seeking to deny the effects of international aid.

2.9   The Only Legitimate Government is a Democratic One

I fail to see how any administration or set of rulers (e.g. a hereditary ruler) that has not been democratically elected can claim to be there "for the people", as this has never been tested. If the rulers are genuinely there in the best interests of the people then they should be able to prove this by standing in free and open elections. If their people concur that they indeed are best for the people then they will demonstrate this by giving them a winning vote.

If the administration hold elections and lose, then by giving the winner the reins of power they will have truly acted in the best interests of the people – as it needs to be up to the people to decide what is in their best interests.

When the administration retains power and doesn't allow their people to vote, then to a large extent they are behaving like auto-colonials and not running the country genuinely in the interests of the people. In other words there is a degree of exploitation with the members of the administration taking advantage of their privileged position at the expense of giving the people what they want i.e. *the government of their choice.*

2.10   Summarising the Country Discussion

I think the key message here is that we need not get too hung up on country and borders and need to see them in terms of their utility and usefulness rather than something of permanence and responsible for identity. Borders are *imaginary* lines on a map, the key word being imaginary which we need to keep in sight. That said, ones tribal identity is of course important and that's the thing to hold onto and not this misleading country concept.

Countries are only of use to the extent that they promote the well being of their inhabitants. If a different setup or configuration could improve well being then the status quo should not be allowed to stand in the way.

Country administrations need to remember that they are only there, and legitimate if they are "for the people" and chosen by the people, if they don't pass this test then other than superficial appearances, they are similar[4] to a colonial power ruling the country autocratically with an exploitative agenda.

> *You'll never have a quiet world till you knock the patriotism out of the human race.*
>
> *George Bernard Shaw*

---

4   The only difference being that the exploiters happen to be from the same people being exploited

3.   A Borderless World

Imagine there's no countries, It isn't hard to do
Nothing to kill or die for, And no religion too
Imagine all the people, Living life in peace...
John Lennon

Countries essentially consist of a collection of individuals who've agreed to come together and function as a single entity on the world stage. However the agreement took place at some distant point in the past, and is that particular grouping and collection of individuals still the correct or most optimal one? There is no reason to assume that because a particular mapping made sense few hundred years ago to our ancestors that it remains the most appropriate arrangement today.

In that sense I regard borders as fluid and only justifiable if they help create value. If a different configuration created more value then we should be bold and open enough to consider it. Just as there are mergers and demergers between companies in the corporate world, leading to better administration and new value being created, similarly we need to be adopt a flexible and utilitarian mindset in the way we view borders.

Having logically established that country borders ultimately, merely reflect the best fit administrative unit, a question has been formulating at the back of my mind for some time now: In our current world of instant communications and the ability to immediately know what's happening all around the world, we are increasingly acting as a single global community, and therefore is the country concept outdated and should we be restructure ourselves as a single global country?

Lets try and see what it might lead to if we did not have any countries i.e. there was just one global country incorporating all of the worlds peoples.

3.1   World Peace

Were we to organise as a single country, at a stroke we would eliminate war, as by definition there being only one country, there would be no other country to go to war with.

The twentieth century had over 25 wars with around 40 million soldiers dying[1]. This huge waste in human life would have been avoided had we had been organized as a single global country.

3.2   Savings on Military

There are in the order of 85 million people working in the armed forces across the world[2]. If the world were to join up as a single country, then clearly we would not need such large amounts of people going into the armed forces, and these peoples considerable talent, ingenuity and energies could be deployed in more productive pursuits.

In addition to the people resource, the world spends $1464 Billion annually on military expenditure. (2008 figure[3])

If all the countries were to come together and form a single global country then at a stroke, that would remove the need for all these separate militaries and their huge spend on weaponry.

Lets try and imagine what we could achieve if the time of those 85 million people and the $1464 Billion were being spent on useful productive objectives. Who knows, we may solve many diseases that are currently untreatable, and lead to thousands of lives saved across the world. Peoples lives could become much richer with better resources in the form of schooling, leisure centres etc. The same figure if spent on building schools, would lead to 46,000 new schools being built per annum worldwide.

3.3   Stopping political psychotic episodes

Often countries have gone through episodes in their history that can only be described as their entire leadership going through a manic period during which

1   1900s Military History Timeline
     http://militaryhistory.about.com/od/timeline/a/20thcentime.htm
     http://users.erols.com/mwhite28/war-list.htm
     http://www.scaruffi.com/politics/massacre.html
2   Armed Force Personnel by Country
     http://www.nationmaster.com/graph/mil_arm_for_per-military-armed-forces-personnel
3   World Military Spending
     http://www.sipri.org/yearbook/2009/05
     http://www.worldometers.info/military/

civilisation and humanity are forgotten and the country goes through a dark period of what can only be called mass hysteria or a mass localised leave of their senses and humanity in pursuit of dubious political objectives.

Examples are Stalin's Purges in Russia, Hitler's Nazi regime and their pogroms against the Jews, the killing fields of Cambodia under Pol Pot, Indonesia at the time of the rise of General Suharto, the Rwandan genocide, Somalia and the Balkans just to name a few from the last century. Millions of people perished during these episodes.

The reason countries could get away with it is that they were shielded by a cloak of sovereignty, a bit like Harry Potter's magic cloak of invisibility, allowing them to carry out their evil deeds while the world looked sideways.

I am reminded of the saying, "If you're not part of the solution, then you are part of the problem".

As a hypothetical example, imagine that in the US, the governor of California started a program of ethnic cleansing, then there would be no need for lengthy hand wringing on the sidelines, debates at the UN and various countries with vested interests vetoing even the hint of criticism – the Federal Government would be in there the very next day and rid the state of the governor and his mess.

Similarly, if the world were one country, then if any local government were to take leave of its senses and have a "political psychotic episode", then the rest of the world would step in immediately and have the misguided political leaders neutralised, saving countless millions of lives.

In essence, if we were a single country the world would acts as a huge stabilising counter weight, forcing each of the states to keep close to the mean, and with the power to act in case any individual state attempted to deviate into a psychotic political state.

3.4   Reducing Corruption

Corruption is one of the key factors preventing countries from developing. It leads to a misallocation of funds and reduces productivity; in effect it's a tax on growth. Since the corruption is often driven by the very people whose job it is to root it out, it becomes extremely difficult to root out.

An example is that of Tehelka.com an investigative journalism website in India. After it exposed corruption in arms procurement in India in 2001, it faced the wrath of the Indian Government and Tehelka.com and its financial backers were investigated by various arms of the government[4], with the result that the company reduced from 120 employees to a mere 4 employees.

---

4   The Economist: Scandalous.   http://www.economist.com/node/1471156

Another example is when Sir Edward Clay, the British High Commissioner to Kenya, accused corrupt Kenyan ministers and officials in 2004 of behaving like gluttons, and vomiting on the shoes of donors.

Further examples are Italy where laws were passed to grant immunity to top members of the Government.

The issue is that Corruption, which is sanctioned or condoned by those close to the leaders of a country, is hard to be extinguished as Sovereignty once more rears its ugly head, and you have the scenario that the gamekeepers are also the poachers.

Having a single world country would remove this shield of Sovereignty, and any misdeeds would be subject to scrutiny from the rest of the world and would be stamped out as the perpetrators could not hide behind their national borders and furthermore would not be free to issue new laws that they could hide behind such as has happened in Italy.

In effect the world would act as a counterweight and stop localised corruption from organizing and taking hold by flourishing under the shelter currently provided by country borders.

Removing corruption would have a huge impact on productivity and growth worldwide.

3.5   Improving Standards of Administration

Although this may sound rather boring, however given that the key raison d'être of a country is to provide administration, it is a key point.

Many countries in the world are simply not administering themselves correctly in terms of education, healthcare, legal, civil service, human rights and infrastructure. The problems are caused by a combination of corruption, poor management, political interference and lack of civil society.

Having a single country for the world would at a stroke ensure that best practice in administration can flow and be spread throughout the world with common standards for openness, access to information, freedom of speech, keeping judicial bodies separate from government etc.

Basically if the hospitals, schools, police forces, legal services, transport infrastructure, water, energy etc in all the currently developing countries could be raised to the standards enjoyed for these services by people in the West, then there would be a huge improvement in the lives of millions of people worldwide.

From the UN Human Development Report 2004, in Norway a child born between 2000 and 2005 will have an average life expectancy of 78.9 years, whereas a child born in Zambia in the same period can expect to live just 32.4 years – a figure lower than that in 1960.

If we were to organize as a single country then there would be no barrier stopping people from directly getting involved and improving things on a world scale and the best practices that allow someone in Norway to live a full life would be exported to other areas of the world with a huge improvement in quality of life worldwide.

3.6   Trade

It's undisputed that Trade is good for the global economy, however with countries keen to protect certain indigenous industries there are still trade barriers despite huge advances in trade from bodies such as the World Trade Organization (WTO).

The WTO has been working to reduce trade barriers, however Trade talks take years to conclude and the recent Doha Trade Round which started in 2001 have stalled in 2008 and have yet to be restarted.

Lack of free trade helps keep some countries poor, as recognized by the Make Poverty History movement; within which people such as Sir Bob Geldof and the Irish rock star Bono campaigned to reduce trade barriers.

The key point is that it's extremely difficult to get Trade negotiated in a way to get agreement from all countries and across sectors there will always be winners and losers. Therefore the do-nothing approach of maintaining the status quo is often perceived as the safest option by risk averse politicians with an eye on short term votes.

Having a single world country would at one single stroke do away with the need for complicated trade talks and tariffs / barriers etc as there would only be a single country and goods and services could travel freely anywhere in the world.

The increase in world trade would lead to a huge increase in World GDP, global prosperity and living standards.

3.7   Remove Limitations on Humanity and the Legitimisation of Inequality

Country borders act as limiters to our natural humanity with our concern for others tending to drop away after crossing a national border.

Whilst there are a host of international organizations and government aid schemes helping other countries to develop, these are tiny compared to what a government will do for its own citizens.

It's quite obscene for people to be enjoying high standards in one part of the world while in other parts of the same world people have hugely reduced life spans and quality of life.

However the fact that they belong to a different country allows us to rationalise that it's not our problem and it's up to them and their governments to do something about it and therefore it acts as a limit on our humanity and allows us to live with our conscience. In effect the country concept legitimises global inequality and inaction, framing it in social and moral respectability.

Were we all to belong to one country, we would no longer have that luxury and would become acutely uncomfortable that our fellow citizens had hugely reduced life spans and quality of life – and be obliged to do something about it.

3.8   Freedom

Having a single global country would give us the freedom to wherever we want to without being beholden to various authorities to give us permission first.

Although it may not seem a major inconvenience, nonetheless it feels perverse that a bird can choose to fly wherever it likes and go across continents in its annual migration. However we as humans, the "intelligent species" don't enjoy that freedom, and need permission and approvals prior to visiting any other part of our planet.

Imagine if in your country the government suddenly changed the law overnight so that you could only move and live within your own region and would need official permits to move to other parts of your country. Predictably there would be riots with people fighting for their rights, and to remove a government which appeared to have lost its senses. However as a race we've done just that to ourselves on a global scale and have calmly accepted it with the same unquestioning mindset that someone born into a ghetto would grow up accepting that that's how life was meant to be.

3.9   Stop Loss of Human Capital and the Birth Country Lottery

Figures for life expectancy around the world[9] shows that Africa has life expectancies in the mid 40s to 50s, compared to around 80 in the West. Even in emerging powers such as India it's a full 10 years less than in the west.

9   UN Human Dev Report http://news.bbc.co.uk/1/hi/in_depth/3894733.stm

The overall lack of education, and reduced lifespan represents a huge loss to the world in terms of human capital. Apart from the humanitarian issue, if the people could be properly educated and had an environment which allowed them to live longer, fuller and more productive lives then who knows what they may have achieved – quite possibly some of them may have had the inventive genius to find cures for hitherto intractable diseases or to make major scientific breakthroughs – we will never know as they never really had a chance.

Organising as a single country would level this out and mean that as a planet we give people wherever they are born the chance to develop and progress, mutually benefitting from their talents, and it would at a stroke eliminate this dreadful birth country lottery[10].

3.10   Elimination of the Tragedy of the Commons

Once you own something you look after it and manage it carefully for the future. However where something is common property, no one person has the responsibility to look after it, yet as it's available to all, everyone has a perverse incentive to maximise their gain from it, creating what's commonly termed the Tragedy of the Commons.

On a world scale, this means that the oceans, the environment and the poles all of which are common property across all nations have got exploited. Global warming has made the situation further crucial.

Were we to move to a one country world then at a stroke this Tragedy of the Commons would vanish as the "one country" would have every incentive to look after the common areas and couldn't shirk its responsibilities or pass the buck.

3.11   Conclusion

As outlined above by eliminating borders, we gain the following benefits:

Peace
Savings on Military

---

10   In the UK when people get different treatments from public bodies, varying by where they live, this is seen as negative and regressive, and termed a postcode lottery. Here I'm extending the concept to country of birth.

Stopping political psychotic episodes
Reduce Corruption
Improve Standards of Administration
Trade
Remove limitations on Humanity and the legitimisation of inequality
Freedom to travel
Stop the loss of Human Capital and the Birth Country Lottery
Elimination of the Tragedy of the Commons

It's easy to criticize this all as naive and dreaming, but I think that's being overly cynical. We need to open our imaginations to the possibilities and not allow ourselves to be constrained or misled simply by the status quo of existing country borders. We should look to actively engage with and encourage our politicians to rise to the challenge and explore ways of bringing about a single global country, without being diverted by false fears of loss of national identity and in the process for them to become world leaders rather than mere political bureaucrats.

> *"You see things; and you say, 'Why?' But I dream things that never were; and I say, 'Why not?'"*
>
> ~ *George Bernard Shaw*

4. Country Unions

The last chapter looked at the concept of a single global country. It will be challenging for people to put aside the trappings of country as we use our country as a form of self-identity rather than the more accurate tribal or regional identities. One can't blame people for that, as politicians seeking cohesion and unity have tended to emphasise the country concept with various invented artifacts such as flags, anthems etc. So lets look at other more pragmatic ways of trying to achieve similar ends i.e. a single global country.

Having a number of countries coming together and forming a free market union for goods, services and people is a great way of moving towards gaining the benefits of a single country approach, with the European Union (EU) being an outstanding example.

Although it has much further to go, I see the EU as a wonderful example of the way the world should develop to get similar benefits as one would from a single country world and it is somewhat fitting that Europe, the birthplace of the renaissance is showing the world a new future.

4.1 Trade and Freedom

As the EU is a common market, all EU countries are free to trade with each other with no restrictions. People are free to move across the EU countries.

There is however still further work to be done though in terms of harmonising standards, ensuring that markets can truly function seamlessly. Perversely the EU gets cast as an administrative bully when carrying out this harmonisation exercise.

4.2   Promoting Standards

New countries wishing to join the EU are required to manage their institutions in a democratic manner as a pre-requisite and holding out the prospect of membership as a prize acts to encourage potential new entrants to modify their country, its regulations, administration and adopt principles of good governance, in the process raising the level of their game to meet EU standards.

Thus the EU is a huge positive force for change in countries wishing to join.

4.3   Dealing with Issues at the right level

It may often be inefficient or less productive to deal with matters at a nation state level. A country union allows responsibility for such matters to be dealt with at the wider country grouping level.

Although some sovereignty is inevitably given up[1] over those aspects of decision-making, in return the countries get increased clout on a global scale and better decisions.

A way to demonstrate this is to imagine America as a separate set of 50 states, each a separate country with its own embassies representing them overseas, and negotiating their own bilateral relationships. Each of the states would have far less power on the world stage than they have now from being part of a much larger entity – the US.

Similarly as a Union, the EU has far more clout on the world stage than its individual member nation states could aspire to, which translates into better deals for the EU.

4.4   Friction with National Governments

As the EU grows, one can imagine country politicians feeling their loss of power leading to friction and turf wars between country level and Union level political players.

---

1   A more accurate term would be trading sovereignty, as each nation state gets some say over what the others are doing, and therefore gains a small part of the others sovereignty in return.

The competitive rivalry needs recognizing and managing and more needs to be done to spread the EU message.

Reverting to the primary role of government, being to administer, the test needs to be what's best for the people rather than the ego of politicians, and to resist xenophobic populist calls for nationalism.

4.5   Is there a need for Country Level Armed Forces?

I can't see why each of the countries in a Country Union needs its own independent armed force. Why not have a single EU armed force comprising of people from all the countries of the EU with the responsibility for defending EU borders.

I can only see nationalistic jingoism and ego that would drive and underpin the need for countries to maintain their own armed forces. But that ego comes at a price, being paid for by reduced services for their citizens.

Therefore the EU should look at merging its armed forces into a single entity.

This would lead to huge savings in manpower and costs, as well as savings in maintaining separate nuclear deterrents, with those savings translating into lower taxes and better infrastructure such as more hospitals and better schools / leisure facilities.

This may provoke all manners of emotional reactions of loss of national identity, but remembering the purpose of a country is to *administer*, as long as the EU armed forces provide us with the same level of security, and if they do it at a lower cost, then it should be a no brainer.

If a single EU armed force were put in place, then the only downside is that any single country would have less flexibility and power to go off and do its own thing on the world stage, e.g. the UK could not send troops off to Iraq without getting the buy in of its EU peers, however with hindsight, that restriction may have been a blessing.

4.6   Monetary Union

There is as yet incomplete monetary union within the EU. If people are to be able to move freely and work anywhere there needs to be a full monetary union.

In its absence, you have the sorry situation of people from the UK receiving pensions in sterling, having bought into the EU message and moved to other parts of the EU now find with currency movements that their pensions have lost purchasing power.

In addition, lack of monetary union creates a small barrier to trade, as it is an extra cost and a factor to hedge for when doing cross border deals.

4.7 EU Reform

Although positive about the EU, there remains a pressing need for EU reform and to improve its workings e.g. the ratification of the Lisbon treaty, and for real executive power to be devolved upwards to EU organs.

To an extent, the EU's role needs to be more fully explained to people in the various EU countries, and the costs/ benefits gone through so that people make their decisions in a more informed manner.

4.8 Moving forward – Deeper Union and Reform

Although the EU could improve further along the lines suggested above, overall I feel it's been a wonderful invention.

People need to publicly debate in a cool manner without letting matters get obfuscated with nationalistic emotions. We need to decide with a purely utilitarian mindset which aspects are best handled at a national level and which can be delegated to the EU level, avoiding giving in to emotional calls such as the one used by the Conservative Party in the UK prior to a general election to "save the pound". Once the cost benefits have been determined, the outcome of the analysis should drive the route-map for change.

A pre-requisite is better information about the EU and how it helps so that it becomes a more informed discussion.

4.9 Expansion in Breadth

Expanding the geographical scope of the EU is the brightest thing I see for our future.

It goes some way towards achieving the benefits[2] that we would derive from a single global country and it does so in a way that's less disruptive to national identity and so may be more acceptable.

I would love to see the EU change its name to GU, standing for Global Union and actively engage with countries in the Middle East, Far East, Africa, South America and North America to put together road maps for these countries to join the GU.

Countries could not join the GU overnight, and would need to work with the GU to prepare themselves for entry – a process which may take years while their civil society and institutions are built up, but it would be the one sure fire way of them being picked out of their current state of poverty, mismanagement and misrule, and the GU should issue an open invitation to countries to join its entry programme. During the transition process, immature institutions in these countries would be built up and strengthened so that the changes become lasting ones and there would need to be some joint power sharing with the GU during the transition phase to ensure that changes cannot be simply undone by the next government. Once they've joined the GU and a strong civil society is in place the GU transition teams role would slowly taper away.

Following this strategy could well make the GU the dominant power in the world, much larger than the United States. I hasten to add that it's not meant to be a competition, and what would be even more wonderful is for the US to eventually join the GU.

The challenge is therefore for EU Leaders to do just that, show Leadership and look to aggressively expand the EU towards a Global Union, and to set their sights beyond their myopic national remits.

4.10   Other Unions

Although the EU is the most successful union, I don't think other countries around the world should wait for the EU to transpose itself into the GU and expand to reach them.

It would be good for countries all over to use the EU template and experience and form their own unions with free movement of goods, services and peoples modelled along EU lines.

---

2   Discussed in detail in the previous chapter

For example there could be a South American Union, African Union and a South Asian Union run exactly along the EU lines.

At some point in the future, the EU and these other Unions could look to merge into the GU.

Lets look at a few of these potential unions and how they could work.

4.10.1 South Asian Union

One can imagine a South Asian Union incorporating Pakistan, India, Bangladesh, Sri Lanka, Nepal as a first stage. Growing in a second stage to incorporate Mynamar, Malaysia and Singapore, and in a final stage to incorporate Japan, China, Korea and Vietnam and Combodia.

With the people having the same freedom of movement as in the EU, and free trade within the SAU borders there would be a huge boost to the regions prosperity and stability.

It would also at a stroke, diffuse the tensions between neighbours such as India and Pakistan.

4.10.2 African Union

An African Union would incorporate the majority of countries in Sub Saharan Africa. A lot of these countries tend to suffer from poor management, and having a strong Union with free movement of people and goods and services would create stronger regional ties and influence and act as a counterweight providing a moderating and stabilising influence.

5. Post Colonial Country Expansion

EU expansion and the creation of new country unions are not the only game in town to lead us towards the ideal of a single global country. Another route would be for successful countries to expand their geographical scope.

Once one accepts that there's nothing sacred or special about a country's borders, then its expansion to merge with other territories should not cause concern and can be seen as a sign of success. Of course it needs careful explaining to the current citizens and their acceptance[1].

For a country to expand, the Colonial model is no longer acceptable or right in today's postcolonial world. However a country with a successful political, social and business model can invite other countries to join and merge with it, thereby sharing and benefitting from its success.

The most promising prospect is for the US to invite other countries around the world to join the United States and for the US to grow from its current 50 states to say 70 states with new parts of the US appearing in the Far East, Africa and South America.

This expansion may seem strange and rather unthinkable, however bear in mind that over a 170 year period the US grew from 12 states to 50 states. Colorado joined the United States in 1876, a full hundred years after the birth of the US, West Virginia joined the US in 1863, Florida in 1845 and Hawaii not until 1959. Therefore for 170 years the US was continually expanding its territories and peoples by adding more states.

Another criticism could be that how could the US expand to include countries that far away from itself. However it's worth bearing in mind that Hawaii is 2000 miles from the mainland USA, and if it can be a state at that distance then so can other countries.

1   as the country is by definition the collection of its current citizens

As the US is already a melting pot of languages and religions, I don't see any cause for concern from a cultural aspect.

There's a certain amount of poetic symmetry in this approach, rather than importing and welcoming the "weary and oppressed" of the world to the US as immigrants, the US could export its successful statehood to them instead.

5.1   The Transitional Period

A country wishing to join the US would need to go through a transition period[2] and modify itself to meet the criteria that the US would set for entry.

This would include ways of running its government and its institutions, education, laws, human rights, and voting procedures.

The transition would take a number of years, and there would be active US involvement and vetting / validation throughout.

However it would be a route that would eventually transition the country and bring it up to become a fully-fledged state within the United States.

5.2   What's in it for the Country Joining?

By joining up and becoming part of a successful entity such as the US the prospective country's citizens would have put themselves onto a steep growth curve in all aspects of life, and lead to a greatly increased quality of life, life span, prosperity and stability.

5.3   What would be in it for the US?

In the short run there would not be too much in this for the US, however it would be increasing its territory and geographical reach and once the people of the new state have reached the same productivity standards as other US citizens, there would be a large increase in US GDP and basically the US would become an even larger and stronger super power.

---

2   In much the similar way as the process that countries wishing to join the EU need to go thru

However the key thing the US would be doing is to make the world a more stable and prosperous place with the obvious advantages that this would bring for the US as well.

5.4   What could derail this approach?

The key things that could derail this approach is that people in the joining countries having a misguided opinion of what a country is about and confuse country identity with tribal identity and become nostalgic for the country paraphernalia such as flag and national anthem[3].

However the biggest factor will be the ego of their political elite. At the top of the pile in their country they are probably already enjoying rather prosperous lifestyles, and by joining the US, they stand to lose exposure to an international stage and get relegated to the status of a state, albeit with greater prosperity. They would also go from a sovereign status answerable to no one, to having to account to the Federal Government. I suspect their ego would get in the way and be a serious obstacle and they would be tempted to give in to their ego, despite the huge benefits to their people from joining.

5.5   Post Colonial Expansion

This expansion would differ from the Colonial expansion, as it would be done with the full agreement of the people of the country joining the US, and the emphasis is on their development and in that sense its sentiments are diametrically opposite to those of Colonial Expansionism.

5.6   Is it Workable?

Germany was split into two in 1949, and both East and West Germany operated as different countries until 1990 when they were reunited. The fact that the two Germany's could join up demonstrates that it is possible to get countries to join up successfully.

To an extent the proposed country expansion is rather similar to corporate expansions where large companies merge with other companies.

---

3   and other such trivia

5.7   So who could the other Post Colonial Expanders be?

I've already indicated that the US is probably best positioned to expand internationally as it is very successful and prosperous and already runs on federal lines.

However it's not only the US that could expand along this path, other successful economies could also take the lead e.g. the UK with its historic ties and the Commonwealth is in a good position, as are India and Brazil.

I haven't mentioned China or Russia as I think a pre-requisite to be attractive to other countries is a strong democratic tradition.

6. Co-Governance

6.1 Why are some countries poor?

The simple answer is Countries are poor because of poor Governments. Poor Governments foster corruption, weak institutions and misguided policies which ensure they remain in a state of poverty.

There is a German saying that a "Fish stinks from its head" and so it is with Governments with the rot descending from inept political leadership.

Lets look at a few examples of this

Figure 1:   GDP Per Capita in $ [1]

	Malawi	Liberia	Zimbabwe	South Korea	China	Madagascar
1960	46.18	181.03	281.44	155.67	92.01	125.38
1970	64.31	251.50	361.26	278.82	111.82	160.42
1980	200.18	510.42	913.65	1,674.38	191.84	445.87
1990	198.83	179.96	831.42	6,153.10	312.41	255.83
1997	251.49	119.30	691.68	11,234.77	774.47	239.38
2000	151.45	182.98	587.47	10,884.45	949.18	239.43
2005	161.10	161.12	262.74	16,387.64	1,720.09	270.88

	India	Hong Kong	Kenya	UK	Singapore	US
1960	83.13	429.51	97.51	1,379.97	394.65	2,881.10
1970	110.37	959.20	142.24	2,222.21	913.87	4,998.73
1980	264.45	5,691.82	446.20	9,517.59	4,859.27	12,185.72
1990	373.08	13,478.33	366.64	17,190.88	12,091.36	23,063.58
1997	424.34	27,169.71	457.90	22,697.51	25,267.96	30,261.10
2000	452.98	25,319.41	414.00	24,150.87	23,077.10	34,599.47
2005	736.11	25,603.82	560.29	36,555.19	26,876.73	41,889.59

1   Nationmaster GDP per historical year http://www.nationmaster.com/red/graph/eco_gdp_percap-economy-gdp-per-capita&date=1960

Figure 1 shows GDP per capita in various countries, and how it's changed over the years. Clearly there's a huge variation between the countries.

Liberia's GDP increased till the 1980s after which the country went downhill and in 2005 its GDP was less than it had been in 1960.

Zimbabwe's GDP was over three times that of India in 1960, but then in 2005, it was about a third of India's GDP, with Zimbabwe going in reverse after it gained independence in 1980.

Kenya in effect went backwards between 1980 and 1990. Kenya started out at an advantage and in 1960 had a slightly higher GDP than China, yet by 2005 its GDP had slumped to a third that of China's.

In 1960 Singapore's GDP was 5 times that of Indian GDP. Yet by 2005, Singapore's GDP was a staggering 37 times that of India's.

The majority of these variations and differential rates of growth are explained by poor governance, mismanagement and corruption these being the real reason why countries are poor.

6.2   Criminal Economic Mismanagement

Politics, n: [Poly "many" + tics "blood-sucking parasites"]
~Larry Hardiman

A definition of Treason is "a crime that undermines the offender's government". On that definition Economic Mismanagement could be viewed as an act of Treason.

If a way could be found to frame the legislation to avoid frivolous and trivial cases, then serious economic mismanagement needs to be treated as a crime against humanity, with its perpetrators and their estates liable for damages in reparation for the human misery caused, with no limit of statutes. Mismanagement in this context refers not just to corruption, but also to incompetence or the following of misguided policies. That would focus political minds on doing not just what is perceived right at the time but also what is going to be defendable as correct in future with even inaction being a potential misdemeanour.

This may seem a bit hard, but a political party pursuing misguided economic policies that impoverishes its citizens are worse than thieves – both have the same impact and reduce the money in your wallet but unlike the thieves who at least acknowledge they've robbed you, the politicians pursuing low growth and poverty causing policies will not even acknowledge the harm they've done to their citizens wealth and future prospects.

6.3   The Corrupting Nature of Power

The nature of Power is seductive and even well intentioned people can get accustomed to it, in the process getting gradually transposed into a completely different being. It's a little like the influence of the "ring" in Lord of the Rings, where the ring amplified any evil tendencies in people, power will do just the same.

In mature economies, strong institutions, judicial independence an educated and aware population and civil society all come together to form a bulwark against politicians straying off course.

However in relatively immature countries that have not yet developed these institutions and social infrastructure, it's not entirely surprising that the democratic process gets captured. With little checks upon them, there are high personal rewards to be made by corrupt politicians and it's seen as a matter of setting themselves up for the future whilst they have a chance at the helm. This given added incentive as the judiciary is often underdeveloped or captive, thereby allowing the politicians to escape with their ill-gotten gains.

6.4   A Poverty Policy Index

As mentioned, countries are poor because of the policies being pursued by their governments.

In effect, it is as if the Government has set as its objective that it is going to keep its people poor, and all its policies are framed to keep its people poor. Of course, no one would put that in writing, but written or not, that is the direct consequence.

There are many reasons for this:

- To get into power, politicians have made certain promises that will directly lead to economic mismanagement.

- Making long term improvements takes time, and politicians fear they will be voted out before the improvements appear, and so why bother handing the benefits to their political opponents on a plate.

- Politicians may be corrupt and more interested in personal short-term gain than in building the long term institutions and policies that will underwrite political stability and economic prosperity.

- Politicians can be genuinely misinformed as to what's the best way to lead the country out of poverty.

- The government may be a weak coalition government including special interest minority parties, and even though the main party knows what needs to be done, its smaller coalition partners are stopping it from taking action.

- Despite knowing what needs to be done, the government may not wish to take on entrenched interests.

The fact that the government is following policies that are destined to keep its people in poverty gets obfuscated amidst all the general noise about what's happening in the economy, its management etc.

I think it would be useful to define a Poverty Policy Index (PPI) which measures how much of a Government's policy is directed towards the aim of keeping its people in poverty.

This would remove the obfuscation and allow people to understand the true nature of their government. It's very easy to hide in woolly words, but an index that took into account institutions, transparency, economic management and government policies as well as other public services such as health, education and infrastructure plans would provide a much needed report card for the government. But rather than a long report, pulling it all together into a single number would focus minds. A suitably qualified independent body would measure the PPI annually.

A PPI would be a predictive or a leading indicator[2], rather than the more traditional poverty index which provides a measure once time has passed, with the PPI able to be altered by governments in the very short term, as it is within their gift to alter policy. Progress up the PPI could itself be made into an election goal because it would be

2   In the sense that a PPI would look at today's plans and policies, in effect becoming a report card on how well the country is being managed

an early indicator of future progress and give the politicians credit in the current timeframe. It would be a useful guide for donors who could insist on a particular rise in PPI as a condition or pre-requisite. The PPI would also be useful for investors, with a rise in PPI signalling future investment opportunities.

6.5   The Importance of Support

If we were to take a teenager and expect them to fend for themselves and get a job and make a life with very little external supervision, it would hardly be surprising to find they've strayed and ended up taking a wrong turn. And so it is with many young countries that've been expected to grow up on their own.

Just like when a tree is growing, it's often tied to a stout piece of wood to give it strength and help it grow straight, it's too risky to expect countries to develop their institutions and social infrastructure on their own, and there needs to be a form of co-governance during which outsiders help the country stay on course and grow strong, following the right direction.

6.6   Should Nationality determine who is fit to Govern?

When it comes to determining who is fit to lead the country and take part in politics it is implicit[3] in most places that the person must be a citizen of the country.

I feel this view is lopsided. Consider how large multinational corporations seek out the best talent to run their divisions regardless of nationality, similarly football teams will root out the best talent from all over the world.

So when it comes to arguably the most important jobs in the country, why should we lock them to outsiders and adopt a xenophobic mindset. Because of their importance, it is an even greater priority that we seek the best people from a worldwide talent pool to do the senior roles in government and government departments.

6.7   A Co-Governance Model

The UN needs to put together a Co-Governance model which countries can opt onto to fast track their development.

3   and explicit in many

The model would bring enhanced levels of aid and special trade agreements with the country being treated as part of the EU and NAFTA (North American Free Trade Association) for trade purposes.

In a similar way to Venture Capitalists taking seats on the board of companies they run, the UN would take half the cabinet posts and half the top posts in all the key government departments including the military. These would be executive posts i.e. with real power and not mere observational roles.

This infusion of talent and expertise would stop any top-level wobbles and stabilise the country during its growth and development, preventing it straying off course.

As the country develops its own strong institutions and processes, the special measures in place would be gradually tapered away, until at some point in the future the country is fully self managing without external aid and with no co-governing posts remaining. However at that stage it would be strong enough and have the social capital to ensure it keeps its leaders in check and democratic traditions intact.

6.8   An Adopt-a-Country Approach

An alternative (or even parallel) approach to the UN providing a co-governance model, is for a more developed country to agree to work together with a less developed country in partnership, providing the Co-Governance support outlined above.

In effect it would be somewhat similar to the developed country "adopting" a less developed country for the purposes off helping it and its institutions grow through the infusion of executive level managerial talent and expertise.

7. Globalising Political Management

7.1 Opening up the Political Management Market

Companies that have developed particular skills and expertise in a field or sector expand around the world creating subsidiaries and joint ventures in other countries to take advantage of their experience and know-how.

If a country wanted to develop its pharmaceutical industry for example, it would look to foster joint ventures with established pharmaceutical companies so that it benefits from the state of the art thinking. The same is true of consulting businesses e.g. engineering, construction, accounting etc

However when it comes to Political Management, there are impenetrable barriers and it's expected that the indigenous people will somehow have the required maturity, skills and expertise to manage their country with little to learn from outsiders.

As mentioned this runs counter to all other areas, where it's normal for sector leaders to have an international policy and set up shop in other countries.

Running a political party requires skills in interfacing with the public, managing constituencies, recruitment and development of a candidate pipeline, managing and making sure their members of parliament are behaving ethically and not conflicted, as well as understanding how to manage the various departments of government and the economy.

If we have a successful political party that really knows how to manage all this, then why should it be constrained to only operate in one country? If the party knows how to do all these expertly, then it should be allowed to set up and foster political parties in other countries where they can leverage the same skills and compete in elections to form a government.

In effect we'd be opening up the Political Management market and making it global.

On the basis that markets help allocate the best resources to the task in hand, and with a country's political management arguably being the most important task there is, it deserves the best possible resource available globally.

If say, the Conservative party in the UK does a particularly good job of managing in the UK, then why should it not be encouraged to put some of those skills and expertise to good use in directly assisting in the governance of some other country.

7.2 What would the incentive be for a Political Party to expand overseas?

The main motivator driving a Political Party to expand overseas is to increase its impact and presence to a global scale, allowing it to do good and help less developed countries grow faster by sharing its political management expertise.

The party would use its expertise and experience to mentor and guide, as well as directly taking part in running political parties overseas.

7.3 The Parties would need to be jointly run with local people

When a Political Party establishes a new party in a different country, then it would need to do so on a Joint Venture basis[1], where it shares the running of the new organisation with natives of that country. I would anticipate something like a 70:30 split in favour of the indigenous population.

This would be necessary as governing a country also involves emotions as well as requiring deep local understanding.

7.4 So where would all this lead to...

Much the same as in any other sector, this would eventually lead to say a dozen dominant global Political Parties who run and manage political parties across all of the countries around the world, ensuring a high standard of political management worldwide.

---

1   International corporate expansion also follow a similar joint venture strategy

If it were ever possible, such a model would lead to efficient politics, and foster greater international cooperation especially between countries being managed by the same Political Party. It would also lead to a reduced likelihood of any future wars, as wars tend to come from extremes of behaviour and egos, and as this model follows a more stable and professional approach, instead of resorting to immaturity and war they would go through some well thought out and agreed dispute resolution process which everyone had signed up to.

Perhaps it might even become slightly boring and dull, but the stability, prosperity and equal opportunities for all would make up for it.

The approach may seem radical, but only within our current mindset. Take football as an example, a few decades ago it would have been unthinkable for the national team to be managed by a foreign manager, whereas now foreign managers routinely manage other countries national teams.

In due course, our current arrangement with each country only seeking political talent within its limited internal talent pool, and cobbling together its own home grown system of governance would come to be seen as anachronistic and passé.

8. India – a case study

I'd like to examine India as a case study to highlight some of the points made earlier.

8.1   No pressing case for Partition

At Independence the young political parties lacked the management skills and political wisdom to see what Partition might mean for the country, and although there was in reality no pressing case for partition, the politicians sleepwalked their way towards it.

The problem was political egos and a lack of strategic thinking on both sides. A last ditch attempt by a British Cabinet Mission in 1946 put forward a plan that preserved the union that was accepted by the Muslim League but not by Congress, which quibbled over the groupings and in effect wrecked the proposal[1].

This lack of foresight would bode ill for both the countries and their future administration.

There is a saying to be careful of what you wish for as it may come true, and so it was with Indian Independence. For the twelve million people who were displaced and a million people who lost their lives during the partition of India the implicit duty of care on the part of the politicians, was neglected recklessly.

I have talked about Co-Governance, certainly this was a case where some third party, perhaps even the British could have stayed on and formed part of the Government of a United India, helping make up for the inexperience of politicians who were effectively learning on the job, as well as creating a buffer of neutrality enabling the two sides to trust and work together and avoid the split.

1   India Partition Hinduonnet http://www.hinduonnet.com/fline/fl1826/18260810.htm
    http://www.hinduonnet.com/fline/fl2218/stories/20050909001107800.htm

8.2   A Health Check at 50

I visited India in 1997, in its 50th year of independence. While in a residential part of one of the poorer areas of Delhi I came across a lady giving a bath to her three children by the roadside. During my short stay, the electricity failed on numerous occasions. I found myself asking was it all for the best, what would it have been like had we remained under the British and might things have been better for the common person.

I was unsure what my answer would be, and therein lay a clue. Despite my desire[2] to believe that independence was for the best, if pressed I would have to reluctantly conclude that the common man in India might have been better off had it stayed under British rule.

In 1947 India's share of world trade was 2.4%, and by 1990 this had dropped to 0.4%, i.e. a drop of 83%[3]. Behind this lay misguided industrial policies such as the License Raj which pretty much strangled enterprise and legislated poverty for its masses.

Had the British stayed in power, then India would not have had these foolish policies and socialist experiments, and would have seen much greater growth and prosperity.

Hong Kong luckily escaped being made independent and continued under British rule and it's worthwhile juxtaposing Hong Kong's development versus that of India's.

Figure 3: GDP per Capita $ [4]

	India	Hong Kong	China	South Korea
1960	83.13	429.51	92.01	155.67
1970	110.37	959.20	111.82	278.82
1980	264.45	5,691.82	191.84	1,674.38
1990	373.08	13,478.33	312.41	6,153.10
1997	424.34	27,169.71	774.47	11,234.77
2000	452.98	25,319.41	949.18	10,884.45
2005	736.11	25,603.82	1,720.09	16,387.64

2   A result of coming from an Indian background

3   India Unbound From Independence to the Global Information Age, Gurcharan Das, page 68

4   Nationmaster GDP per historical year
     http://www.nationmaster.com/red/graph/eco_gdp_percap-economy-gdp-per-capita&date=1960

Figure 3 shows that in 1960 India's GDP was $83 versus one of $429 in Hong Kong. By the time Hong Kong got its "independence" in 1997, India's GDP had risen to $424 however Hong Kong's had risen to $27,169. Within that period, India's GDP rose by a factor of 4 versus Hong Kong's rising by a factor of 62.

I think it's a safe bet therefore that had the British remained in charge then India's share of world trade would not have reduced and it would have seen a much higher growth rate and prosperity.

To try and put a number on it, lets assume that an India being managed by Britain would have prospered similarly to Hong Kong, a reasonable assumption as both were being managed by similar British administrations. That would lead to a per capita GDP for India in 1997 of $5258 or roughly 12 times higher than under self-rule. Put another way, the earnings of the average person are only 8% of what they might have been had India remained under a Britain administration.

One can argue that it's worth trying new approaches such as socialism, however by 1970 when India was clearly falling behind economies such as Hong Kong and South Korea which had both doubled their GDP, then the penny should have dropped in India's politicians minds. Sadly it took another twenty years before partial wisdom dawned[5].

With hindsight, the misery of partition was indeed a foreboding of more unnecessary hardship and suffering that was to follow through economic mismanagement, and is why I make the assertion that poor governance and mismanagement are the biggest reasons for poverty.

8.3   Freedom is a double-edged sword

The preceding section may lead the reader to believe that perhaps I'm against freedom or secretly harbour a return of Empire. Nothing could be further from the truth. I'm a firm believer that people need to be free in all aspects including that of self-rule.

However freedom is a double edged sword and using a motoring analogy, after independence Indian politicians had the freedom to control the car and could choose to step on the gas and increase speed moving to the fast lane of development,

5   even then it was under duress and pressure from the IMF that enabled the License Raj scheme to be shelved

however instead they chose to use their freedom to drive onto the hard shoulder where they discovered the reverse gear.

I'm confident that had they driven wisely, they would certainly have made it into the fast lane, i.e. had India followed an economic liberalism approach right from the start then it would have prospered far more than had it stayed under the British however that would have required much better political management, of which sadly even at the time of writing[6] there is little sign of.

8.4   The Tipping Point

In 1991 facing a foreign exchange crisis and under pressure to obtain a loan from the IMF the Indian Government liberalised its industrial licensing policies and instituted trade reform and removed import controls.

In effect the government removed the padlocks that had chained "free enterprise" and released it. The results were the economy grew at 6.5% per annum in the mid 1990s, fiscal deficit halved and foreign exchange reserves rose to $20Bn from $1Bn over a two year period[7]. All this caused India to be seen as an awakening tiger, and since then India has been on a much higher growth rate.

This however begs the question, if it only took two years to implement these changes, and they had such a dramatic effect on the economy, then why did the country wait till its back was to the wall before implementing the change, and had it done it say 30 or 40 years earlier, then the benefits of a higher income and growth would have been enjoyed by so many more people who were forced to endure unnecessary poverty.

Although it's better late than never, but there remains a case to be answered for by earlier politicians.

8.5   Leopards and Spots

> *"We learn from experience that men never learn anything from experience."*
>
> ~ *George Bernard Shaw*

6   2009
7   India Unbound From Independence to the Global Information Age, Gurcharan Das, page 222

Inertia and old habits die hard and once the initial reforms had had its impact and brought increased economic growth, it appears to have reduced the imperative for further reform and the pace of reform duly went down to an gradual / increment reform, with many factors still actively slowing down India's growth potential and further prosperity.

India pays a price for this inertia and gradualism by having a lower growth rate of 7% compared against China's 10% growth rate[8].

One of the key areas of mismanagement are its Labour laws, which are among the most restrictive in the world, and restrictive laws in Agriculture both relics from its discredited past that continue to do damage. Its taxation regime varies across the states and fragments what ought to be a single market with lorries having to endure long delays at interstate checkpoints. In effect Indian politicians legislate unemployment and poverty for its citizens through their inactivity to remove damaging and misguided statutes. Other areas requiring attention are poor public services such as education, health and water, infrastructure and a bloated public sector.

As the saying goes, you cannot cross a chasm in two steps and the incremental approach to reform is in reality rather obscene, as it's unnecessarily extending Indian poverty. It's like an ambulance driver knowing he has to attend an emergency but then choosing to drive at a sedate 10 miles per hour.

Apart from complacency and unwillingness to take on vested interests, another reason for a low rate of reform is the phenomena of weak coalition governments where a coalition partner ties the hands of the ruling party. The answer to this should be clear from Chapter 1, where we established that the purpose of a country was "for the people". If the ruling politicians knows what needs to be done, but cannot proceed because their hands are tied by a coalition partner, then they needs to remember they are not in Government to simply occupy an office and enjoy the trappings of power. It's far better they explain the issues to voters and resign forcing an election than tacitly accepting lower growth and prolonging the poverty of millions.

8.6   Prognosis – what should India and the region be doing?

The immediate no-brainer is to remove the own goals of misguided restrictive legislation in labour, agriculture and fiscal regulations fragmenting the market.

---

8   The Economist, India on Fire http://www.economist.com/finance/displaystory.cfm?story_id=8625681

Follow that with privatising the bloated public sector, raising and releasing much needed capital that should be channelled into infrastructure as well as improving the climate for private sector involvement in infrastructure.

These are not rocket science and most political managers would propose a similar medication regime.

However lets move beyond the obvious, and to the starting theme of this chapter, Partition. That was a mistake, however to assume that things once done can't be undone would be to make a further mistake and one needs to remember the argument in Chapter 1 about borders being imaginary and in reality existing only in people's minds.

I'm not proposing a messy re-unification along the lines of East and West Germany, however I think a Union solution along the lines of the European Union that encompasses India, Pakistan and Bangladesh at its core, but pulling in other countries such as Nepal, Afghanistan and Sri Lanka would be a wonderful step forward. By modelling along EU lines it would end up with free movement of people and goods and monetary union.

At a stroke it would diffuse the situation between India and Pakistan leading to a peace dividend, and create an economic momentum and dynamic for the region.

I see that only as an initial phase, and just as the EU expanded, this South Asian Union (AU) would expand to include the South Asian countries of Singapore, South Korea, Malaysia, Cambodia, Thailand, Indonesia, Vietnam and Japan. In short a replica of the EU but for South Asian countries.

Whether it happens and when, will be a test of their collective leaderships and statesmanship, and would be contingent on politicians' abilities to rise above petty local politics to make and take a place in world history.

"Our aspirations are our possibilities."

~ Samuel Johnson

9. The Democracy Illusion

Democracy is only a dream: it should be put in the same category as Arcadia, Santa Claus, and Heaven.

~ H. L. Mencken

For some time now, I've been uncomfortable with the concept of Political Parties and the manner in which elections are generally contested with first past the post systems. I'm not at all sure that it is in an electorate's best interests to have Politics organised as contests between political parties and feel there are a number of potentially fairly serious drawbacks both with Political parties and first past the post systems.

In his farewell address of 1796, George Washington advised against political parties, however his foresight appears to have gone unheeded[1].

If there are drawbacks, then how come we still have political parties and they've not given way to other more efficient ways of governing politics? I suspect the answer other than inertia is that there are benefits to the politicians in power to continue with political parties and being astute individuals they're not about to undercut an arrangement that gives them power and prestige. So we can't look to Politicians to sort it out by themselves any more than expecting Turkeys to vote for Christmas.

Lets take a closer look at the potential issues and some solutions.

9.1 First past the post is undemocratic and crowds out minority views

A democracy is nothing more than mob rule, where fifty-one percent of the people may take away the rights of the other forty-nine.

~ Thomas Jefferson

---

1   George Washington, Farewell Address 1796
    http://en.wikisource.org/wiki/Washington%27s_Farewell_Address#8

With a first past the post system, in effect we ignore any votes cast for the losing candidates. The parties of the losing candidates get no recognition or say in parliament and the votes cast for them are therefore simply ignored.

Recognising this people are much less likely to vote for small minority parties as they will probably never get enough votes to win a seat, and so it kind of a waste. Therefore people then vote for their second choice.

Lets say we have 650 Members of Parliament, if a minority party gets 5% of the popular vote, but this is distributed evenly across the country, then they're unlikely to win any seats in Parliament. This directly disenfranchises and ignores the views of 5% of the population, and in a fair system they should have got 5% of 650 or 32 Members of Parliament to directly represent their views.

The absurdity of this was shown in the United States where in 2000 George Bush got half a million fewer votes than Al Gore and yet he won the election to the US Presidency[2].

It's in the interests of the major established parties to keep the First Past the Post system, because it keeps their competition out of politics and in effect acts as a barrier to entry into the Political Arena, keeping newcomers out. But it is a monopolistic and anti-competitive system as well as being deeply undemocratic. Furthermore if minorities can't get their views heard in parliament because the system is stacked against them, then they far are more likely to become extremists.

In Chapter 1, we established that the core role of a country is it's there "for the people", however if the administration systematically ignores a section of its people then ultimately it is behaving illegitimately, as it is no longer being true to the "for the people" clause, as it's denying them representation and their share of voice in decision making.

Politics too suffers, as the way to keep newcomers out is not to fix the system against them, but to come up with good and innovative politics that people want. In short, like in all other walks of life, competition will be good for the providers of political administration as well.

This is therefore something that is simply wrong headed and foolish, and needs fixing urgently. It's not rocket science and can be fixed pretty much overnight, as outlined later. Given that it's straightforward to fix, why hasn't it been fixed? The

2   Infoplease, US Election Results in 2000 http://www.infoplease.com/ipa/A0876793.html

common reason is First Past the Post leads to strong governments – which it does, but at the cost of systematically disenfranchising large parts of the electorate.

9.2   First Past the Post can lead to Direct Action and Terrorism

By systematically ignoring small but not insignificant views within the electorate, the system closes its doors to a peaceful and democratic process of debate and engagement, and there is the risk that minority groups will either get cynical and disillusioned or else end up taking direct action including in extreme cases terrorism to get their agenda on the table.

Having a fair system would remove the need for direct action, and lead to a healthier society with the government more in step with the people.

9.3   Fixing the First Past the Post System

Fixing the First Past the Post system is fairly straightforward. What is needed is that in deciding the number of Members of Parliament from each political party, the "Total Votes" cast by the electorate for a party needs to be added up across the entire nation, and then the number of seats available be given out to the Political Parties in exact proportion to the total overall votes they received.

This would mean that votes cast for minority parties no longer are a lost vote, and we would get a lot more new entrants into politics, and people voting for a minority party will finally get their basic right of representation in parliament.

To keep the system fair and predictable, if a Party wins a majority in say 140 constituencies, but after allowing for proportional representation it can only have 120 MPs, then the MPs would be selected in the order of the proportion of their constituency that voted for them. This would apply for each party so that the relatively most popular MPs get chosen. It does however mean that an area may get a different MP to the one that actually got the majority in their area. To create an element of selection from the constituency, there could be a runoff in the area between say three candidates of the party that is to represent the constituency.

Addressing this would lead to a far more representative and democratic government with all people's views being considered and would be an intrinsically fairer system.

9.4   Female Representation in Politics

> *The reason there are so few female politicians is that it is too much*
> *trouble to put makeup on two faces.*
> — *Maureen Murphy*

Although half the population of the world is female, across the world on average national parliaments only have 18% females[3], i.e. there are four men to every woman in politics.

In the UK, 19.5% of the MPs are female, amounting to 126 female MPs out of a total of 646 MPs in Parliament. (2009)

This is clearly undemocratic and not justifiable. The female perspective is important and different to a males and not having it is a loss.

The top 24 countries in the UN's list of countries by Human Development Index[4] have a female MP ratio of 27.2 % i.e. half more than the world average (table 1). It's difficult to determine whether this is a cause or an effect, however I suspect a virtual circle exists where the greater proportion of women in politics has led to better and more representative politics and a change of priorities with more balanced decision making at the national scale.

Therefore the lack of females is not only undemocratic, it probably is leading to poorer politics and less development as demonstrated by the UN Human Development Index.

9.5   Female Representation in Politics – the Quick Fix

In the UK it's been a stated aim of all Political parties to see an increase in the number of women in politics and people have wrung their hands and lamented that at the current rate of progress it will be many decades before there is gender equality.

---

3   Women in National Parliaments http://www.ipu.org/wmn-e/classif.htm
4   UN Human Development Index
     http://wapedia.mobi/en/List_of_countries_by_Human_Development_Index#1

Table 1:   Female Ratio in Parliament for the top 25 countries in the UN
Human Development index.

HDI Rank	Human Development Index (2008 data)	HDI	Ratio (%)	Females in Parliament Rank
			Female Ratio in Parliament	
1	Iceland	0.97	33.3	15
2	Norway	0.969	36.1	11
3	Canada	0.967	22.1	46
4	Australia	0.966	26.7	32
5	Ireland	0.962	13.3	86
6	Netherlands	0.96	41.3	5
7	Sweden	0.959	47	2
8	Japan	0.958	9.4	104
9	Luxembourg	0.957	23.3	42
10	Switzerland	0.957	28.5	25
11	France	0.956	18.2	66
12	Finland	0.956	41.5	4
13	Denmark	0.955	38	7
14	Austria	0.953	28.4	26
15	United States	0.95	17	71
16	Spain	0.949	36.3	10
17	Belgium	0.948	35.3	12
18	Greece	0.947	14.7	80
19	Italy	0.945	21.3	52
20	New Zealand	0.947	33.6	14
21	United Kingdom	0.947	19.5	60
22	Hong Kong (SAR)	0.945		
23	Germany	0.945	32.2	18
24	Israel	0.937	17.5	69
25	South Korea	0.933	20.1	57

However this is pretty hypocritical as there is a quick, simple and inexpensive way of fixing this overnight. We need to change the political representation system so that every constituency elects two MPs to parliament – one male MP and one female MP, each of them representing the constituency, which ends up with two representatives.

With this one single change, we would immediately get a balanced and more representative democratic government. This would have a modest cost of £76M per annum which represent two hundredth of one percent of GDP (0.02 %)

Having one male and one female representative per constituency should be a universal principle world wide for all elections to governing bodies. This simple principle would immediately ensure gender equality at the political level across the world.

Women's organisations nowadays take for granted the rights hard won through the efforts of women in the female Suffrage movement. However there is a need to see that earlier struggle only as the first phase, with the second phase being equal representation in Parliament.

Women's organizations worldwide need to be actively addressing this agenda, taking their lead from courageous women such as Emmeline Pankhurst and Lady Constance Lytton who played leading roles in the female Suffrage campaign in the UK[5].

---

5   Womens Suffrage in the United Kingdom http://en.wikipedia.org/wiki/Women's_suffrage#United_Kingdom

10. Politicians Party On ... but who picks the bill?

Some men change their party for the sake of their principles; others their principles for the sake of their party.

~ Winston Churchill

There are quite a few reasons why I feel political parties are not in the best interests of democracy and society at large. Lets examine some of the concerns.

10.1 Creates Voter Apathy / Disengagement with Politics

Political parties need to publish a Manifesto, outlining their views on a range of topics, thereby allowing voters to know what they're voting for.

Most people will have desired outcomes/ expectations in many policy areas, and you would not expect to find any single party's manifesto neatly maps onto their desired outcomes. In the real world one party may meet a couple of their requirements, another would meet a few more and a third party meets the remainder of the requirements.

Therefore whoever gets in power the voter is bound to be disappointed because the party has already made their manifesto clear beforehand. Also irrespective of who wins, the average voter will get some of their requirements addressed.

This creates a sense of indifference as to who wins, because regardless of which party wins, the voter is going to have to accept a compromise. As it's often not that important to them which particular set of compromises they end up making, it leads to them becoming apathetic about which party wins.

10.2   Compromises Politicians Views

> *How can one conceive of a one-party system in a country that has over two hundred varieties of cheese?*
>
> ~*Charles de Gaulle*

Politicians looking to join a political party will have a range of views on number of issues. It's rare for them to find that any one political party exactly maps onto their particular set of views. They too will find that some of their views map onto one party, and other views map to one or more of the other parties.

They need to compromise on some of their views when deciding which party to become part of. But by so doing they're in effect being a little dishonest to themselves and having to support views that they themselves don't actually believe in.

The Political Dishonesty acts as a form of internal friction that saps the energy from them as they are no longer able to be true to themselves at all times.

10.3   Concentration of Political Power leads to lack of democracy

Power in a political party is concentrated amongst the key people at the top of the party. It's these people who set the broad strategy and approach, and get the rest of the party on board.

Whilst nominally the entire party will work through and support the agenda, in reality ambitious junior politicians wishing to climb the greasy pole will end up deferring to and supporting the leadership and its agenda.

Furthermore, when voting in parliament each party expect its members of parliament (MPs) to vote in line with the party. Thus the real power both in government and opposition parties lies in their respective leaderships with the rest of the MPs simply falling in line with the party view.

This behaviour greatly reduces the power of the individual MPs and concentrates power in the hands of the party elite, and is not democratic.

10.4   Creates Divisions and Splits the Electorate

> *"It (parties) agitates the Community with ill-founded jealousies and false alarms; kindles the animosity of one part against another, foments occasionally riot and insurrection"*
>
> *~ George Washington*

Political parties need to find some unique proposition that allows them to differ from the other parties and find a way to appeal to voters. In order to promote themselves they often resort to false criticisms and exaggerating the faults with the other parties, creating splits and animosity in the electorate.

As people have strong attachments to their religion, tribe / ethnicity and local geographic region, Parties looking to explore all ways of attracting voters find it hard to resist the lure of these attachments, and many end up defining themselves along religious, ethnic and/ or geographic lines.

Once they've defined themselves along such lines, it creates a dynamic and gathers momentum leading to divisions and jealousies between communities with the ultimate result of social unrest, anger, resentment and a broken society.

George Washington's prescience was shown by events in India, where in the run up to independence the politicians split along religious lines into the Muslim League and Indian National Congress, and this led them to focus on their own sections of society, ignoring the wider population, eventually leading to a million people losing their lives during partition and the splitting of the country into two parts, Pakistan and India.

10.5   Parties Facilitate Corruption and Cover Ups

Having power concentrated in a ruling elite makes it much easier for corruption to take place. If a third party such as a company wants a particular favour then they only need to deal with a very small number of people at the top, knowing that once they've concluded the deal the leadership has the power to deliver. Furthermore the fact that they only have to deal with a small group reduces the risk of detection, as only a few people are involved.

This leads to a lowering of the transaction costs in seeking favours and means that the party system creates an environment more likely to foster corruption.

If one of the MPs in a party does a corrupt deal without the party leaders knowing about it and it's found out, then there arises a conflict of interest for the party. Should it bring it into the open, or quietly sideline / retire the MP for "personal reasons" and cover up the corruption to avoid any political comeback on the party.

10.6 Parties lead to a waste of political talent

Ministers heading government departments are selected from the ranks of the winning political party, while the politicians in the other parties sit out the term on the opposition benches.

This represents a fundamental waste of political talent and energy as we have talented and able elected politicians frozen out of government and reduced to finding flaws in the current government approach.

A certain politician in a minority party might be much better suited for heading up a particular government department but is rendered unsuitable as a consequence of their political party, with the result that someone less able but belonging to the "right party" gets the role.

This misuse and waste of political talent and energy is bad for the nation and the politicians concerned.

10.7 Manifesto's reduce flexibility of Action

As the Government will be formed by the winning party, Parties need to have Manifesto's outlining what they intend to deliver over the term of the next parliament.

On the face it appears reasonable, as people need to know what they're voting for, however from another perspective it reduces flexibility. Deciding beforehand what the key policies are going to be means taking a view on what the future may bring, which is difficult, and spelling out intentions in advance may unduly restrict the government from taking the right steps in future.

If during the term of a government, new insights arise or the environment changes requiring a particular policy to be altered, or dropped, or given a lower priority compared to other more pressing issues that have cropped up, then the government may find it awkward to change their approach if they had already made a manifesto commitment.

In effect having a manifesto acts as a constraint on flexibility to respond to changing circumstances and events, and creates a delay in following the right approach.

10.8   Manifesto's can lead to bad campaign promises

During the heat of a campaign, to gain popularity with particular voters, a party may end up making manifesto promises favouring particular groups of voters to get them on side. Their opponents can respond in kind, with the result that their manifestos contain sops to various special interest groups.

This can rapidly descend into political farce with parties vying with each other to win voter affections through various ill-considered political sops.

An example is India, where in the state of Maharashtra farmers were given free electricity, which drained resources from the state coffers and eventually had to be withdrawn. In other states such as Karnataka parties have tried to attract voters by promising to lower the price of rice.

The result of all this is poorly thought out policies that favour particular groups and ultimately are bad economics diverting resources from better uses.

10.9   Parties lead to stagnant "do nothing" periods

Parties suffer from stagnant periods when nothing much happens and normal government progress comes to a near standstill. This generally happens because the incumbent leader has fallen out of favour with their own party and the electorate however has still got time on his hands before a general election is due.

In this situation the party is in a dilemma, because if they move too fast to oust the existing leader by pointing out the mistakes then that may comprise an own goal of sorts. In addition as the leader has lost credibility and authority, very little new policy initiatives are raised with the people in his party mostly busy planning and jockeying for the period when a new leader is in place.

Examples are when President Clinton was investigated for relations with Monica

Lewinsky, which lasted nine months from January 1998 to September 1998. Other examples are John Major who faced internal divisions in his party leading to his famous call to "Back me or Sack me" and a leadership election. President Bush too had a similar period towards the end of his second term.

The key point here is that normal government business and major government initiatives gets put onto a backburner during this period as all the politicians are preoccupied with the forthcoming change. This "dead" period therefore represents a huge wasted opportunity.

10.10 Parties have Egos that creates delays

Parties are like people, they have egos, and don't like admitting that they got things wrong. Changing their policy radically would be tacit admittal that they had got it wrong earlier. Thus they have a tendency to cling to their own perceived wisdom for too long even though the rest of the world has realised there's a problem with it.

This "ego effect" creates an inertia that makes policy making sluggish and slow to change. It also makes experimentation difficult, as the party ego doesn't want to be seen making mistakes.

10.11 Parties crowd out new Political Ideologies and maintain the Status Quo

Although in most democratic countries there are generally no restrictions on new political parties, in most places two or three major parties will form the serious contenders for power. Any new up and coming politicians therefore need to be thinking of joining one of these top three parties or else be reconciled to the political wilderness.

Therefore all the new political talent tends to be sucked up by the big three parties and the remaining parties remain minnows on the sidelines, creating a self-fulfilling prophecy.

The big parties in the meantime tend to have their well-established direction and sets of policies and the new comers need to fit in with this.

All this creates a strong force in favour of keeping the existing status quo and crowding out new political ideas, and a general ossifying of politics.

10.12 Parties lead to Dynastic Behaviour

Political parties often lead to political dynasties. This is caused by the people at the top grooming their offspring for succession, and the top people around them acquiescing to the succession.

The best example is India, where a single family, the Nehru's has been in power starting from Jawaharlal Nehru, his daughter Indira Gandhi, her son Rajiv Gandhi, and now it's increasingly looking likely his son Rahul will at some point take the reins. A member of the family has been prime minister for 37 of the last 62 years i.e. 60% of the time[1]. This rises to 42 years if you add in the five-year period during which Sonia Gandhi deferred the top job to Dr Manmohan Singh.

Other examples include the two George Bushes in United States, Laurent and Joseph Kabila in Congo, Kim Il-sung and Kim Jong-il in North Korea, Hafez al-Assad and his son Bashar in Syria, Zulfikar Ali Bhutto and Benazir Bhutto in Pakistan.

The point of this is that how can it be that a country such as India with a billion people cannot find top political talent outside of a single family? Clearly a party system leads to a monarchy type of leadership where the monarch passes on their throne to their offspring.

In no way can this be democratic, or efficient – as it's vitally important that the best qualified person occupies the top job.

10.13 Parties can lower the quality of Candidates

A political party acts as a Brand, and can bestow credibility onto a candidate. This reflected glory allows defects in the candidate to be overlooked by the electorate who may find themselves buying into the message of a party and its policies rather than the qualities of any specific candidate. This lowering of candidate quality also lowers the quality of political thought and debate and leads to a general downgrading of politics.

---

1   Indian Prime Ministers   http://www.webindia123.com/history/modern/pm.htm

An example is the Indian elections in 2009, where in the state of Eastern UP, 17% of the 272 candidates had criminal records. However in three of the large parties 44% of candidates were tainted. The criminality rate[2] in the two main parties was 25%. The fact that the larger parties had a criminality rate higher than the average shows that the party acts as a cloak to mask the candidates background, allowing a greater proportion of less savoury candidates to come through.

10.14 Parties can end up giving too much power to a minority group

To get into power parties may need to enter into a political union with a minority party. This can often lead to the situation of the minority group punching far above their weight, and is fundamentally undemocratic and can hold back the will of the majority.

However the ruling party may have to put up with this as a necessary evil in order to remain in power.

An example is the Congress Government of Dr Manmohan Singh in India, which had a coalition with the Communist party, who had been attributed with blocking further liberalization of the economy and applying the brakes on proposed changes in labour laws[3].

It needs restating that the objective is not for a party to "remain in power" but is to enact government policies for the sake of the people and what's best for the people. It's a major flaw of the party system that a minority view can hold the balance and block progress.

10.15 Parties are susceptible to Media Influence

Political parties act as Brands, and in common with all other branded products or services their popularity is affected by media promotion.

This gives media owners' huge influence over the political process and which party

2   The Economist, April 18th 2009-05-03 India's Election "The untouchable and the unattainable"

3   New York Times http://www.nytimes.com/2007/10/09/world/asia/09india.html?fta=y

gets elected. Improperly exercised such influence can distort and even hijack the democratic process in favour of special interests.

An example is Italy, where every Italian under 30 has grown to political maturity in a country where Mr Berlusconi and his family control half the television output, one of four national newspapers, one of two news magazines and the biggest publishing house[4].

10.16 Parties an abstract view

In this section I'll take a rather abstract view of political parties.

In essence, each local MP is providing a political service to their constituents and can be seen as a Political Service Provider (PSP).

As in the provision of all other products and services the Political Services market is ultimately a market with the MP of a locality implicitly contracted to represent his/her locality and provide them with a political management service.

What appears to have happened is that rather than remaining independent and distinct political service providers, the MPs have grouped into large groups, in effect acting as quasi monopolistic providers with a stranglehold on political power, effectively keeping out outsiders.

Were this to happen in any other service provision such as accountancy or law, there would be anti-trust issues raised and investigations by bodies such as the Monopolies and Mergers Commission to see whether the concentration of power was in the consumer interest.

10.17 Parties lead to sub optimal outcomes

A party will select a set of policies upon which to base its manifesto. However no single political party will always have the best set of policies. It may be that the best / most knowledgeable or creative person to formulate policy in an area belongs to another political party.

4   The Economist, April 30th 2009, The Berlusconisation of Italy

Taking parliament as a whole, it's likely the people who are best placed to make policies in different areas will be distributed across all the parties. Therefore it's simply not possible for any one party to have the best possible set of policies and by definition the policy set of any party has to be less optimal than the best set of policies possible.

10.18 So why is there no change?

With the long list of potential drawbacks outlined above, the natural question is – how come the political system hasn't been modified and changed?

The principal reason is the political parties in whose gift change lies are the same ones benefiting from the dysfunctional setup, and expecting them to do something about it would be like expecting turkeys to vote for Christmas and pull the stop cord on the political gravy train.

> *All of us who are concerned for peace and triumph of reason and justice must be keenly aware how small an influence reason and honest goodwill exert upon events in the political field.*
> ~ *Albert Einstein*

11. A new political order

"Under democracy one party always devotes its chief energies to trying to prove that the other party is unfit to rule – and both commonly succeed, and are right."

~ *H.L. Mencken, 1956*

Our Political structures might appear permanent however it's worth remembering they are virtual constructs – in theory able to be changed overnight in response to peoples' desires if sufficient people change their minds.

With that in mind, let's outline the core elements of a political system to overcome the shortcomings of political parties discussed in the previous chapter and apply them to the mother of all parliaments, the UK parliament.

As many countries around the world have followed the UK structure, the suggestions would be generic and apply in other countries as well.

11.1 Representative Democracy

I think we are right in dividing the country into areas, each selecting its representative or MP to go to the House of Parliament. There does need to be a direct link between the people and the legislators.

However we need to change from the current system of one MP per area, to a new system where we elect one male *and* one female Member of Parliament from each area.

In the UK, currently only 19.5% of the MPs are female, amounting to 126 female MPs out of a total of 646 MPs in Parliament[1].

---

1   2009 figures

Changing to one male and one female MP per area would fix the issue of gender inequality overnight, and the five-fold increase in number of female MPs would bring a moderating influence and a different set of priorities into parliament and be a more democratic system.

11.2   Term of Representation

Once elected, barring gross misconduct, MPs need to stay the entire term, giving them space to take bold or unpopular steps without having to keep looking back over their shoulder for approval.

11.3   The Party's Over

In the new system we should ban all political parties as they suffer from the large number of weaknesses outlined in the previous chapter.

People in constituencies would vote for individuals and not for any Parties. This would open out the political market for many more people to be able to stand for election and have a real chance of being elected, compared to the current situation where it's in effect a two or three horse race. Ultimately this would make Parliament far more diverse with a much greater proportion of people rooted in the real world entering politics as compared to the present stagnant pool of career "Westminster Village" professional politicians.

As there would be no parties, each MP would vote in the interests of the areas they represent and for the nation as a whole, in the manner that they personally see fit.

MPs should not be allowed to form any alliances or enter into quid pro quo arrangements as these would distort their judgement and they should approach and vote on each issue solely on its individual merits.

11.4   Forum Selects the Executive

As people haven't voted for any party (party being a banned concept), there is no de facto executive or manifesto in place either.

The elected representatives form a forum[2] and their key first task is to choose an executive from amongst themselves.

All this may appear rather uncertain and scary, but I see it liberating as it opens out the possibility of genuine change. If people are worried about this approach letting a genie out of the bottle with no telling what policy gets selected, we need to remind ourselves that just as we trust Juries to get it right, the forum will also ultimately make the right decisions.

Every MP in the forum is free to formulate policy and vision for any aspect of government, however they need to get a minimum number (say twelve) of other forum members to back them as a candidate for Policy Leader. The candidates would then pitch their policies to the forum in a kind of beauty parade and it's up to the forum to decide which of the candidates to vote for.

If there are more than two candidates in the running for a particular Policy Leadership post, then unless the first candidate has received an absolute majority, I envisage a two-stage selection process with a second ballot between the top two candidates.

The selected candidate would become the Minister with the job of delivering the vision they presented to the house. If they need supporting junior ministers then it's up to the Minister to select them and one would expect them to be from their campaign team.

Following this process allows any MP who feels they can lead in a particular area the freedom to pitch for it. It therefore exercises and exposes all the arguments to scrutiny, creating genuine debate leading to the most popular vision being adopted.

In our current system the best person to lead in a particular area could happen to be in a minority opposition party and therefore they would never have the chance of leading the policy despite being the best person to do so. The proposed system however allows the best policies and people in each area of government to surface and therefore would lead to far greater progress.

11.5 The Cabinet

The group of Ministers selected for the various portfolios would come together to

---

2   As there are no political parties in this model, to make the distinction I'm using forum instead of Parliament.

form a Cabinet that would work as a team to collectively deliver the set of visions on which each of the Ministers' was elected by the forum.

I don't see the need for a permanent Prime Minster, because that leads to an excess of power embodied in one person, who becomes in effect an "elected King". We need to move forward from the middle ages and away from single King like figures!

I see the role of Prime Minister being rotated amongst the Cabinet Ministers, each holding the post for one session, so that by the end of the Parliamentary Term each Minister would have performed the Prime Ministerial role once.

Having such an arrangement would promote joined up government because the Cabinet would need to work as a team.

In this arrangement the Prime Minister becomes a working leader, and if a Minister needed to be changed then this would be for the Cabinet to recommend to the Forum, which would ultimately decide.

11.6   Benefits of the Proposed System

The proposed system will invigorate and refresh politics by making it possible for a whole range of new people to enter politics without having to get past party gatekeepers. Not only could they enter politics but they would also have the opportunity of presenting a vision and being selected to Ministerial level, leading to a dynamic political environment.

Elected MPs will be free to hold their own opinions on all subjects and not have to compromise their views to suit a party line. This would lead to more conviction politics and a much greater interest in and respect for politicians who would upgrade from political puppets being operated by the strings of party whips to people with their own individual complex set of opinions and beliefs.

As there will be no political parties, the question of power concentrating in a party elite simply doesn't arise.

As there are no parties, there will be no divisive splits in the electorate that happens when parties seek to exploit or exaggerate divisions in society in order to create their political proposition. The forum is there to represent the whole nation and would work in team mode as a single entity.

With each MP in effect being on their own and voting as they see fit rather than following a party line, it's much harder for broad corruption to take hold as power is no longer concentrated in a small party elite responsible for setting policy. Possible seekers of influence would have the logistical difficulty of targeting a large number of MPs to influence how the forum voted.

The proposed system would allow the MPs' with the best vision to rise and take a leadership role ensuring that the best person for the job does it.

Parliament would have a lot more flexibility as no specific manifesto has been promised in advance to the people, and so there's room for manoeuvre and of selecting the best competing vision. Ministers however are bound to deliver the vision they sold to the House, but as circumstances change the House can alter that vision without the need to refer back to the electorate or fear of breaking manifesto pledges.

There would be no stagnant periods of lost opportunity due to an incumbent leader having lost popularity. If a Minister fails to deliver then they can be readily changed for a fresh one from the forum with little loss of energy or time – in fact rather similar to the way a footballer can get substituted towards the end of a game if they're running out of puff.

As there are no parties, there are no political egos standing in the ways of new ideas and change. It'll also be a lot easier for new ideas to be raised and jostle for attention leading to a greater diversity of opinion and ultimately better and more creative ideas being implemented.

Political dynasties would become a thing of the past, as the forum would choose Ministers based on the policy vision they present rather than patronage.

With each MP standing for election on their own individual merit, rather than in the reflected glow of a party, the electorate would be choosing a person rather than a party, and this would lead to an increase in the quality of the selected candidate.

As there are no parties, the situation where a junior coalition partner wields a disproportionate amount influence would never arise.

Media would find it harder to influence the outcome of elections' as election's would be fought at a local level between individuals and not at the national level between parties.

The proposed system would unlock and release the political system from its entrapment by parties and open it out for more democratic, dynamic and flexible management leading to greater and faster progress.

> *I have come to the conclusion that politics is too serious a matter to be left to the politicians.*
>
> ~ *Charles de Gaulle*

12. Immigration

People coming to work from other countries are often viewed negatively with distrust, and phrases such as "the country is being swamped" or "being overrun" by immigrants often appear in the popular media in the UK. Another example is Enoch Powell's infamous "Rivers of Blood" speech prophesying doom.

Immigrants gets a bad press and the concept is misunderstood, with politicians often taking a populist approach rather than addressing it head on.

12.1   Who is the "Our" in "Our" Country?

When I hear people say this is "our" country, I have to stop and shake my head, do they really understand what they're saying and how can any country belong to a set of people. If we take all the people in the country today and somehow stand them in a field, then over time the number of people in the field would decrease as people die and pass away, and a day would come when that field would be empty as everyone had passed away.

My point being that a day will come when everyone alive today will no longer be alive. So the concept of "our" country is a temporary one. In reality we are only passing through and momentarily occupying the country and in that respect it never really belonged to us.

Once we grasp the concept that the country doesn't really "belong" to us, then it's a small step from starting to question what right we have to stop other fellow travellers through life from entering "our" country.

12.2   The Freedom of Movement

We are all inhabitants of the same planet, and it seems a basic birthright for us to be able to travel to any location on our planet without being artificially constrained by bureaucracies.

As mentioned earlier, birds have the right to travel freely, and so how come we, the more intelligent species have limited ourselves into country sized corrals?

12.3   We are ALL Immigrants

> *Remember, remember always that all of us, and you and I especially, are descended from immigrants and revolutionists.*
> ~ *Roosevelt, Franklin D.*

If we go back far enough, then scientists have discovered that we all originated from a small number of tribes that moved out of Africa[1] around 70,000 years ago. That in effect makes all of us immigrants – the only difference being the time duration since we migrated.

It's worth remembering this, before seeking to close the gate to new immigrants.

12.4   Genetic Factors

People generally tend to be risk averse and avoid change, preferring the low stress option of sticking with the familiar.

Migrants however are willing to cross some fairly high hurdles in their quest for a better life abroad. Ranging from people from North Africa risking their lives in leaky boats to cross the Mediterranean, to people being smuggled inside lorry containers or even under lorries to cross the English Channel. All this displays huge amounts of resilience and personal courage.

I think therefore there is something special about migrants, and their ambition and risk-taking propensity are much higher than the norm. A recent study has found that when people go and live abroad they tend to become more creative[2].

---

1   Out of Africa, 2009, Dr Alice Roberts, BBC
2   Cultural borders and mental barriers: The relationship between living abroad and creativity. Maddux, William W.; Galinsky, Adam D, Journal of Personality and Social Psychology. 2009 Volume 96, Issue 5 (May)

Those genetic factors, when merged into the population will have a positive impact and make the host nation more ambitious, creative and able to take risks.

It is no surprise therefore to find the United States – largely made up of immigrants to be the world leader in terms of creativity and enterprise, leading with advances such as space travel and the internet, with world beating companies such as Google, Microsoft, Intel, Ford Motor Cars and Coca Cola to name just a few.

What is surprising is that people have not realised the source of their success and migrants only get a grudging acceptance rather than being recognised as being rather special.

12.5   The Cause and Effect of Migration

Ultimately very few people like to leave the place where they've grown up and developed social contacts, and yet for them to be obliged to do so is indicative of a failure by their country's administrators to do their job and provide citizens with the basics of a decent life.

Just as water flows naturally and relentlessly from high places to low spots, similarly migrants will flow from countries with high poverty levels to areas with low poverty.

The real culprits in all this are the politicians mismanaging their countries through corruption and shortsighted policies and thereby obliging their more enterprising fellow citizens to leave and seek better prospects overseas.

Thus migration will only reduce once countries become better managed and develop real prospects for their citizens.

Developed economies too are to blame here, as argued earlier, it's insufficient to simply shrug one's shoulders and say they're a sovereign country and it's up to them as to how they manage things.

There need to be more intelligent and proactive ways of ensuring that countries around the world move onto and keep on a path of growth and stable development and ways of stopping them from imploding should a bad government take over.

12.6   The real "Cure" to Negative Migration

Migration for the right choices – to see the world and experience other cultures is wonderful and positive, however to be forced to do so through a lack of development in one's home country is not right as then it's no longer a free choice and is one forced out of economic desperation.

I see the solution to removing negative migration lies in improving our global governance by implementing some of the concepts discussed earlier such as expanding the EU, adopting co-governance schemes and improving the standards of politics and eventually moving in the direction of a single country world.

Of these EU expansion offers the best short-term prospects, as it creates a positive dynamic in the prospective new entrants' to get their act together in terms of social structures and organizations, attitudes towards women, political standards and transparency etc.

> *"But then I came to the conclusion that no, while there may be an immigration problem, it isn't really a serious problem. The really serious problem is assimilation."*
>
> ~ *Samuel P. Huntington*

13. Race to the Bottom

"I hope that people will finally come to realize that there is only one 'race' – the human race – and that we are all members of it."
~ *Margaret Atwood*

When I was eleven, I was on a ship travelling from Venice to Bombay via the Cape. At Cape Town I went with my father to post some letters and on finding him join a rather long queue in the post office I pointed out that he had overlooked a much shorter queue some feet away, however he declined and stayed in the same queue and so as any eleven year old would I simply shrugged and left it at that. I then went to use the toilets and as I was coming out a white man walked in and glared at me sternly, somewhat disconcerted I thought weirdo as I left.

It was only many years later that these rather two rather strange incidents made sense as something as unnatural as apartheid would never have occurred to me at the time.

13.1   Race is a Four Letter word

I find "race" a confusing and a somewhat dangerously misleading concept. As human beings the differences between so called races appear only to be minor adaptations to local circumstances.

When someone white goes to a warm country then they'll rapidly develop a tan and become very brown, but that doesn't mean that they become part of another race. So why do people in whom a dark skin colour is more permanent get seen as being from another race?

As human beings, our external organs differ from others and we have varying eye, hair and skin colours. We've used skin colour to define race, but why didn't we choose eye or hair colours? I can see that asking that question may make people uncomfortable, but in reality there's very little logic to use an external organ's colour, as that's simply a response to the environment.

The danger is that by saying we're from different races, we start viewing each other as somehow being from a different group or type. The Oxford Paperback dictionary includes the definition of race as "a genus or species or breed or variety of animals or plants". People can thus interpret it to imply that different people have developed along different paths and that the differences are non-trivial and some might be superior to others.

The reality, proven by genetic analysis is that we're all descendants from a common tribe originally coming from Africa[1] some 70,000 years ago which then spread around the world adapting to the various environments and we are a single species, homo sapiens.

Race has a huge potential for misleading people, especially those who're less well read, simply mischievous or seeking to use it to gain an edge for a subset of the community.

I think therefore "race" is a word I would like expunged from the dictionary as it creates artificial differences when in reality none exists. Its usage belongs to a period that ought to have ended with the Nazis.

Interestingly this approach puts me at odds[2] with people wanting "racial harmony" as my view is that there is only one race – the human race.

13.2   In Praise of Diversity

Imagine a world in which we all were of the same skin colour, lets also all of us have the same eye and hair colour and grow to be the same height. Continuing with this theme, lets all of us be of perfect beauty with not even a single blemish – and so that we're all at this same level of perfection, each of us facially looking almost identical to everyone else.

Imagine too that we all ate similar food, liked similar music and had the same views.

---

1   Out of Africa, 2009, Dr Alice Roberts, BBC
2   in the sense that people wanting racial harmony have implicitly admitted that there are different races

Now imagine that world, is it really one you would like to live in? Personally it w̲ be completely boring and a living nightmare.

Diversity with all its varieties is so much more interesting and fun with never a dull moment. We should all keep the nightmare I've just described in mind and celebrate our diversity.

13.3   It's not all Black and White

One day, whilst doing my MSc, Martin a fellow student from Kenya, asked me where are the "white" people. Slightly bemused I humoured him and replied all around you – just look. Martin persisted and asked me to name one. So I mentioned Les who was an Irish student on our course. "Aha" Martin exclaimed, and pointing out of the window at the falling snow, enquired, "Is he that colour?" I replied "No", at which Martin exclaimed with a broad smile "Then he's not White!".

At that point the penny dropped for me and I got it. There were no "White" people.

A direct corollary of that is that there are no "Black" people either, as I have not come across anyone with the skin colour equal to the colour of a lump of coal.

So why would we describe different communities using labels which are inaccurate and emphasize and exaggerate the differences?

My feeling is that these labels are rooted in the days of slavery. At that time light skinned Europeans were taking dark skinned Africans to work as slaves in plantations in America. The Europeans however would have had a human side, and many would be religious and church going. By using labels such as White and Black, they were seeking to exaggerate the differences between the people and position them on opposite ends of the spectrum not just of colour but by inference human development, thereby opening the path to treat them as a different race of people and somewhat justifying that it was acceptable to enslave them.

I wince when I hear someone dark skinned describe themselves as "Black", so complete is the brain washing and unquestioning acceptance[3] of what is ultimately a carry over from the days of slavery.

3   I confess to having used the term black myself earlier in the book. This was to avoid having to go through this discussion at an earlier stage.

Similarly when I see a European with a bright pink complexion or one who's just come back from holiday sporting a tan, it's curious that they don't appear to question applying the patently inappropriate label "White" to themselves.

13.4   Labels Matter

Labels really matter and are not just semantics. Anyone doubting this need only reflect for a moment the rationale behind hard nosed multinational consumer marketing companies spending millions on research choosing a new product name.

As a further illustration, lets consider that the fact that the majority of people on the planet are so called non-white, with the term "coloured" also being used at one point to describe them. However as "coloured" people are in the majority, being coloured is the norm and an alternative logical naming convention would be to describe the "white" people as lacking in colour or as colourless.

Apart from for illustrative purposes, I'm not proposing this term, but were we to adopt the term "colourless" to describe white people, it would somehow brings some negativity into the scene, and anyone described as colourless would feel they were immediately missing something and lacking in some way, and therefore implicitly feel at a disadvantage.

Although not a neurologist, my background in computing gives an insight into processing and ultimately our brain functions as a biological processor. Were a computer to work out meaning, it would have to recover all possible meanings and apply each of them to the context and score the fit, and then moving on to choose the best fit within any given context. I suspect our brains must do much the same in a flash and mostly at a lower subconscious processing layer.

With that model when a word such as "black" is used, then at a subconscious level our brain will retrieve all possible meanings of the word and parse through them working out which meaning best fits the context and then deliver that meaning to our conscious. When the word has many negative connotations then simply bringing the other negative interpretations into our brain's processing area, risks leaving a shadow of negativity akin to a type of hysteresis or memory effect, which can persist as a backdrop or scene setter altering our outlook.

Therefore labels matter, and using labels such as black, which are not only factually incorrect, but risk bringing a general negativity into one's contextual mindset is a major issue and not mere semantics, and I'm keen that we drop this historical baggage.

13.5   Colour as a basis for Classification

It feels somewhat inappropriate to use colour as a basis for classification of people as people in Southern Europe e.g. Italy, Spain often have similar colours to people from northern India.

Someone from the UK who's moved to Spain will often have a deep tan, and is therefore much darker than say someone from Japan.

Colour therefore is a rather blunt instrument for classification, and given its ability to mislead and create biases due to its historical baggage, I'd prefer we stop using colour as a classifier or definer of peoples and stick to broad geographical classifiers.

13.6   Pigmentation

If however we still wish to classify people based on the colour of their skin, then it's worth being precise.

As there is no one who is pure black or pure white, we need to stop using these unnecessary extremes as they polarise and exaggerate differences, and we should use other names which more accurately reflect the actual colour shades.

The reason we appear of different colours is that the skin has different amounts of pigmentation in it, so a medically precise descriptor would be the amount of pigmentation. With that schema, white would translate onto low pigmentation, brown to mid-pigmentation, and someone dark skinned would have a high pigmentation. These could be further shortened colloquially into lopig, mipig and hipig labels for low, medium and high pigmentation respectively.

The reason I'm drawn to the pigmentation approach is that it's completely neutral with no historical baggage and plays down the differences, and given the problems in this area in the past it would be nice to have a clean break.

It's worth having an open debate to move away from provocative labelling of people because sadly, less educated or thoughtless people are unable to separate the labels from their historical baggage and get influenced adversely. Having neutral labels would draw the sting from this issue and allow us all to grow up and have mature relationships between different communities.

> *Let us all hope that the dark clouds of racial prejudice will soon pass away, and that in some not too distant tomorrow the radiant stars of love and brotherhood will shine over our great nation with all their scintillating beauty."*
>
> *~ Martin Luther King, Jr.*

Section 2
Global Bodies

14. International Bodies and Agreements

I've made clear my strong belief that there needs to be a single global country which would count as its citizens all human beings. That needs to be our aim, and in reality there is nothing of any real substance stopping us – remember all our structures are just that – artificial dreamt up methods of organization.

However people get taken in and seduced by illusions of country, neighbourhood and falsely ascribe permanence to these concepts. Hence I don't anticipate a shift overnight towards the ideal approach. In the interim there is a real need for countries to work together and a whole plethora of international bodies and agreements have cropped up. In this chapter I'd like to examine the workings of some of these as well as see if we can identify any shortcomings.

14.1 Timescales and Procrastination

One of the major issues with international bodies, is the sheer time that it takes to get agreements. Everyone knows an agreement is needed and everyone wants one, but getting to an agreement proves elusive and difficult due to the numerous different agendas of the various players.

A case in point is the failed attempt to form an International Trade Organization in 1948, and after numerous trade rounds, finally approximately 50 years later, 1995 saw the creation of the World Trade Organization. During the intervening years a provisional agreement the General Agreement on Tariffs and Trade (GATT) was used and this steadily became more liberal through various rounds of trade negotiation[1].

---

1   Understanding the WTO: The GATT Years from Havana to Marrakesh
    http://www.wto.org/english/thewto_e/whatis_e/tif_e/fact4_e.htm

The timescales and the efforts that it takes to put these agreements in place are huge, and as yet it still remains a work in progress with the Doha round in 2008 failing to reach an agreement. This demonstrates the inherent weakness of trying to put in place complex multilateral agreements. This is not an academic point, had the WTO arrangement been in place since 1948, the world would today be a far more prosperous place and the common citizen would be a lot better off, and so these delays have caused real hardship and extended poverty and suffering in various parts of the world due to the lack of free trade opportunities and trade barriers. It's worth noting that trade was one of the aims of the popular Live Aid concerts.

Although I've chosen an example of trade, in other areas the procrastination also leads to an incubation of problems allowing them to grow rather than be nipped in the bud. A specific example is that of Global Warming. As a global community we're still trying to work out multilateral agreements on curbing climate change, with the backdrop that the longer it takes to sort out, the worse the eventual problem becomes.

If we were organized as a single global country, then that would remove at a stroke all the need for these tedious and turgid negotiations and as a world we could get on and work as a team to solve the problems and because we would all be working as a single country it would reduce conflicts of interest and allow rapid progress.

14.2   Achieving Faster Multilateral Negotiations

> *A politician thinks of the next election; a statesman thinks of the next generation.*
>
> ~ *James Freeman Clarke*

Ways need to be found to enable multilateral negotiations to proceed at a quicker pace, thereby reducing the damage caused by lack of agreement.

Removing Short Term Political Bias

One factor that complicates decision-making is that governments have an eye on their voter power bases and this skews their priorities.

In effect when evaluating a potential agreement, the agreement is parsed through a country filter, but then also through a party political filter for issues.

One way to achieve faster decision-making is to take the politicians out of the picture entirely. Each government should elect an apolitical team of experts who are given the mandate to negotiate on behalf of their country. Once appointed to a negotiating team, members cannot be removed and have the sole discretion to negotiate without any input from their national government.

The only role of the government then is to ratify the final draft of any agreement. However ideally they should be kept out of the negotiation stages (by physical means if necessary) and should only be asked to accept / reject the final output package.

This process lets the government somewhat off the hook of offending their stakeholders and by taking party political considerations out of the negotiations, will speed up the process.

Increasing the cost of Intransigence

Another idea would be to limit each country to a maximum of three vetoes after which they would need to either accept the agreement or pay to purchase further vetoes. This would raise the costs and stakes of taking an intransigent stance and help focus political minds. It would help to stop negotiations drifting as drift has a real tangible cost in terms of needing to continually buy vetoes. The cost of the Veto would be linked to the country's GDP.

Negotiating on the level of transitional support and not on the terms of the agreement

Often it's clear what the ideal agreement needs to be, however countries will still take incremental steps towards that ideal, and progressively move closer to the ideal in a sequence of agreements over time, for example the way the GATT agreement moved forward with various trade rounds over 45 years.

This slow incremental approach is easier to adjust to as it's a gradual change. However there is a saying that one cannot cross a chasm in two jumps. A way of changing the mindset would be not to negotiate on the structure and workings of the agreement and to base the agreement on what the ideal agreement / end game needs to be.

However where negotiation should come in is over the level of compensation and support to the various governments in moving over to and accepting the new agreement. So the negotiations would be over the transitional support rather than on compromising the actual terms of the agreement.

Applying this to the GATT trade rounds, one would go for free trade and open up all markets, however rather than allowing countries that are affected to make special cases and constrain the agreement, instead these countries would receive a transitional relief to make it easier for them to adapt to the new situation.

14.3 United Nations General Assembly

The UN General Assembly is one of the main organs of the UN involved with policy making with wide scope, and has initiated political, economic, humanitarian, social and legal actions affecting the lives of millions of people.

I am concerned though that such a central body does not appear to be structured democratically.

Each of the 192 countries in the General Assembly has one vote. Therefore tiny Iceland with its population of 306,000 has the same voting rights as the 1,166,079,217 people of India. In effect a single Icelander has the same voting rights at the General Assembly as 3,810 Indians. This appears to be grossly undemocratic.

Moving to a more democratic General Assembly

The General Assembly should represent the views of the peoples around the world, and each global citizen ought to have the same amount of voting rights. Therefore in the first instance countries should be given voting rights in proportion to their populations, lets call this V.

Democratic Adjustment Multiplier

However simply giving each country voting rights in proportion to their population would be insufficient and wrong headed. If a country is undemocratic e.g. a dictatorship or a single party state, then their politicians cannot claim to represent the views of their people as that claim has never been tested and proven, i.e. politicians from a dictatorship or single party state are really only representing their own clique of ruling elite. Therefore a Democratic Adjustment needs to be applied as a multiplier to their basic votes, and a dictatorship might have its votes reduced to 50% e.g. would have 0.5V votes, and a country that is fully democratic would have its votes increased by a multiplier of 2, i.e. would have 2V votes. Countries falling in-between the two extremes would have multipliers of between 0.5 to 2.0.

The Democratic Adjustment would change as the conditions of a country alter, and would act as a natural incentive for the country to move towards democracy. On the other hand if it slips towards one party rule, then it's only ri͜g͜ deserves a smaller role and influence on the world stage, which would occu͜ naturally as a result of the democratic multiplier decreasing.

Level of Enterprise Multiplier

When it comes to giving people rights to vote, consideration needs to be given to how industrious and enterprising the people are. So for example a country that is being poorly managed with a low level of national income are contributing less to the global scene than a country where the people are industrious and creating a lot of wealth.

Therefore a multiplier based on relative per capita Gross Domestic Product (GDP) needs to be defined. e.g. if a country has a per capita GDP equal to the world average then it gets a multiplier of 1, if it is four times the world average per capita GDP then it may get a multiplier of 2, similarly if it is half the average GDP then it may get a multiplier of 0.5.

Global Maturity – Human Rights and Gender Equality Multiplier

Consideration also needs to be given to the country's record on human rights, gender equality and keeping to International Commitments. Once again a multiplier would be defined and applied to its voting base that reflects how the country manages these.

The idea is that a country that is well behaved on these factors is proving that it is mature and has earned the right to have a greater say in the running of the world than a country that is misbehaving itself on these factors and in effect has been acting as a spoilt and immature child.

Earning the right for a greater voice on the world stage

Although the numbers I've proposed are just for illustration, the key point is that the voting rights at the General Assembly need to reflect the population, suitably modified by the levels of democracy, enterprise and human rights/ global maturity.

In effect those countries that are democratic, hard working and enterprising, respecting human rights and gender equality and meeting their international commitments have earned the rights to a much greater voice on the world stage than a country of the similar size population but lagging on level of democracy, industriousness and observance of human rights.

There is also the possibility that making the global expectations clear may motivate countries to follow good behaviour as that in turn gives them the chance to have a greater say and influence on a global basis.

14.4   United Nations Security Council

The UN Security Council is probably the most important organ of the UN. While other organs of the UN only make recommendations to Governments (who can then take their own decision), the UN members countries are obligated to carry out the decisions of the Security Council.

The Council is composed of five permanent members: China, France, Russian Federation, United Kingdom and United States and ten non-permanent members elected by the General Assembly for two year terms.

The "Great Power Unanimity" rule confers a veto to the permanent members, since any substantive matter must have the concurring vote (or abstention) of all five permanent members[2].

The current structure of the UN reflects the power status quo back in the 1940s after the end of World War II, and I feel it's completely undemocratic to give permanent member status to any particular countries.

Furthermore to give these permanent members the right to veto anything they dislike is effectively enshrining a "schoolyard bully" principle on a global scale and is completely wrong headed.

The Veto power is ultimately not good even for the countries that have it, because it means that they can exercise their Veto and keep a problem on hold indefinitely avoiding having to face the issue, in effect keeping a stalemate alive for decades. One such example of this is the US support for Israel, where the US has exercised its Veto power on numerous occasions[3].

I simply cannot see the need or legitimacy for any single country to be able to Veto and in effect act as a block to the rest of the world. It's wrong headed and egotistical and needs to be removed.

---

2   UN Structure and Membership http://www.un.org/sc/members.asp
3   US Vetoes http://www.globalpolicy.org/component/content/article/196/42647.html

Replacement of the Veto with a Significant Majority

The Veto concept needs to be removed as it's outdated and unjust, and replaced with the need for a significant majority in favour before substantive action is approved. Although it's debatable on what constitutes a significant majority, I would expect it to be 12 out of 15 i.e. an 80% majority to be reasonable. If more than 3 countries have doubts then their concerns need to be examined.

Democratizing the Permanent Membership

I agree with the concept of permanent membership of the Security Council, as this gives it a certain amount of stability and continuity. However we need to move away from using the status quo of the 1950s to determine who should be a Permanent Member. What is needed is to have clearly laid down democratic criteria of who is eligible to become a Permanent Member of the Security Council and *any* country that meets these criteria should immediately receive Permanent member status.

The criteria would work both ways and if due to internal changes a country no longer meets the criteria then they could find themselves being asked to relinquish their permanent member chair in the Security Council. Obviously there would be notice periods involved but the principle remains that there is a democratic, open and transparent set of rules on who is eligible to be a permanent member of the Security Council.

If it turns out that the Security Council starts having a lot more permanent members, then the solution is fairly straightforward – periodically make the criteria more stringent to keep its member count manageable.

Criteria for Admittance to Permanent Member Status

In the previous section on the General Assembly, it was proposed adjusting voting rights of each country to factor in their population, level of democracy, economic development and global maturity / participation. When deciding on the criteria for becoming a Permanent Member, these voting rights would be a good place to start from as they reflect the gravitas that each of the countries has on a global scale.

However as we're concerned with security, which brings in the armed forces, I would include a couple of factors to reflect their bias towards military power e.g. the size of their armed forces and spending on their armed forces both on a relative basis for their size and economy, as well as on an absolute size basis globally.

Once the General Assembly voting rights have been modified for their armed forces strength, then the resulting score can be used to determine which countries have the right to be permanent members of the Security Council.

Having a process such as this would be adaptive in the sense that as new countries grow and develop they earn the right to join and become permanent members of the Security Council. Equally if a country decides to "play bad" and either goes downhill or misbehaves globally then it could find itself losing its coveted seat.

It would then become a far more democratic and dynamic system, and much better than the current fossilised, closed and unresponsive system.

14.5   The International Criminal Court

The International Criminal Court (ICC) was set up in 2002 to try people accused of crimes of genocide, war crimes and crimes against humanity. It's based on a treaty and has been joined by 110 countries and is a court of last resort acting only where a case is not being progressed by a national judicial system.

At the time of writing, the ICC was dealing with cases involving war crimes in the Congo, crimes against Humanity in Central African Republic and Uganda.

Although it's early days, the very fact that the ICC exists, sends a clear message to people running countries that they are not free to do as they please, protected by their sovereignty. It establishes that there are some universal principles that they need to obey, and crucially puts in place the mechanism to take the perpetrators to task.

It's easy to talk about the wrongs of genocide, war crimes and crimes against humanity, however by putting in place a permanent mechanism for dealing with these moves shows that the international community is serious and has moved dealing with these crimes from warm fuzzy words to a new practical reality.

One thing I find somewhat dismaying is that China, Russia and the US have not signed up to the ICC. With their special positions in the UN Security Council where they act as permanent world leaders tasked with helping ensure peace and stability, it would only be right to expect them to take a lead role in the ICC. By staying outside of the ICC it gives the wrong message, almost like they don't want to be called to account by the rest of the world. These large powers can use their veto in the Security Council to deflect anything aimed at them, and by remaining outside of the ICC once more they appear to be evading being put in a position where they are called to account. Anyone who feels they are above the law and therefore untouchable is actually doing themselves a disfavour as well, as they lose the moderating effect that being held to account provides, in turn breeding elitism and alienation.

In an earlier section I talked about the need for a rules based approach for deciding who becomes eligible for Permanent Membership of the Security Council. One worthwhile rule is that anyone wishing to play a role in the Security Council needs to be a member of the ICC.

14.6   International Conventions and Agreements

On December 10, 1948 the General Assembly of the United Nations adopted and proclaimed the Universal Declaration of Human Rights[4]. This spoke of various lofty aims including education, health, right to life, no-one to be tortured, freedom to change religion, freedom of expression, no one held in slavery etc.

Despite the convention there have been various outrages commited around the world, Cambodia under the Khymer Rouge[5] in 1975 with a death toll of 1.7 million over three years, the Balkans conflict in the 1990's, ethnic cleansing in Rwanda with around a million Tutsi's killed, Zimbabwe's mismanagement of its economy and expropriating property, the mass murders and rapes in Darfur in Sudan starting in 2003, to name just a few.

Major powers such as India and China too have acted in ways showing little heed to the convention. Approximately 50 years after the convention was signed, a report[6] to the US House of Representatives quoted Government of India figures of 20 million child labourers with non-governmental organizations (NGOs) estimating it at 50 million, this despite Article 26 enshrining the right to education for everyone. The killing of hundreds of the demonstrators in Tiananmen Square[7] by China in 1989 showed little regard to Articles 3 and 20 concerning the right to life and free association.

---

4   Declaration of Human Rights http://www.un.org/en/documents/udhr/
5   Cambodia under Khymer Rouge
     http://news.bbc.co.uk/1/hi/world/asia-pacific/country_profiles/1244006.stm
6   Child Labour in India http://pangaea.org/street_children/asia/carpet.htm
7   China, Massacre in Tiananmen Square
     http://news.bbc.co.uk/onthisday/hi/dates/stories/june/4/newsid_2496000/2496277.stm

Clearly despite the lofty words of the General Assembly, the reality faced by people on the ground is completely different. I've come to the view that international conventions and agreements are just so much hot air and simply not worth the paper they're written on. In the end it's action that counts.

Each agreement needs a detailed implementation plan to ensure compliance; with clearly laid out escalation procedures and predefined mandated penalties with personnel fully resourced and in place to carry out all the compliance and enforcement work.

Without such an implementation plan in place, it may be better not to have any agreement at all, since an agreement lulls people into a false sense of security and creates an illusion of something being done masking the reality that the exercise is simply a talking shop. Perversely, the existence of a sham agreement means world attention moves away from the issue and it stops the creation of a firm and enforceable agreement.

"Talk is cheap. Words are plentiful. Deeds are precious."

~ *H Ross Perot*

15. Missing Organizations – World Defence Organization (WDO)

The release of atom power has changed everything except our way of thinking... the solution to this problem lies in the heart of mankind. If only I had known, I should have become a watchmaker.

~ Albert Einstein

15.1 The Birth of a Police Force

Imagine that police forces have not yet been invented, and there have been a spate of burglaries in your area. Householders getting unnerved, respond by employing security guards with each householder having their own security guard exclusively guarding their property.

This works well, and burglaries decrease. However it's costly keeping all these security guards in place, and householders have to forego luxuries such as expensive holidays and new cars in order to afford them.

Then one day, at a community meeting, they decide that wouldn't it be more efficient to pool their resources and create a local police service, with each householder finding the only spend around 5% of what they were otherwise spending on an individual burglar deterrent.

Moving over to a shared policing service, allowed the homeowners to save 95% of their current spend yet maintaining an effective level of policing.

Once they had the Police force in place, homeowners looked back in bewilderment, shaking their heads, wondering what foolishness and need for a "personal security guard" had made them develop their own individual deterrents and waste money for all these years.

15.2 Is there a Need for Armed Forces at the Country level?

The era of true peace on earth will not come as long as a tremendous percentage of your taxes goes to educate men in the trades of slaughter.

~Reginald Wright Kauffman

The previous story was of course dreamt up, however I feel when it comes to the armed forces, we are exactly in the same wasteful situation as those householders each with their own "individual burglar deterrent".

I see no good answer why each country needs to have its own individual armed forces.

Let's look at this more closely by examining the purposes of an Armed Force; there are five main purposes:

a.   Defending the country's territories against outside attack.
b.   Help to repatriate the country's nationals from an overseas danger zone.
c.   Assist in the case of national disasters such as earthquakes, floods etc.
d.   To join together with other countries as allies and fight a common enemy.
e.   To unilaterally attack another country.

If we were to completely disband all our armed forces and to totally rely on a single shared armed service funded by the various participating countries, then we would still be able to meet the first four objectives (a to d).

It's only the last objective, that of having the freedom of unilaterally attacking another country that we would be unable to do – and that frankly is something most would say three cheers to. If our rationale and the facts are such that we are unable to justify and convince our allies of the need to join us in making war, then there must be some serious deficiency in our argument and it is not a war that we should contemplate.

15.3 WDO

I see the WDO as a single military entity whose personnel derive from all of the constituent countries that have opted into the WDO. They would have a charter outlining their responsibilities, which would be points (a) to (d) of the previous section. Each of the WDO participants would share the costs of running the WDO, and the WDO itself would have military assets distributed across its member states.

The WDO command would not take directions from any single nation, it would need to carry out its duties impartially as required by its charter, however it would be answerable to a council of its member states who would ensure that it's correctly carrying out its charter responsibilities.

15.4 The Defence Dividend

> *Every gun that is made, every warship launched, every rocket fired signifies in the final sense, a theft from those who hunger and are not fed, those who are cold and are not clothed. This world in arms is not spending money alone. It is spending the sweat of its labourers, the genius of its scientists, the hopes of its children. This is not a way of life at all in any true sense. Under the clouds of war, it is humanity hanging on a cross of iron.*
> ~ *Dwight D. Eisenhower, 16 April 1953*

The world spends $1464 Billion per annum on defence[1], equating to $219 per person (figure 4), and directly employing 85 million people.

World Spend on Military	1,464,000,000,000	Sipri
World Population	6,692,030,277	World Bank
World spend per person	218.77	$ per person on defence
World income per person	880	$ per person, South Asia

Figure 4: World spend per person on Military (2008)

With the average South Asian earning $880 per person[2], that represents 25% of their income.

My estimate is that the WDO would only require around 10% of the current spend,

1   World Military Spending
     http://www.sipri.org/yearbook/2009/05 http://www.worldometers.info/military/
2   World Bank regional Gross National Income figures
     http://siteresources.worldbank.org/DATASTATISTICS/Resources/reg_wdi.pdf

thereby releasing 76 Million people worldwide and $1300 Billions to be reallocated to more useful work.

The world would also become a safer place, because as countries demob their armed forces and opt into the WDO the external threat would steadily diminish as there would be fewer countries with their own armed forces capable of aggression. In theory if every country in the world joined the WDO then there would be zero threat of external attack from other countries and the WDO would only need a minimal or zero force to carry out this aspect of its role.

15.5   Objections to the WDO

> *If you want to make enemies, try to change something.*
> ~Woodrow Wilson

There would be major objections to the WDO forming coming from a broad front.

People working in the Armed Forces
With 84 million people in the armed forces worldwide, they would fear becoming unemployed and redundant and being used to fighting, would fight politically for their survival, stoking fears in people's mind and getting politicians to support their cause.

Firms manufacturing weapons and military hardware
The $1464 Billion being spent worldwide supports many weapons and military hardware companies. They too would respond aggressively to their market disappearing and lobby politicians and the general public to their cause and seek to conjure up false fears and exaggerate threats.

Politicians whose constituencies contain large weapons manufacturers
Politicians whose constituencies contain major weapons manufacturers would feel it their natural duty to protect the livelihoods of their constituents (and their vote base).

Politicians jumping onto the bandwagon and garnering cheap votes
Many politicians would see this as an opportunity to gain cheap votes, and use the issue to whip up misguided patriotism and jingoism.

Political Egos
Many politicians would see the loss of their own armed forces as a blow to their

egos and standing in the world, as it removes their power to take unilateral action.

People getting fearful and having a misplaced sense of patriotism and ego
With a plethora of confusing messages arising from the various stakeholders, it's only natural that a section of the general public would get fearful and have their patriotism whipped up, resulting in them opposing the WDO.

15.6   Transition to the WDO

As outlined, the WDO would involve significant structural change and stress, and in order to minimise the discomfort and objections any move to it would need to be accompanied with large amounts of transitional support to retrain and equip armies of people with the new skills to take up meaningful and respectful civilian jobs with dignity.

There would also need to be transitional support for industries affected by this to make it easier for them to convert to civilian uses.

I would prefer a quick solution, and in principle see no sound logical reason why we should delay on setting up the WDO.

However if the objections mentioned in the last section prove too difficult to overcome in one go, then an alternative would be for the WDO to be initially set up by the European Union whose 27 members have already pooled some sovereignty, and once it is in place, the WDO could then expand by incorporating countries from outside the EU.

> *A day will come when a cannon will be exhibited in museums, just as instruments of torture are now, and the people will be astonished that such a thing could have been.*
>
> *~Victor Hugo*

16. Missing Organizations – Space Defence Agency (SDA)

I couldn't help but say to [Mr. Gorbachev], just think how easy his task and mine might be in these meetings that we held if suddenly there was a threat to this world from another planet. [We'd] find out once and for all that we really are all human beings here on this earth together.

~*Ronald Reagan, 1985*

16.1   Is there Intelligent Life On Other Planets?

The question has been asked numerous times, lets try and reason it out.

The very fact that we are able to ask the question means that there is a greater than zero probability of life being present in the universe, lets call it P. P may be a very small number, but when multiplied with the large number of planets in the entire universe we would end up with a small finite number of planets with the conditions to support life. That finite number could be just one, or equally it could be greater than one, say ten or twelve or even fifty.

The point is we don't know, however we cannot rule it out as a possibility.

In 2007 a group of leading British astronomers[1] told the British Government that they believed intelligent extra-terrestrials almost certainly exist on distant planets beyond our solar system.

16.2   How might an Intelligent Extra-Terrestrial (alien) respond to us?

How would an advanced intelligent alien species from another planet respond to

---

1   Guardian, Is there life out there? UK Scientists report
    http://www.guardian.co.uk/science/2007/jun/06/spaceexploration.uknews

us? This is a difficult question to answer, since it depends on their culture and outlook towards life and their level of development.

I think it's best answered by looking at some of our own behaviour in the past.

Viewed as Resource Occupiers

In the 19th century, the plains of America were populated with Bison, however people took over and hunted the bison nearly to extinction and taking the land for ourselves.

One response therefore could be that an alien species may view human beings much as we viewed the bison, as a lower species occupying valuable resources and seek to expropriate the resources for themselves by clearing us from the planet.

Viewed as a Resource in our own right

An alternative view might be that the alien species could view us, much as plantation owners viewed native Africans, a resource to be enslaved and put to work in their equivalent of plantations, in short human beings would become a resource to help support their lifestyle.

Viewed as a Peer Civilisation to Trade with

They may however be an intelligent and sensitive culture, and view us as peers, and as a species from whom they could both learn and help develop and trade with.

16.3   Impact on Policy Making

Ultimately, which of the three scenarios would prevail is anyone's guess. Perhaps we may be the more advanced civilisation, and so it would be us making the decision.

The key point is that we don't know, and it would be foolhardy to assume. I am surprised that we have not seriously addressed this issue and have prepared to defend ourselves against an alien species. To wait until something happens to start preparing is taking a rather huge and unnecessary risk.

We're like a group of countries who cannot see beyond their own particular horizon, and busy infighting amongst each other, completely blind to any external invading force until it is upon us, at which point it may be too late to do anything about it.

This is why I feel we need to innovate the Space Defence Agency (SDA) into existence.

Whilst this may all be resources wasted, nonetheless I don't think it right for us to be simply unprepared due to a collective failure of imagination or complacency, and the plaintiff epitaph "It hadn't happened before..." would not be a fitting one for the human race.

16.4   The SDA Mandate

The SDA would conduct research into defending earth against attack from aliens, and sponsor weapons and communication systems that would operate in space.

It would have its own military personnel and would establish outposts that would act as bases and space refuelling stations hosting early warning systems.

16.5   Funding the SDA

As discussed in the last chapter implementing the WDO would release large amounts of economic resources as well as technical research and manufacturing capabilities and a portion of these resources could be channelled towards the SDA.

> *If you fail to prepare, you're prepared to fail.*
>
> ~*Mark Spitz*

17. Missing Organizations – World Elections Commission (WEC)

Whenever a man has cast a longing eye on offices, a rottenness begins in his conduct.

~ Thomas Jefferson

17.1 Conducting Trials – A Scenario

Lets imagine that after seeing some serious miscarriages of justice, people have got very concerned that there should never again be a miscarriage of justice and they come up with a proposal for a new system.

The new system proposes allowing the accused to select and employ the trial lawyers, the judge, as well as all the court officials.

Almost everyone would balk at the naivety of such a system as it gives the accused huge scope to abuse the system and put in place puppets to ensure their acquittal.

17.2 Great Expectations

Nobody would take more than a moment's reflection to reject the proposed trial system just outlined. However when it comes to elections we cheerfully use a similar system to the flawed one just described above and expect it to deliver the goods.

An election is similar to a trial, with the citizens forming the jury, and the media playing the role of the trial lawyers posing questions to the various competing political parties.

In countries that lack deep and longstanding civil societies, there are huge incentives for the ruling party to introduce bias and rig the election, behaving as the accused in the earlier example.

The ruling party has huge powers at its disposal to introduce bias and rig an election, ranging from phantom voters, the discarding of valid votes for the opposition, to simply lying about the results by having corrupt officials.

With the huge rewards possible from the side benefits of holding office, there are large incentives for the ruling party to cheat if they feel they can get away with it. Even if the outside world suspects and disapproves, the ruling party can hide behind sovereignty leaving the outside world to simply tut-tut its disapproval until eventually pragmatism takes over and it's business as usual.

Therefore in closed / tightly controlled societies with less developed civil societies there is always a high risk of elections being rigged and stolen.

This is only natural, and it is unreasonable for the world to expect otherwise.

17.3   Recent History

Looking at recent history, there have been numerous elections with disputed results: Iran[2] in 2009, Kenya in 2008, Honduras, Zimbabwe and Afghanistan to name just a few recent cases, with Mynamar deserving special mention.

These outcomes bear witness to the flawed logic underlying the current approach towards elections in countries lacking mature institutions and electorates.

17.4   Impact on the Global Community

> *Those who are too smart to engage in politics are punished by being governed by those who are dumber.*
>
> ~Plato

A stolen election in a country is a tragedy and disaster for the country itself, but it's also an issue for the wider global community. People living elsewhere may not always appreciate this.

2   Iran 2009 Election http://news.bbc.co.uk/1/hi/8102400.stm

Less Control and Extremism

As the government has reduced its ties to its people – it's able to win elections without their direct approval – there are reduced constraints on the government and it's more likely to veer towards extremism.

Reduced Cultural, Economic and Technical Development

As the government has reduced dependence on its electorate, it feels less of an incentive to promote their well-being and overall the country would suffer reduced cultural, economic and technical development. This impacts the world too as the country turns inwards and contributes less to the world.

Migration

People would tend to flee the repressive regime and go to other countries, and this too can create an issue for other countries social infrastructure in having to deal with increased demand.

17.5   World Elections Commission

It's for these reasons that I believe we need to invent a World Elections Commission (WEC) with the direct responsibility of organizing and carrying out elections throughout the world.

Countries that have signed up to the WEC would no longer have their own Election Commissions; instead the WEC would organize all aspects of their elections including the resourcing of equipment and systems and be responsible for declaring the election result.

Elections require specialized equipment, infrastructure and communications and the WEC would utilise its own equipment to conduct elections and reuse the same equipment in different countries.

17.6   Benefits of the WEC

> *"I consider it important, indeed urgently necessary, for intellectual workers to get together, both to protect their own economic status and, also, generally speaking, to secure their influence in the political field."*
>
> ~*Albert Einstein*

Fair Elections

The most significant benefit of the WEC would be to ensure that elections are uniform and fair, and that the party the citizens truly wish to see in power wins the election.

Fairly run elections would bring more people into politics as they would now feel that they have a genuine chance of winning as the election is no longer being rigged.

Responsive Government

Once political parties know that they cannot rig their way into power or keep power falsely, that would create an incentive for them to put in the hard work needed for good sound government and policies that would genuinely win the confidence of people.

Progress

Being properly managed, countries would make more progress in all spheres ranging from cultural through to scientific development.

Greater Investment in Systems whilst saving Costs

The election equipment would be used much more intensively, as with 150 countries in the WEC, the same equipment would be used in 30 elections per year, as opposed to being used once every five years. This level of reuse allows much greater investment in systems, equipment and anti-fraud practices. However despite the greater investment in systems the costs per country would drop significantly due to the systems being shared.

17.7   Objections to the WEC

The main objection would be that countries want their "Sovereignty" and would view the WEC as outside interference. However they would be entirely wrong in this respect as no sovereignty is ever transferred, all that's happening is that the Election Commission has been outsourced to ensure a completely open, fair and transparent election.

In any case, if the election process is not fair, then the sovereignty it bestows is stillborn, as the peoples wishes have been ignored and their right to self-determination compromised.

In the absence of justice, what is sovereignty but organized robbery?
~ Saint Augustine

18. Missing Organizations – World Compliance Organization (WCO)

In Section 14.6 I spoke about the problem of international agreements where the parties agreed to adopt conventions such as the Human Rights Convention, but then ignored their responsibilities and paid little heed to the agreements; the proposed solution was for all agreements to have a detailed implementation plan with pre-defined escalation procedures and mandatory penalties.

I see the role of a new body, the World Compliance Organization to ensure that countries worldwide carry out their responsibilities under the various agreements.

The WCO would play a pro-active role by directly monitoring compliance and on finding deviations agree with the country in question action plans to bring them back in line. The WCO would have the ability to fine the country as prescribed in the agreement being enforced. WCO officials would have global visas valid for travel to any country that's signatory to the WCO, and could not be denied access.

The WCO would have an additional enforcement role in those agreements where human life is threatened[3]. Thus the WCO would have its own enforcement force including a military force that could be rapidly deployed without needing permission from other bodies or countries. In short the WCO acts to police and ensure countries stick to their commitments and when life is threatened it can directly intervene.

Compliance and Enforcement require particular skills and mindset, and it's more effective to have the skills and resources concentrated in a single organization than diluted and dissipated across a number of teams monitoring particular agreements.

3   When human life is in threat, due to the time pressure, a fast track mechanism to ensure compliance is
     required, namely a rapid deployment military force that plays an enforcement role

An an example, China recently[4] imprisoned Liu Xiaboa, for organizing a petition for greater political freedom. Liu appeared to have been exercising his rights to freedom of opinion and expression under Article 19 of the Universal Declaration of Human Rights. So in this case, I would expect the WCO to take the matter up with the Chinese Government, and expedite his release as well as fining the Chinese Government for infringing their international responsibilities.

With its global passport, the WCO could deploy to hotspots at a moments notice in order to uphold international law and agreements, without needing to gain administrative approval and visas, hopefully helping to ensure that episodes such the genocide in Rwanda never reoccur.

The key point is that Sovereignty should not mean immunity from having to carry out ones responsibilities and the WCO would be somewhat like a global policeman ensuring that countries play fair and keep to their agreements.

4   December 2009

19. Missing Organizations – World Dispute Resolution Organization (WDRO)

I recoil with horror at the ferociousness of man. Will nations never devise a more rational umpire of differences than force? Are there no means of coercing injustice more gratifying to our nature than a waste of the blood of thousands and of the labour of millions of our fellow creatures?

~Thomas Jefferson

19.1 Law of the Jungle

Lets imagine a country where courts of law, lawyers, juries and trials have not yet been invented. Lets also imagine that there is no king or ruler whom you could go to settle differences.

In this country, how would people settle differences? If their initial negotiations fail, and one party remains stubbornly obdurate, then differences are likely to fester unsettled.

At this point there are three options:
(i) Accept and live with the status quo, putting up with the injustice
(ii) Find an indirect way of putting pressure on the other party to change
(iii) Resort to direct action and force

Asked to describe such a country, it would be fair to characterise it as "Might is Right" situation and effectively the law of the Jungle.

19.2 Earth's Jungles

The country described above would be seen as backward, foolish and lacking civilisation and most people would only need a moment's reflection to denounce it.

Were a political party in power to ever suggest doing away with its domestic judicial system, its citizens would rightly rise up and evict such a foolish party from power.

Yet, when it comes to the domain in which our countries operate – they (our countries) are entities operating in a very similar backward and uncivilised regime.

It's not an exact comparison as there is the International Court of Justice in The Hague[1], this being the principal judicial organ of the UN. However it has restricted jurisdiction with both states involved in a dispute needing to agree to bring the case to the Court and to accept its jurisdiction.

Imagine in a dispute with a builder who's done shoddy work on your house, you decide to take the builder to court, however the court says we can only act if the builder agrees to accept our jurisdiction – there would be no prizes for guessing what the builder would say!

There have also been some recent moves in resolving trade disputes with the WTO, however overall there is a missing legal entity which has jurisdiction over all countries[2] and where disputes between countries can be efficiently and fairly resolved.

Therefore to some extent, our countries are operating in a jungle, and the fact that we have tolerated this for as long as we have should be a matter of shame for all politicians.

19.3   What's stopping clearing up the Jungle?

> *"One of the great attractions of patriotism it fulfills our worst wishes. In the person of our nation we are able, vicariously, to bully and cheat. Bully and cheat, what's more, with a feeling that we are profoundly virtuous."*
>
> ~ Aldous Huxley

---

1   The International Court of Justice http://www.the-hague.info/court/
2   i.e. its jurisdiction would override sovereignty.

Human beings are remarkably clever and intelligent and we've built complex domestic legal systems with vast case laws. So why have we singularly failed when it comes to developing a compulsory judicial system for the settlement of international disputes with the ability to hand out binding judgements?

The answer can only be, because the powers that be don't want it. In a "Might is Right" jungle, big beasts can roam the world with little to check or penalise them and a formal legal system for countries that would take over dispute resolution between countries and which could impose compulsory judgements would clip their wings.

Ultimately the reason is certain large countries prefer their freedom to act as unconstrained bullies on a world stage.

19.4   World Dispute Resolution Organization (WDRO)

> *The direct use of force is such a poor solution to any problem, it is generally employed only by small children and large nations.*
> ~David Friedman

It's time for the world to mature and realise direct force is never a lasting solution and for the bullies to put away their slingshots. The world community needs to invent the World Dispute Resolution Organization (WDRO) that would act as a formal legal entity to which countries could bring their disputes to be resolved. The WDRO would have the jurisdiction to impose compulsory and binding judgements on both countries, overriding sovereignty.

In addition to disputes between countries, the WDRO would also be able to help resolve disputes involving a single country and a particular geographically defined community or tribe, with the precondition that the community would accept as binding any judgement.

I see the WDRO as using a Jury system to make the judgement instead of a fixed panel of legal experts. The reason for this is that I trust a jury of normal everyday people to come up with a common sense and fair decision, and as juries work well in domestic law then there is every reason to expect the same in an international sphere. Juries would be drawn at random from ordinary people from around the world and kept in quarantine throughout the trial to ensure there are no attempts at biasing them. Each side would bring its expert witnesses to ensure the juries are fully aware of all the relevant issues prior to deciding.

The countries involved in the dispute should have a minimum period to attempt to settle the dispute amicably between each other on a bilateral basis with no outside involvement of any kind, and I anticipate this to be eight years as that represents at least a couple of governments in power. However if after eight years the dispute is still unsettled, then either of the countries should have the right to bring the dispute to the WDRO for resolution, with both sides mandated to accept its jurisdiction and judgement.

19.5   Benefits of the WDRO

The key benefit of the WDRO is that it offers countries an alternative to war and a timely route to a binding and final peaceful settlement.

In the case of disputes between a community / tribe and a country, it offers the community an alternative to direct action (or terrorism).

It is free of outside political lobbying and interference and would be a way of achieving a just settlement rather than leaving the issue to fester as both sides balk indefinitely at facing the inevitable and prolong festering of a poisonous status quo.

I don't agree with terrorism and would never condone it, however I can understand that facing a seemingly permanent stalemate with little hope of progress, people feel painted into corners and tempted to resort to direct action, becoming terrorists. Having the WDRO would help lance such boils before they leak their deadly puss and create terror networks.

Politicians on both sides could let the WDRO take the politically unpalatable decisions that they themselves have balked from and not had the courage to expend their political capital upon. In that sense they could find themselves implementing what they might privately admit needed to be done, whilst in public letting the WDRO carry the can for it and be the target for any flak from their publics, thereby avoiding political suicide.

As private citizens we accept there are constraints on our behaviour and however aggrieved, we can't take the law into our own hands and need to resolve matters peacefully and rationally through the courts. The WDRO would force countries to come to the same realisation and behave in a more civilised and mature manner.

I am certain that had an organization such as the WDRO existed, the dispute between India and Pakistan over Kashmir, and the dispute between Israel and Palestine would have been resolved many years ago with the saving of countless lives.

> *All wars are follies, very expensive and very mischievous ones. In my opinion, there never was a good war or a bad peace. When will mankind be convinced and agree to settle their difficulties by arbitration?*
>
> *~Benjamin Franklin*

20. Extensions to the Universal Declaration of Human Rights

Although an excellent document, the Universal Declaration of Human Rights was drafted over sixty years ago and like all documents need to be reviewed and updated time-to-time to ensure its relevance and new ideas and thoughts get incorporated.

In this section I look at some of the extensions I would wish to see in the Declaration of Human Rights.

20.1 The right for an individual to choose their clothing and hairstyle at all times

The right to choose what to wear needs to be declared a fundamental human right, to be decided exclusively by the individual. The only exception is that the attire should not be of a form that a majority would find obscene and likely to give offence.

This right is needed because increasingly religions are veering towards fundamentalism and dictating dress code and hairstyle and coercing people into observing it, in the process oppressing people and taking away their freedom.

Clothing is a fundamental way of expressing oneself, and having to follow a rigid code is psychologically oppressive and the removal of personal choice affects a person's sense of dignity and self-worth and takes away some of their identity and individualism.

To an extent this right is already in the Declaration of Human Rights as Article 19 states: "Everyone has the right to freedom of opinion and expression", and choice of clothing can be seen as a form of personal expression. That said, it is an important area, and for the avoidance of doubt it's best to be explicitly stated.

20.2 The right for any group of citizens to devolve from their country and to set up their own state or independent nation

The only justifiable purpose of political institutions is to ensure the unhindered development of the individual."

~ *Albert Einstein*

Lets imagine we happen to live in a large extended family. So the grandparents, parents, their children and their children's children all live together in this very large house.

After a while, people being what they are, differences develop and one of the family members thinks that they can form a better life for themselves by living outside the extended family and decides to leave.

In this situation, no one would try and pressure them to stay, or to paint them as being a rebel because of their desire to do their own thing, and were anyone to try to do so, most people would regard that as repressive and a bad move.

When a group of people wish to devolve from their mother country and form their own small independent nation, then the situation is analogous to someone wishing to leave an extended family or seeking a divorce, albeit on a larger scale. Just as we would not pressurise someone to stay in an extended family or in a marriage, we should not seek to force people to remain as citizens in a country against their will.

This right may seem controversial, as we tend to be blinded by patriotism and a false sense of duty and historic identity – forgetting that these are fabricated concepts and ultimately abstract creations of our minds. What actually matters is that the maximum numbers of people have the greatest chance to increase their potential and if that's to be achieved by splitting into smaller countries then that's absolutely fine and to be encouraged as a way towards greater progress and happiness.

Therefore *any* group of people should have the right to devolve from their country and set up as an independent nation – if that is what a significant majority of them want.

One might argue that this right can also be arrived at by extrapolating Article 4 of the Declaration of Human Rights, which states "No one shall be held in slavery or servitude". If a large group of people within one part of a country wish to be self managing and form their own independent state, then for the majority in the country to deny it to them, is a form of tyranny and treats them as inferior or in servitude in the sense that they are being denied the freedom that they desire and held against their will in an "extended nation family"

Natural justice also implies the need for this right, as democracy dictates that people should have the right of self determination and to attempt to impose some other management system onto them is undemocratic as it leads to one group of people seeking to dictate to another group of people against their will.

Having this right on the statutes would put pressure on national governments to deliver and become more inclusive in their management of the country in the knowledge that if they ignore extremities or sections of their nation then the people there may up sticks and devolve into a separate nation.

I have argued for this purely from the perspective of a fundamental democratic right, since am strongly of the view that countries and nations are divisive and negative constructs that keep people apart and as mentioned earlier I would ideally like to see all national borders dissolved and the world move towards a very small number of large Country Unions such as the EU, with complete and unhindered freedom of movement of people, goods and services and a common currency, in short for the political management layer to recede transparently into the background much as a common utility or plumbing service.

20.3   The right to be governed by politicians free of corruption, and for Political Mismanagement to be classed as a crime against the individual.

Corruption

> *Politics is supposed to be the second-oldest profession. I have come to realize that it bears a very close resemblance to the first.*
> ~ *Ronald Reagan*

Were a gang of thieves to break into a public hospital and steal expensive hospital equipment, there would be an immediate outcry at how this was allowed to happen with people rightly upset about the loss. However when a group of politicians siphons off millions of dollars from their nations funds through crooked deals and corruption, that crime manages to stay in the background failing to achieve the same level of exposure with people almost accepting a level of corruption as a necessary evil and a fact of life.

However the millions siphoned off could have built and completely equipped many new hospitals and schools. Comparatively speaking, the crooked politicians are a far greater and insidious threat than the thieves, as their crime tends to go unnoticed and on a greater scale.

A rare example is the expose[1] by the British High Commissioner Sir Edward Clay of corruption in Kenya, where it was estimated that the missing money could fund anti-retroviral treatment for every HIV-positive Kenyan for ten years.

Wrongheaded Policies

> *Politics is perhaps the only profession for which no preparation is thought necessary.*
>
> ~ *Robert Louis Stevenson*

Corruption is not the only form of political mismanagement. An even greater political mismanagement is allowing inherited wrongheaded policies that stifle economic and social progress to remain in place, or to initiate new policies that inadvertently have a negative effect on economic and social progress. I see it as greater political mismanagement because it systemically and silently chokes progress.

In Chapter 6 and 8.2, I outlined how political mismanagement has kept a number of countries impoverished and stunted their growth. As mentioned in 6.2 this mismanagement is effectively a crime perpetuated against every individual in the country, silently removing monies from everyone's purses and wallets and forcing them to accept a less prosperous life. Therefore political mismanagement needs to be seen as a crime against humanity.

When accountants, management consultants, financial advisers etc provide their service they are open to being sued for giving wrong advise. The same is true for doctors and lawyers who can be sued for malpractice. I find it odd that in politics one of the most important professions, the only sanction is to fail to be reappointed at the end of their term. Politics need to be brought in line with other professions with

---

1   Kenya, Corruption
     http://www.economist.com/world/middleeast-africa/displaystory.cfm?story_id=E1_PGVQSDG

politicians able to be sued for continuing with policies that hold back economic and social growth. There needs to be a twenty year period after they leave office during which they are open to being sued for political malpractice and mismanagement.

This will worry a lot of politicians and make politics a far riskier profession. I see politicians having to take out political indemnity insurance, and having to get more formal qualifications for the job (that would reduce their insurance premiums). However all that is a good thing if it puts some people off and makes others take the role more seriously and make greater preparations for it. That said, there will need to be safeguards to protect them against frivolous or vindictive cases. Ultimately though it's about increasing accountability and getting politicians to take responsibility. Knowing that they may pay a price later would ensure that they act more responsibly and professionally and ensure they are able to defend their policies with sound reasoning.

20.4   The right of any individual or group of individuals to challenge bad political policy and practice

I have come to the conclusion that politics is too serious a matter to be left to the politicians.

~*Charles de Gaulle*

If a government is following bad policies, and they have an unsophisticated electorate then where would the voice of reason come from to turn them back onto the right track? Traditional thinking would suggest it should come from their political opposition who ought to take the opportunity to point out mistakes and build their own credibility by suggesting corrective actions. However what happens if the opposition is ineffective or its politician benefits from the same wrongheaded policies. The media is another source able to act as referee and expose mismanagement, however that too can be supine and for its own interests choose to fall in line with the government of the day.

Therefore I think it's important for any interested person or body to be able to challenge bad policy in the courts. Once again there need to be safeguards against frivolous or mischievous cases.

Put another way, although governments have the right to make laws, it would be perverse to grant them the right to make bad law and follow bad policy, and therefore any law should be able to be challenged in the courts, and if after expert witnesses have given their testimony, a jury is convinced that the law is in fact perverse, then it would be right for the government to be obliged to reconsider.

Traditionally this is the function of a second or upper house, but they can often play a rubber stamp role or vote along party lines and let bad policy through and so the right to challenge bad political policy needs to be considered as a safeguard and basic right.

The only exception to this is where the policy has been arrived at in a referendum.

20.5   The right of every individual to decide whom to marry and the decision can only be taken when the individual has reached a minimum age.

Marriage is probably one of the biggest decisions taken by an individual and will shape a major part of their life and future. I'm deeply concerned that in some societies the decision on whom to marry is taken by the extended family with the target obliged to "go along" with their choice. This is fundamentally wrong and inhuman, and akin to a form of slavery in that the person is not treated as an individual with rights. Individuals need to have the right to make their own decision on such an important issue.

In some cases[2] girls as young as eight have been married off by their families. As they were a child at the time and in no position to give consent, this is completely wrong and there needs to be a universal minimum age prior to which no individual may consent to marriage, and marriages where one of the parties was under the minimum age would be automatically considered null and void.

2   Saudi Women Can Drive. Just Let Them
     http://www.washingtonpost.com/wp-dyn/content/article/2009/08/14/AR2009081401598.html

21. War and Weapons

I dream of giving birth to a child who will ask, "Mother, what was war?"

~ Eve Merriam

21.1 The Nuclear Race

Nations have recently been led to borrow billions for war; no nation has ever borrowed largely for education. Probably, no nation is rich enough to pay for both war and civilization. We must make our choice; we cannot have both.

~ Abraham Flexner

Imagine a couple of neighbours on your street fell out with each other, and each became suspicious that the other would throw white paint onto their lawn, and started stockpiling cans of white paint to retaliate, each continuing until both had filled their entire garages with cans of white paint. You would immediately dub them as nuts without a moment's hesitation.

Yet when the actors change from being a couple of neighbours to two superpowers then the charade has continued unabated for almost four decades!

The Nuclear Weapons Race has been rightly called "Mutually Assured Destruction" with its apt acronym. Between 1940 and 1996 the United States spent at least $5.5 trillion on its nuclear weapons programme[1]. As the USSR had a similar arsenal a good working assumption would be that it too spent in the same ballpark. Hence the two super powers spent $11 trillion on building items that each of them would do their best to never use. Like the two fools and their cans of paint, the superpowers each built up an arsenal of 10,000 warheads[2]. With only two bombs

1   Atomic Audit: The Costs and Consequences of U.S. Nuclear Weapons Since 1940
     http://www.ipb.org/Schwartz%20presentationText.pdf
2   Nuclear Arms Race   http://en.wikipedia.org/wiki/Nuclear_arms_race

being needed to convince the participants to end World War II in the Pacific, what were they thinking of when extending their arsenals to 10,000 warheads.

Had the $11 trillion been spent on education and scientific research one can only imagine what benefit it could have provided to humankind, rather than being squandered on a fool's errand.

Hindsight makes things easier, however as the issue was one of trust, surely the leaders of these superpowers could look back and see how people dealt with lack of trust in the past. In the middle ages kings used to cement ties with other countries by getting people in their family married to someone from the other country's royal family. Perhaps we should have had the top 1000 politicians in the US get one member of their family to marry someone from the family of the top 1000 politicians in the USSR, with half living in the US and the other half in the USSR. It may seem unorthodox but if it saved $11 trillion then it was worth a second thought. Other options would have been to station a US officer as an observer in every barracks and ammunitions factory in the USSR and vice versa. If it saved $11 trillions and helped make the world safer then we needed to be thinking of alternate risk reduction scenarios.

Thankfully there now exists a new US determination[3] to reduce levels of nuclear weapons, however with the two superpowers having 23,000 out of a world total of 24,000 that is still far too high, but it's encouraging to see the political will there to eventually eliminate all nuclear weapons.

What I still find puzzling is why the common person in the street tolerated the madness for so long[4]. There were pacifists complaining about it, but it needed the majority to protest in sufficient numbers to help the politicians gain courage to venture outside their limited mindsets.

21.2 Is it hypocritical to prevent other states from going nuclear?

This is a question that's been vexing me for some time. Is it hypocritical for countries with nuclear weapons themselves to prevent others from going nuclear?

The short answer is yes, it is. However it's not that straightforward. If the country

3   Barack Obama's new offensive against nuclear weapons
    http://www.guardian.co.uk/world/2009/apr/04/barack-obama-nuclear-weapons
4   One of the reasons I wanted to write this book was to highlight the numerous other madness's we
    continue to tolerate.

in question is not a democracy, then in theory its actions are not expressions of the free will and desires of their people and are merely the expression of the will of the group that have somehow seized power and held onto it.

Therefore as they're not necessarily the will/ desires of the people of the country, there is less need to accord respect to those desires and therefore I feel it's right to seek to prevent non-democratic countries from going nuclear.

The only qualms I have with this argument is that a number of countries that are not democratic already have nuclear weapons, so it remains open to a charge of hypocrisy if one were to seek to stop others on the basis of a lack of democracy.

I am particularly worried about undemocratic countries where religious leaders hold political power, because they tend to have different value systems from normal countries, money is of less importance and religious dogma more important than human rights.

On this basis I felt it was justified to seek to prevent Iran developing nuclear weapons, as Iran is not merely undemocratic, but it's religious leaders play a broad and deep unelected role in government, including vetting who can stand for parliament.

Of course were Iran to move to a proper democracy and shed their non-democratic religious baggage then my view would change.

21.3   World Defence Organization

> *We have failed to grasp the fact that mankind is becoming a single unit, and that for a unit to fight against itself is suicide.*
> ~ *Havelock Ellis*

I've discussed at length[5] the need for the World Defence Organization (WDO), in which countries disband their national armies and pool together their armies to create a single WDO to provide a defence umbrella for them and their overseas interests.

Were the WDO to become a reality, and all the countries in the world to join it, then in theory as no country had a national army anymore, then no country would

---

5   Chapter 15

need to fear aggression – there being no national armies with which to launch aggression.

In addition the WDO would release huge amounts of resources worldwide that could be used in other areas of human development.

This is something our leaders should be addressing as a matter of priority.

21.4   Nuclear World Defence Organization

Organized slaughter, we realize, does not settle a dispute; it merely silences an argument.

~James Frederick Green

In our joined up world, I am unable to understand the rationale for countries to have their own independent nuclear deterrent. For entirely the same reasons given for the WDO, it makes sense to have a shared defence organization protecting against nuclear aggression.

However even if the WDO were aimed at the top 60 countries in the world, it would take time to establish and put in place and get working due to the large number of countries involved and demobilising all their armed forces, retraining etc.

Hence I see the need for a separate parallel effort, the Nuclear World Defence Organization (NWDO) that functions as a WDO for nuclear weapons. All existing nuclear countries would transfer their weapons into the NWDO that would take over their management and ownership, and gradually reduce its stockpile of weapons as the nuclear threat diminishes.

With the NWDO in place, the earlier question, on whether it's hypocritical to try and prevent other countries from developing nuclear weapons, would never arise, as no country apart from a pariah state would seek to have its own nuclear deterrent.

As an example of the benefits that would flow, in Britain there's been a controversy over the need to replace its Trident nuclear deterrent at a cost of £65 Billion[6] over 30 years. Were an organization such as the NWDO to be invented, then Trident

---

6   Trident replacement costs put at £65bn over 30 years
    http://www.independent.co.uk/news/uk/politics/trident-replacement-costs-put-at-16365bn-over-30-years-427149.html

would become redundant, and the monies saved could be spent on creating 16,250 new leisure centres instead i.e. a new leisure centre for every 1200 households[7].

21.5   Global Terrorism

> *We all have to be concerned about terrorism, but you will never end terrorism by terrorizing others.*
>
> ~ *Martin Luther King III*

The World Community's Behaviour

I'm not comfortable with the word "Terrorism". It carries an implicit suggestion that the people practicing it are irrational and not to be taken seriously due to their preference for violence.

A search for the definition of terrorism yields: "the calculated use of violence (or the threat of violence) against civilians in order to attain goals that are political or religious or ...". This definition holds the key, that although violence is being used it is "calculated" in order to achieve their ends, and calculation means some logic and analysis and sifting of options when formulating strategy, and not the work of some irrational psychopaths.

The question that leads to is why have these groups turned to violence and not sought other approaches? The short answer clearly is they feel they're more likely to achieve their aims with violence, but what is it in our society that makes groups come to this conclusion?

This may appear very naive, however my view is that the majority of people are intrinsically good, even terrorists but they get socialised and channelled into these behaviours, and then a tit for tat culture takes over until eventually it's a way of life.

As an example, Nelson Mandela has been feted for his statesmanship, leadership and noble behaviour, and was awarded the Nobel Peace prize in 1993 and the highest honour in Johannesburg, the freedom of the City. Yet for 27 years he was in prison with the South African state seeing him as a threat and accusing him of sabotage and treason. This illustrates how one person's freedom fighter becomes another person's terrorist and the label used really just depends on your political perspective.

---

7   Cost of a Leisure Centre is £4 million. Cost study: Chipping Norton leisure centre
http://www.building.co.uk/story.asp?storycode=1026279

It's for this reason I dislike the term terrorist as it discounts the possibility that there is a real cause there and categorises people as belonging to a lunatic fringe and therefore not to be dealt with seriously – as who would talk to a mad man.

What happens if a group of people have a dispute or grievance with a country due to a disagreement over its politics and behaviour, where are they to take their grievance for resolution? The group in question need not necessarily be citizens of the country in question. If they go to the courts within the country, they first need to find a judge foolhardy enough to take on the case. Assuming they are able to get their case heard, there's every chance the courts will side with the government who will do their utmost to politically fix the outcome or have the case declared out of scope due to its political nature. The group can't take their dispute to courts in other countries as that would cut across sovereignty. Therefore the group don't have that many formal established channels for settling their grievance. By denying them options we're painting such groups into a corner, and in a sense encouraging them to become vigilantes and take direct action, transforming into terrorists.

The nub of the problem is that we've created a world where countries are laws onto themselves and under the badge of sovereignty can strut around like cowboys in the Wild West.

The WDRO described earlier[8] would be an important vehicle to reduce terrorism by offering a real practical alternative for resolving disputes. I don't think people like being blown up to bits, and as in private life we overwhelmingly choose to go to court rather then grabbing a gun and taking the law into our own hands, similarly the majority of groups would shun terrorism if there were a real, just and pragmatic alternative framework in place.

The WDRO would need real teeth, and the ability to make and enforce decisions that a country and its people may not like. Just as all of us as ordinary citizens are entities governed by the law, and answerable to it in case of disputes then why should country entities be treated any differently. Similarly just as we trust the courts to come up with the correct decisions, a country entity needs also to have the same trust and cannot argue that the outcome could be biased, imagine the complete chaos that would follow if we as citizens took the same irrational line and argued courts could be biased. In any case, that's why Appeals courts exist and the WDRO would have a secondary higher court performing an appeals function.

I believe one of the reason's nothing like the WDRO has been put in place is that it suits countries to live in the "Wild West" because it allows them to get away with things without being answerable to others. That needs to change, and countries move to a more civilised formal framework where they are accountable and not a law onto themselves. In due course, history will regard these as the "bad old days" much as we look back at the Wild West.

> *"War is what happens when language fails"*
>
> ~ *Margaret Atwood*

The Terrorist's Behaviour

As just discussed, I believe we lack the formal political structural frameworks to deflate and prevent the raison d'être of terrorism, however I think there are also major faults on the part of terrorists.

The ends can never justify the means, and even a single drop of blood is simply too high a price to pay.

Terrorist leaders have taken the intellectually lazy route and are guilty of miscalculation and misleading their people. They may also have been cynical in calculating that a crackdown by the authorities will easily become heavy handed and stir up emotions, acting as a recruiting Sergeant for them to expand membership.

I say misleading because although they can dent large democracies and give them a bloody nose, that's really where it stops because democracies will fight back and until the terrorists change their ways, ultimately they're simply prolonging the misery of their followers, and in that sense are leading their followers into a dead end. It can be self-defeating for the terrorists too, since with each innocent life they take, a small part of their own humanity disappears.

Although more difficult to implement, peaceful non-violent action is ultimately far more effective as demonstrated by Mahatma Gandhi, and nowadays in the world of mass media, terrorists need to convert their old world thinking and realise it's a battle for minds that needs to be won. I have often felt that although I had sympathy for a cause, the way they were going about it was completely wrong and risked losing my sympathy, and they had simply not understood the power of the media and were losing huge opportunities to advance their cause through mismanagement and a fatal addiction to armed struggle. Anyone heading up a terrorist organization ideally needs to send all their senior people onto a marketing and public relationship course as that's where the real battleground lies and those are the weapons they're so desperately short of.

> *The terrible thing about terrorism is that ultimately it destroys those who practise it. Slowly but surely, as they try to extinguish life in others, the light within them dies.*
>
> ~ *Terry Waite*

21.6   War Crimes

> *Stripped of ethical rationalizations and philosophical pretensions, a crime is anything that a group in power chooses to prohibit.*
> ~ *Freda Adler*

We human beings are a remarkably inventive and ingenious race. Whilst this is normally beneficial, we can misuse this gift to concoct justifications for morally reprehensible actions. In each of the major genocides of the last century in Germany, Russia[9], Cambodia and Rwanda, the ruling party's had justifications for their actions at the time.

If a loophole exists that allows a country to legitimately declare war, then sooner or later our race's inventiveness will be used to rationalise and fabricate a justification to wriggle through the loophole. They can use this inventiveness to attribute crimes onto the other country, thereby justifying their action. This manifested itself with the war against Iraq[10], where we were in the somewhat bizarre situation of starting a war in order to ensure world peace and our self-defence; or with Israel going to war against the Palestinians yet again labelling it as "self defence".

Therefore as a global community we need to close this loophole and make it a criminal action for any country or ad-hoc group of countries to unilaterally declare war on any other country, with no exceptions.

This need not affect the rights of direct self defence, for example if a plane enters a country's airspace and is seen as a threat then of course the country has the right

---

9   Ukraine's Holodomor
10   2003, U.S led coalition invades Iraq

to defend itself – but only against that specific plane, and it cannot use that as an excuse to send its forces across its borders in retaliation.

The only way that a country should be able to declare war on another country is if it is specifically granted the right to do so by the world community[11]. Any other declaration of war needs to be treated as a criminal action undertaken by its political leaders.

> *Never think that war, no matter how necessary, nor how justified,*
> *is not a crime.*
>
> ~ *Ernest Hemingway*

11   as a last resort

Section 3

Commerce

22. Trade

Trade is often seen as a mixed blessing with people ambivalent about it, some fearing globalisation from an exploitative angle and others fearing its effect on their jobs – whilst as consumers simultaneously enjoying its benefits.

Because of this ambivalence, it's easy for Trade to become hijacked by political opportunists playing to people's fears. It's worth therefore taking an in-depth look at Trade and its surrounding issues.

22.1 Trade as Global Bonds

Peace is a natural effect of trade.

~ Charles de Montesquieu

Each time someone in a country trades with someone in another country, it involves a number of factors. The parties need to communicate and negotiate, meet and trust each other, often involving travel to the other's country. After the trade has concluded their mutual trust increases. Over time these trading linkages convert into friendships, and the travel increases mutual understanding of each other's cultures.

In effect therefore each trade can be regarded as an international link or bond of friendship between the two countries, with each party having a vested interest in both countries being at peace with each other. When multiplied across a large number of people and organisations, it creates a web of friendships holding the two countries together.

Free Trade therefore is a powerful force for the development of peace and stability across the world.

If a trade link can be viewed as a bond of friendship, then its opposite, the denial of trade can be viewed as stopping a bond of friendship developing, and from that perspective a somewhat cold and hostile act with each trade stopped viewable as a miniature act of enmity.

Trade Sanctions have been used to try and get countries to change their behaviour, e.g. the sanctions against South Africa during the apartheid period. If there were still any doubt, Sanctions expose the fact that restricting Trade can be a form of punishment or weapon.

Restricting trade therefore needs to be viewed as an expression of hostility and a form of economic warfare and making the world a more fragmented place.

22.2   Trade and Globalisation Benefits

Peace Dividend
By making the world more peaceful and stable, Trade brings a huge peace dividend for the world – manifested in a reduced need for armies, weapons and personnel.

Technology, Skills and Mindset
As companies expand around the world, they bring new technology and skills with them, helping others to develop faster and grow in prosperity. It also brings a new way of thinking and mindset, and helps developing countries to learn and grow at a faster pace.

Capital Investment
A country at an early stage of growth may not have all the resources itself to invest in new infrastructure and plant, and so Trade also brings in Capital from global investors, creating new employment and helping fuel growth.

Improved Living Standards
Global business tries to optimise each aspect of production process, so that the end product gets produced in the most cost effective manner. Each step is examined and executed in the most efficient way possible on the planet, keeping costs low and productivity high. This has led to a huge improvement in our living standards.

It's difficult to compare living standards across time, however as living standards improve, it would be natural to expect the better standards to lead to an increase in life expectancy and therefore life expectancy can be used as a proxy for living standards. In the United States life expectancy[1] changed from 47 years in 1900, to 68 years in 1950, rising to 77 years in 2000 an increase of 64%.

22.3   Anti Globalisation

I must confess I simply don't get the anti-globalisation[2] lobby.

The only issue I can appreciate is that multinationals should not be free to exploit local people, however am puzzled how giving people jobs at standards comparable or better than those being enjoyed by their compatriots working for other local employers, can be seen as exploitation.

However the situation could arise that a country goes soft on a particular multinational in order to attract them to the country, with the multinational using it to extract favours such as reduced environmental obligations or a more relaxed health and safety environment with the implied threat to move their operations elsewhere.

Alternatively the country may have less developed environmental / health and safety legislation, and therefore allowing the multinational to exploit the loopholes.

Those could be real concerns but they're easily resolvable details and shouldn't be allowed to derail the huge benefits of globalisation and trade, which would be like throwing the baby out with the bathwater!

To address the issues I'd be in favour of a global minimum standard (GMS) for Environment, Health & Safety, Employee development and Management that all multinationals would need to comply with when operating overseas. That would ensure that even if the country had very low standards, the multinational would still be obliged to meet the higher global standards. To ensure that this was not just a paper exercise, there would also need to be a monitoring body ensuring compliance.

1   Table 26. Life expectancy at birth, at 65 years of age, and at 75 years of age,
    by race and sex: United States, selected years 1900–2005
    http://www.cdc.gov/nchs/data/hus/hus08.pdf#listtables
2   As an aside, the issues that the Anti-Globalists are worried about only arise because we're fragmented into a number of countries each with varying standards that can be arbitraged. I argued earlier for the need to reform as a single country with worldwide scope – were this to happen it would remove this form of arbitrage. This leads to the somewhat ironic conclusion that the anti-globalists should support the single country world concept!

22.4 The Legacy of Trade Restrictions

Imagine in your country the politicians decide that in order to encourage local sourcing of goods and services they're going to partition the country into four regions and companies would face tax charges and quotas if they wish to move goods across a regional border into the next region. How would you respond? Predictably there would be a huge outcry from business community as well as consumers.

Business leaders would point out that their markets would reduce and they would have lower economies of scale leading to higher costs. In addition they would have a smaller choice of suppliers and with the reduced competition they would face increased input costs.

Consumers would point out that this would lead to increased costs as a result of lower competition. The reduced competition may also lead to a reduction in innovation and quality as firms feel they have more of a captive market and so less of a need to innovate and maintain quality.

Citizens would view the proposed partitioning as completely unacceptable, and agitate with the government eventually obliged to climb down or face riots.

If we now take a step back, and look at the planet as a whole, then from that perspective our current trading system is similar to the doomed partition idea of the government in the preceding scenario. Despite this, the common person doesn't feel the same agitation and emotion sense of a wrong being done.

In this regard, we're a bit like a child that's been brought up in a prison and knows no better. The child will play happily oblivious to the prison walls, as the walls have always been there.

If cigarettes had not been invented, but were to be invented now, there would be an outright ban from a health viewpoint. However they're allowed because they're a legacy item. In a similar way trade restrictions are harmful and do economic damage but they're tolerated and accepted as the way things are due to our mental inertia, in effect they are a legacy item causing harm, which needs to be slowly weeded out of existence.

> *By means of glasses, hotbeds, and hotwalls, very good grapes can be raised in Scotland, and very good wine too can be made of*

them at about thirty times the expense for which at least equally good can be brought from foreign countries. Would it be a reasonable law to prohibit the importation of all foreign wines, merely to encourage the making of claret and burgundy in Scotland?

~ Adam Smith, The Wealth of Nations

22.5   Sanctions

Should we ever have Sanctions and do they work? On the face of it, Sanctions appear an attractive policy option, a way of inflicting some pain onto the other country without a single shot being fired.

If they worked then sanctions may well be a good policy, but I have serious doubts about how pragmatic they can ever be.

Sanctions will cause pain on the country but will the country actually shift its policy as a result. It's a bit like throwing a tiny spear at a wild animal, it will cause it some pain but it's not going to make it roll over and give up the fight. The same is true of the country; it most likely will absorb the pain and learn to cope with it.

In a fragmented world community, it's normally asking too much for all countries to sign up to the sanctions, and there almost always will be some countries that don't sign up to the sanctions and continue trading, as is their sovereign right. If you can't achieve full multilateral sanctions then the effectiveness of sanctions becomes further weakened and questionable.

 The people who suffer most from sanctions are likely to be the common citizens of the country, and if a regime is that deviant that others feel tempted to apply sanctions, then the regime is probably not likely to care much about the sufferings its citizens are going to face.

 Sanctions can perversely be used by the regime as a way of stoking up nationalism against "unprincipled outsiders" trying to punish the country, and create a siege mentality in which people get distracted and patriotic. The regime could use this to shift people's emotions and attention away from internal politics, paradoxically helping them consolidate and remain in power.

I talked of trade creating bonds of friendship, imposing sanctions means those bonds are lost. One is more likely to be influenced by friends than by people we dislike. With friends there is dialogue and communication and one's guard is not up and a chance for advocacy exists. However by going down the path of aggression predicated by sanctions, dialogue and friendship go out of the window along with our influencing ability. In effect Sanctions also imply a sanction on ideas and the trading of thoughts, leading to cultural isolation, which the regime can exploit, with its own propaganda to fill the vacuum conveniently created by sanctions. Increased trade would however mean that a large portion of the country has dealings with us and are more likely to be influenced by our way of thinking.

It's always hard to predict, but for the reasons above, I feel that ironically one of the reason's that Cuba's regime has survived for that long in its original form is the sanctions imposed against it by the US.

I think therefore that although superficially attractive, Sanctions are a form of cold war and almost always a negative and poorly thought out idea, and a lazy way out of continued dialogue.

> *War is never a solution; it is an aggravation.*
> ~*Benjamin Disraeli*

22.6 Trade Aid

Aid is welcome when sudden disasters strike, or for dealing with specific shortcomings such as helping bridge gaps in knowledge and know-how. However it can be a double-edged sword, and aid can destabilise the market, in the product being given as aid. How can local producers of the product compete with the same product coming in for free via an aid route? The aid may make them retreat from that market sector leaving the country more vulnerable and dependent on aid in the future.

Countries have often complained about "dumping" when a firm from overseas sells its items at prices that appear lower than cost. They've retaliated by creating anti-dumping restrictions. To an extent, Aid has the characteristics and consequences of dumping – as it's being given away free. To stop the dumping consequences, it's preferable to give aid via a "trade wrapper" by sourcing and buying all the items to give as aid in the recipient country's local markets, so that the aid intervention takes on some of the properties of trade.

Chronic Aid can trap countries in a cycle of corruption[3] because governments can remain inefficient or corrupt and fail to grow their economy, and rely on the free money coming via the Aid route to remain in power. In that sense, Chronic Aid is a bit like keeping someone brain dead or in a coma on life support, if it's not willing to "wake up" perhaps it's better to let the patient pass away and give chance to a new regime built on sounder principles. However that will not happen while the aid life support is on, effectively blocking anyone else from getting to grips with the situation.

Just as Aid can be negative, Trade is its mirror image and is positive, improving dignity and self-respect. Trade also forces the government to raise its income by taxing citizens rather than getting handouts from foreign governments, this taxation leading to an increased accountability to the electorate.

The Live 8 campaign held ten concerts[4] across the world, one of the things they wanted to draw attention to was that despite having 12% of the world's population, Africa's share of world trade[5] was only 2% in 2002, having fallen from a 6% share in 1980. For each additional 1% share of global trade, Africa would earn $70 Billion in extra exports each year. If Africa could revert its share of world trade to 1980 levels, that would mean an additional $280 Billion per annum.

I outlined earlier how restricting trade is in fact a form of hostility and aggression. By subsidising farmers through rich world programmes such as Europe's Common Agricultural Policy (CAP) the rich world damages and restricts trade in the very areas where developing countries such as those in Africa have a competitive advantage.

It's worth repeating – Trade Restrictions are an act of hostility. On the one hand rich countries are actively being hostile by restricting trade, whilst on the other hand are trying to "help" by giving aid. This is dishonest and hypocritical and if they were really genuine about wishing to help, then the best way would be to remove restrictions on trade by stopping harmful subsidies and quotas.

> *Free trade is not based on utility but on justice.*
>
> *Edmund Burke*

3   Why Foreign Aid is Hurting Africa http://online.wsj.com/article/SB123758895999200083.html
4   July 2005
5   Live 8 Concert   http://www.live8live.com/makepromiseshappen/#

22.7 Approval of the Arms Trade

With the global arms trade[77] worth over $50 Billion per annum, a phenomenal amount of resource is being spent upon items ultimately meant to kill our fellow human beings. It's immoral and wrong headed to spend this level of resource on such a negative mission, and in earlier chapters I've outlined more efficient ways of organizing our defences requiring far fewer weapons.

If a person at a bar has drunk a lot of alcohol, and is clearly out of control, then it's expected the bartender should refuse to sell them any more alcohol, and the bartender would be regarded as being irresponsible if they served them any more alcohol.

In a similar way, a country that is repressing some of its people and not observing human rights can be seen as being "out of control". To continue to supply the country with weapons that it can then use for further repression of its people is irresponsible and similar to supplying the alcoholic with more drinks.

Anyone supplying weapons to such a state must share some responsibility for the repression.

Countries currently make their own decision on whether or not to allow their companies to sell arms to particular states, basing it upon their overall national interest.

However I feel this shouldn't be an issue of national interest, rather it is a matter of global interest in protecting human rights, and any individual supplier country's national interest should not factor into the decision.

We therefore need to invent a neutral international body, the Weapons Trade Approval (WTA), whose mission is to decide whether or not to allow the trade of weapons to particular countries, each decision based upon the country's observance of human rights. All countries within the UN would need to observe a WTA ban or restriction on weapons sale to a particular country, preventing the refuelling of repression.

When a country has a lot of trade or other interests in a country guilty of repression, it becomes vulnerable to economic threats to its other business interests, and can

6   The financial value of the global arms trade
     http://www.sipri.org/research/armaments/transfers/measuring/financial_values

be arm-twisted into supplying weapons. However if the WTA bans weapons sales then it takes the onus away from the supplier country, which can use the WTA ruling to argue its hands are tied. Therefore it becomes easier to refuse to supply weapons, as there would be less of a fear of it impacting other trade.

22.8   A Poisoned Chalice of Oil

The qualities that get a man into power are not those that lead
him, once established, to use power wisely.

~Lyman Bryson

"May you be cursed with plenty of wealth" sounds unusual as far as curses go, however for a less developed country natural resources such as oil can paradoxically be a curse[7,8].

In most economies the government gets its income from tax on its citizens activities, however in a resource rich and less developed country the government derives much of its income from exporting its natural resources. The government can get the monies to stay in power and keep the core essentials of army and police running without needing to look towards its native population for income. To an extent therefore one can view this situation as a state within a state. Those in the inner state being well off with all their needs being met, while those in the outer state having a meagre subsistence living on the periphery. With the monies coming in from outside the politicians at the top of the inner state have an unprecedented opportunity to siphon off income and stash away personal fortunes, protected by sovereignty from any tiresome investigations.

The government may regard those in the outer state as an inconvenience, it doesn't need them to stay in power and they can almost be viewed as chattel grazing the countryside. There is the fear that if it invests and educates those inhabiting the outer state they might just wake up to the injustice and demand their share of the nation's wealth and hold the politicians to account. From a game plan perspective it's entirely in the inner state's elites' interest to maintain the status quo and drag its heels on bringing in democratic institutions and do the bare minimum to avoid the ire of the global community.

---

7   The Curse of oil: the paradox of plenty
     http://www.economist.com/businessfinance/displayStory.cfm?story_id=5323394
8   The Resource Curse http://en.wikipedia.org/wiki/Resource_curse

Accordingly, studies have found that economies with abundant natural resources have tended to grow less rapidly than natural resource scarce economies[79].

The issue is that in countries with less developed civil society and democratic institutions, and whose citizens have had limited access to education then it's relatively easy for the political classes to amass wealth, with few checks and balances to stop them. Expecting them to voluntarily change is simply naive and expecting too much, with the global community not facing up to common sense.

Although there are initiatives to try and bring additional transparency such as the Extractive Industries Transparency Initiative[80], they rely on the country itself taking the initiative and putting in place procedures to ensure transparency. This misses the point that the problem lies with the people wielding power in these countries. It's no surprise therefore that such initiatives have moved at a glacial pace with very few countries being compliant. No individual country is going to want to lose face by denying or moving out of such programmes, but behind the scenes will ensure that progress slows to the point of becoming inconsequential.

If you were planning to bequeath a fortune to a teenager, there would be some checks and balances in place to ensure they manage and spend their inheritance wisely. It would be foolish to simply transfer the monies to the teenager's account – which would be asking for trouble with the teenager likely to blow it away living the high life. However if a mature 42 year old were doing the inheriting then we would be quite willing to simply hand over the inheritance.

I think countries need to be treated in the same manner, those that have not yet developed strong institutions and civil society need to be treated differently to those that have developed such institutions. Ideally we need to classify countries along a curve of political maturity and be willing to treat them differently as they move through the various categories of political maturity. This is not denying their Sovereignty but just accepting that their institutions are vulnerable to capture during the early stages of development. Although this is the ideal situation, it's not practical as each country would argue over the level of their political maturity, and a more robust approach is needed. The relative level of development of a country's non-extractive-resource economy can be used as an indicator of its development and maturity.

---

9   Natural Resource Abundance and Economic Growth http://www.nber.org/papers/w5398.pdf

10   EITI: Extractive Industries Transparency Initiative http://www.eiti.org/countries
     http://en.wikipedia.org/wiki/Extractive_Industries_Transparency_Initiative

We need to invent an organization, the Extraction Trade Intermediary (ETI) whose function is to act as an interface layer sandwiched between the country and international companies acting as an intermediary on all financial transactions dealing with extraction industry trade. On financial matters the oil and mining companies would have no direct contact with the country, instead they would be mandated to go via ETI, which would act as a transparent conduit between the two, not adding to or distorting the communication but merely noting it before passing it on. ETI's value-add would be that all financial transactions between external companies and the country would be recorded and published, ensuring complete transparency.

ETI would be needed where a country's trade in extractive industries is greater than a particular threshold, say 15%. Once ETI is in place for a country, then it would be illegal for any company to handle any product extracted that hasn't been produced under an ETI supervised contract.

Once the country has developed other parts of its economy, so that its revenues from extractive industries falls below 15% of total revenues, then it would become free to trade directly without needing to go via the ETI layer. The key point being that in order to develop other sectors the country will have had to eschew the perverse state within a state strategy and develop other parts of the country's infrastructure and human capital and involve all citizens in the economy.

22.9   Moving to a Free Trade Agreement – a Ten Year Blueprint

The world has been going through a series of Trade Talks for over fifty years now, leading to the formation of the World Trade Organization (WTO) in 1995. Despite considerable improvement trade liberalisation remains a work in progress with the most recent round[81] failing to reach an agreement.

To attempt to get agreement between 153 countries on trade is a colossal task, and it's no surprise the Doha round failed to reach an agreement and that it's taking such a long time to reach an agreement.

There's a saying, you cannot cross a chasm in two steps; in this case we appear to be trying to cross the chasm in multiple steps and the strategy to get to an agreement appears flawed. Trying to make deals and trade concessions bit by bit is simply too

---

11   Doha, 2008

complex when there are 153 countries involved each with their own individual lobbies and political calculations. We need to find a simpler and more effective way to reach the goal.

I'll outline what I regard could become the basis of a simpler and effective way of moving towards a complete free trade regime worldwide.

There should be no disagreement over the fact that we would all like a world free of all trade restrictions. So the first step is to decide on a timescale, and I would propose 10 years as a reasonable time frame, but this could be altered to 15 or 20 years.

If we assume at the end of ten years every country will have zero trade restrictions and quotas, the task becomes a simpler problem of how should each country move towards that goal so that by year ten they arrive at it. The simplest solution is we take an audit of today's trade restrictions and each country reduces barriers by exactly 10% every year for the next ten years so that by year ten every country will have reduced its trade restrictions by 100%, and be at a zero restrictions. As everyone relaxes restrictions by the same proportion annually, it appears a fairer process for politicians to sell to voters.

There may be the need for a transitional fund, which would help countries with particular issues adapt to the changes. Each country would put a tiny portion of their GDP (e.g. 0.25%) annually into the transitional fund.

Import duties are easy to handle, and would simply drop by 10% (of the first year value) each year so that by year ten they have dropped to zero. Quotas behave differently and would need to be increased annually so that by year ten the quota figure for the country is equal to the total market size for the product / service in that country. Once the quota figure is equal to the total market requirement there's no need for quota's as the entire market can be satisfied from imports. Subsidies would also be reduced by 10% per annum so that there are no distorting subsidies left in ten years.

As this is a completely mechanistic way of moving forward, once the principle and approach are agreed, it's straightforward to work out, apply and monitor and guaranteed to lead to a complete worldwide free trade regime with the changes applied in small incremental steps. If 10% reduction per annum is seen as being too high, then simply move the time frame out to 15 or 20 yielding 6.7% and 5% per annum decrements. The point however is that once everyone has signed up to it, it becomes like a train moving at an agreed speed on a track, it's bound to reach the other end of the line at a known time.

A major source of objection to a free economy is precisely that it ... gives people what they want instead of what a particular group thinks they ought to want. Underlying most arguments against the free market is a lack of belief in freedom itself.

~ Milton Friedman

23. Private Sector Organizations

There appears to be a divergence of views over the best way to put together and run commercial organizations. One of the main questions hinges over whether they should be in private or public ownership, with capitalism still seen by many as exploitative and seizing control of the economy for its own ends. In other cases capitalism is allowed in certain areas but deemed improper for other sectors. In this and the next two chapters I'd like to explore this area and try and get to the heart of the matter.

23.1 Every Day is Election Day in the Consumer Democracy

> *The consumer, so it is said, is the king... each is a voter who uses*
> *his money as votes to get the things done that he wants done.*
> ~ *Paul Samuelson*

The main benefits of the private sector is that it empowers the Consumer, giving them complete freedom and choice on where they spend their money. If sufficient numbers of people want to spend their money on a particular item then sooner or later a market will spring up to meet their needs. In that sense money acts as a voting mechanism to get things done.

In other words the private sector is a Democracy with the power residing with people to make their own individual decisions as to what to choose to buy and what to leave on the shelf.

The fact that power rests with the consumers is the key strength of the private sector. Each purchase decision is at a micro level, a vote of confidence cast in the organisation providing the product/ service, and summed up over the economy become a nationwide poll on the organization.

Provided markets are working well, and have not degenerated into monopolies, the fact that there are multiple suppliers means that each day is an election day in the consumer democracy with votes being cast for which products are better and provide greater value add, with those failing to make the grade ending up remaining unsold and ultimately loss making.

23.2   Continuous Innovation emulates Natural Evolution

This continuous polling creates a relentless drive for product and service improvement and innovation, manifested in extra features, cost reduction and continual progress. The fact that something is good is no longer sufficient, it must be better value add than competing offerings from other suppliers. In effect it puts suppliers on a nonstop treadmill to improve their products and services and if they pause for breath or rest on their laurels, they face extinction.

This continuous innovation means that companies are constantly seeking ways of getting an edge for their products / services and experimenting to find what works and what doesn't, all the time learning from the feedback and incorporating successful changes and rejecting unfruitful ones. This process emulates nature's evolution and feedback pattern[1], which led us to evolve from simple single celled organisms into complex biological beings with trillions of cells.

By emulating nature, the free market private sector model is based upon and following what's probably the most important and powerful pattern in existence.

23.3   Survival of the Fittest – Creative Destruction

Necessity, who is the mother of invention.

~ *Plato*

It may be seen as a rather ruthless model, but ultimately it delivers continuous improvement and innovation whilst simultaneously reducing costs and ensures that only the fittest companies survive, with those less able to adapt falling by the wayside somewhat as the dinosaurs in the biological history of our planet[2].

---

1   The Secret Life of Chaos, Professor Jim Al-Khalili, Furnace films shown on BBC 4
    http://furnacetv.com/programmes/secret-life-of-chaos
2   The most popular theory for extinction of the dinosaurs is an asteroid hitting the earth, however its worth noting that cockroaches which existed around the same time, were able to adapt and survive

As the process mirrors natural evolution, it's no surprise that it has a similar outcome of survival of the fittest.

Private sector companies and the people working in them know that if they stop driving forwards relentlessly then there are plenty others there waiting to grab their lunch. That necessity creates a continuous internal pressure and motivation on staff and managers to try and improve their product / service and innovate.

23.4   Self Regulating Networked Brain Decision Making

The entire system is self-optimising and regulating in the sense that thankfully it does not require quangos of "wise people" making decisions on products / services and companies.

Although I say self regulating, in reality it's more than that, it's a form of networked intelligence and decision making, where in effect everyone's thoughts have been silently polled and the results pulled together, the same decision would have been arrived at if we could have networked all our brains together to arrive at a decision.

In this way we can regard a market decision as a decision taken by putting together and networking our individual brainpower, and this will always trump the decision taken by any government department or quango.

23.5   Greed is Good

> *If you would attain to what you are not yet, you must always be displeased by what you are. For where you are pleased with yourself there you have remained. Keep adding, keep walking, keep advancing.*
>
> *~Saint Augustine*

The phrase by Gordon Gekko in the film Wall Street has been immortalised, however it was meant to be symptomatic of how things had become lopsided with people losing their sense of balance over money. It's become fashionable to look down on greed and write it off as a negative trait, however to do that would be throwing the baby out with the bathwater, and I think it's time greed was brought in from the cold.

Of course the greed that makes people behave in a corrupt or fraudulent manner is completely wrong, and equally any uncharitable behaviour driven by greed is distasteful, however these are not the kind of meanings I ascribe to greed when I say it's good.

I see greed as the basic human desire to better themselves and their family, i.e. to improve their way of life. It's greed that leads to people being ambitious for themselves and drives them to achieve great things, the greed of fame. Similarly greed for knowledge has lead scientists to work endless late hours and achieve major breakthroughs in science such as the discovery of penicillin or X-Rays. Again it's greed that pushes people to invent new things and file patents as well as creating new companies that offer customers better value and choice.

In all these examples greed is good and a real motivator for people to get involved and push themselves forward and is a major factor that's helped create the world we live in today. Were it not for greed then we would be satisfied with the way things were, and lose the drive to change things and perhaps the industrial revolution might never have happened!

When designing systems and structures one need to take account of the characteristics of its building blocks, on that basis any organizational approach that tries to deny the basic human instinct of greed is simply foolish and wrong-headed as it's trying to deny one of the most powerful motivators of humankind, and to ignore it is a bit like trying to make water flow uphill.

23.6   Healthy Profits

> *It is a socialist idea that making profits is a vice; I consider the real vice is making losses."*
>
> ~ *Winston Churchill*

People often regard profit as something bad, with a whiff of exploitation about it, with the implicit view that if someone's making money then it's at someone else's expense. It's also used in a negative connotation to imply that people are taking away resources from an essential sector with the implication that the sector is going to be soon starved of resources and whither.

However this misses the key points and significance of profits. Profits may be seen as a measure of the usefulness of an enterprise and how well it is being run, and in that sense act as a Report Card on the organization delivered by society at large.

The real villains are those enterprises making losses as ultimately they're doing something wrong and wasting resources. If a company has misjudged what people want, they will have very low sales income and end up making a loss – the loss made directly points to the fact that the company got its marketing wrong and are producing items that are simply not needed and therefore wasteful. Alternatively they may be needed, but the company happens to be inefficient at marketing and its competitors have designed more compelling packages. Whatever the reason, the key point is that they have not been efficient in meeting their customers needs, with the result that they have not made enough sales. Thus the resulting loss reflects their poor marketing skills.

Lets say they now fix their marketing skills, and the product specification is exactly what people want, but if their manufacturing or purchasing remains inefficient and they cannot make it cheap enough, or their quality is poor, then again customers will either balk at the high cost or poor quality and once again shun the product. The profit will drop once more yet again providing a direct report on the fact that they have poor manufacturing.

If the company has got its marketing right and are producing goods/ services that their customers want, with good management in place to get the item manufactured in a quality manner efficiently at a competitive price, then they will end up making a profit.

The key point is that profit provides a key indicator on the health of the enterprise, right from how well it's anticipating and meeting customer needs, through to how its manufacturing and operations are being managed. In effect profit provide a report card and health check on the organization.

By operating in free markets and posting profits, private enterprises are subjected to a continuous "profits" health check and knowing their performance is clearly visible, keeps them on their toes and at all times striving to excel. Thus the profit motive drives companies forward down a path of continuous improvement.

23.7   Privatisation is not sufficient

Although there are a number of benefits accruing from being a private enterprise, that by itself is not sufficient. It's important the enterprise operates in a free market with healthy competition. The key factor that pushes the company is competition. In the absence of competition, in theory the firm could name its price and make money regardless of its operational efficiency.

That's why to get the private enterprise benefits, it's not sufficient to simply take a state company and privatise it, it's crucial that it's privatised without creating a monopoly.

I'll illustrate by giving an example of a poor privatisation, that of the rail system in the UK. Various rail lines were licensed off to different train operating companies, however each line formed a perfect monopoly on its own route with resultant high fares. A quick check reveals that it would cost £190 for a return train ticket to travel the 180 miles between Manchester and London. I then checked the price of a return airline ticket to cover the 4230 miles between Manchester and Delhi which came at £324 – inclusive of a £40 economy long haul air travel tax, resulting in £284 for the ticket itself. The train cost of £1.05 per mile was 30 times the £0.03 airline cost per mile[3], the huge difference being attributed to the intense competition in air travel compared to the relative monopoly in train services.

When privatising companies and industries that tend towards being monopolies, governments have put in place regulators whose role is to ensure the company doesn't veer towards monopolistic behaviour. Although better than nothing, there's great danger that the regulator may get captured and go native. Even if they resist this, they will never be able to match the influence that a strong competitor would exert.

Had the UK government given multiple train companies the rights to run trains on the same stretch of line then the fares would have been much lower.

A more successful example is that of telecommunications. In the early 1990's it cost £1.25 per minute to dial India from the UK, now in 2010 one can dial India for as little as £0.02 per minute. This demonstrates the massive benefits from privatisation of British Telecom and opening the market to competition, which was a process started by Margaret Thatcher, with the British endearingly true to national character, never really giving her recognition for her far reaching changes.

3   Return fare of £284 divided by (2 x 4230)

23.8   Regulation

If we had a football game without rules, it would quickly degenerate into a free for all with fights breaking out and people getting hurt, eventually bringing the game into disrepute. Similarly capitalist companies are giving it their all when competing in a market and there needs to be some regulations governing the rules of the "game".

Setting the regulatory frameworks and standards is a legitimate and vital role of governments, in effect setting the rules of the game. Just as without rules and a referee, football would degenerate, similarly capitalist companies and free markets run the risk of getting overheated and their players burning out in the desire to outcompete. Regulations are where the markets and government meet in mutual dependence and define the interface between the two.

Governments need to set the rules, and act as referee ensuring the rules are being adhered to. Failure to do so would be derelict of them, and somewhat like a referee sleeping on the sidelines.

If the Government drags its feet and fails to update regulations to keep up with market innovations, or gets that awe struck or corrupt that it fails to monitor and apply the existing regulations effectively, then this is to a large extent a public sector failure. However the consequences might be market failure with poorly regulated firms burning out through making catastrophic mistakes unchecked by the lax regulation, or becoming that large that they stifle any new competitors leading to low innovation and the market stagnating, providing poor value for customers. Ironically though, the naive conclusion often drawn is that the markets have failed, and that perhaps the firms should be brought into the public sector – completely missing that the public sector regulatory failure was the initial catalyst and possibly even the prime cause[4].

One caution to watch out for is that standards and regulations should not get hijacked and used as a ploy to erect proxy barriers to trade.

If a country is at an earlier stage of development and hasn't put in place its regulatory frameworks, then a lack of standards shouldn't imply a free for all, and

---

4   I say prime cause, because it's in the nature of firms to take risks as well as having a fiduciary responsibility to seek advantage including via lobbying government. However it's up to government to take a balanced view, framing and applying intelligent regulations and not to cave in.

as mentioned earlier[5], I'd floated the idea of a Global Minimum Standard that would apply when local standards are overly lax or nonexistent.

> *Every individual...generally, indeed, neither intends to promote the public interest, nor knows how much he is promoting it. By preferring the support of domestic to that of foreign industry he intends only his own security; and by directing that industry in such a manner as its produce may be of the greatest value, he intends only his own gain, and he is in this, as in many other cases, led by an invisible hand to promote an end which was no part of his intention.*
>
> ~ Adam Smith, The Wealth of Nations

24. Public Sector

24.1   Performance is obfuscated and hard to measure

> *"When you can measure what you are speaking about, and express it in numbers, you know something about it, when you cannot express it in numbers, your knowledge is of a meagre and unsatisfactory kind; it may be the beginning of knowledge, but you have scarcely, in your thoughts advanced to the stage of science."*
>
> ~ *Lord Kelvin*

In the private sector one can deduce a lot of things from a company's profitability such as its ability to meet customer needs and efficiency in sourcing inputs and converting them to goods/ services at a competitive price. All these have bearing on a company's profits. If the company is efficient in manufacturing but has got it's marketing wrong then its goods will remain unsold on the shelf, resulting in a loss. Similarly even with the best and most compelling customer proposition if its manufacturing is off the mark and there are quality or cost issues then too the goods are likely to remain unsold, leading to a loss. It's only when a company manages everything right will it be able to post healthy and sustained profits. Thus profit is a way of distilling the entire company's performance into a single statistic, and apart from fraud, it's hard to conjure up fictitious profit.

Due to their nature and setup, Public Sector organisations don't have profits, and so their performance and efficiency gets obfuscated, with it becoming difficult to measure their performance, creating difficulties in managing and ensuring value for money.

Governments have invented various bodies such as Oversight Committees, Audit Committees, and inspection regimes with a view to ensure Public Sector performance. These aren't useless, but by definition they can never provide a regime as thorough or demanding as the ones private enterprises are subjected to. Each time someone buys an item from a private company they are in effect like a "micro level inspector" looking at the company's products and comparing with other firms offerings, and marking their approval by their purchase. This continuous daily minute-by-minute market inspection that a private company has to deal with is orders of magnitude harder than the occasional visit from an audit committee or chief inspector!

As it's hard to measure a public sector organisation's efficiency and productivity, it becomes entangled in political ideologies that further muddies the water and confuses the issue.

A way around that the UK Government has tried is creating a whole plethora of benchmarks for performance, and to measure the public organisation's performance in meeting the benchmarks. Although benchmarks can be good they can also become distorting as focus and attention shifts to the benchmarks and things not being benchmarked tend to suffer and become neglected. The consequence is that although benchmarks make things better at one place it deflects the problems to other areas. It also makes things hugely bureaucratic, spawning an administrative layer to measure and administer the benchmarks and deal with performance issues. In the private sector no administrative layer was needed – the customer having performed their own inspection at the point of sale and voted with their feet.

Benchmarks did not serve the Soviet Government well either, with Soviet managers becoming expert at manipulating their factories to excel at whatever the going plan criteria was. Often benchmarks were based on gross output criteria such as weight, and Nikita Khrushchev once complained[1] of chandeliers so heavy "that they pull the ceilings down on our heads".

24.2 Low Innovation and Growth are the result of an unnatural design

A civil servant is sometimes like a broken cannon – it won't work and you can't fire it. ~ George S. Patton

1 Lodi News Sentinel, Thursday September 21 1995, page 4, Misleading Indicators by Thomas Sowell
http://news.google.com/newspapers?nid=2245&dat=19950921&id=nNw0AAAAIBAJ&sjid=
OCEGAAAAIBAJ&pg=5593,2451504

Employees in government jobs are pretty secure[2]. When the government decides to provide a particular service it tends to become a monopoly provider with few competitors, leading to government agencies having captive clients. Unless the employee does something really drastic, they're in a job for life, with pay scales often set by national level agreements.

Private sector companies and their employees, facing relentless competition and daily inspections by their customers, have to relentlessly search out innovations and new sources of differentiation and value add – or risk being out on the scrap heap.

However in the Public Sector with their existence pretty much guaranteed, there simply isn't the same level of personal hunger and drive to innovate and push the boundaries, and to actively take on the stress of change. This results in a structural bias towards low innovation and low growth in public sector organizations.

Therefore the intrinsic design of Public Sector organizations flies in the face of everything we learn from nature. Nature makes us fight for existence, in the process evolving and growing stronger. However with their existence guaranteed, public bodies are exempt from this discipline and relatively tend to fossilise.

The situation is further exacerbated by Public Sector organizations often having key decisions made from the centre, creating delays in decision making, leading to them behaving like massive tankers, slow to respond and change course.

Although anecdotal as an illustration of the different mindset, when I was a consultant working in local government, after 3:30 on a Friday the office tended to be deserted with almost everyone having left for the weekend. In comparison, at commercial companies I found work normally continued till at least five on Fridays.

24.3   Poor service and error prone due to complacency and attenuated feedback

If a private company makes a major mistake then the publicity will lead to a major loss of credibility and business and cost it heavily, perhaps even closing it down or forcing a takeover. This makes them identify and manage risk, keeping a close eye

---

2   Apart from the special circumstances when a country facing a sovereign debt crisis is forced into taking drastic action and major restructuring

on anything deemed mission critical, with the whole organization getting involved as the impact could effect everybody.

However in the public sector, survival is never in doubt as the government is underwriting it, and although one or two individuals might get disciplined and sidelined, the impact on the majority of personnel and organization is minor compared to the potential impact had it been a private company. Therefore sanctions and feedback on the organization after making a serious mistake are considerably attenuated.

As they know their jobs are never on the line, it creates an attitude of complacency acting as a catalyst for poor service and error prone behaviour.

In nature, feedback is an essential element playing a key role in our evolution[3], with positive feedback encouraging good evolutionary traits and negative feedback stamping out poor traits. Similarly in engineering systems feedback is vital to keep systems behaving predictably, with weak feedback loops leading to erratic outcomes and behaviour falling outside the accepted bounds.

With its weak feedback, public sector organizations are not designed to evolve or wired to behave predictably and it's not a question of if, but rather when, the next over / undershoot occurs along with its attendant tragedy.

Put another way, with the lack of sanctions, people don't treat things as mission critical and fail to internalise the lessons. The result being that public sector organizations tend not to be learning organizations and history keeps repeating itself, with public officials earnestly and solemnly promising to "learn lessons" as each new mistake unfolds. The real lesson is the one we need to learn about the intrinsic nature of public organizations.

As an example, in a recent trial of two brothers in Doncaster, UK, who had brutally tortured two young children, it was judged[4] to have been preventable, with the Social Services missing 30 opportunities to intervene.

As another example of the poor service mindset, at a recent neighbourhood

---

3   The Secret Life of Chaos, Professor Jim Al-Khalili, Furnace films shown on BBC 4
     http://furnacetv.com/programmes/secret-life-of-chaos
4   Doncaster child services criticised
     http://www.guardian.co.uk/society/2010/jan/18/doncaster-child-services-brothers-report

meeting, it was found that quite a few of our neighbours had written to the local council, myself included, but months later no one had received a reply.

24.4   Poor Cost Control – it's easy to be generous with someone else's money

Who owns a public sector organization? The simple answer is the public, i.e. everyone in the country. However if everyone owns it, then each person's ownership is an infinitesimal amount and mentally this gets approximated to zero, with the net result that no-one actually feels any real sense of ownership, and these organizations tend to drift blown by the prevailing political winds.

In private companies, the directors are keenly aware of the costs and closely manage them, however with a lack of ownership mindset in the public sector there is less oversight and emotional involvement in managing costs, it being easier to be generous with someone else's money, with the net result that costs are higher in the public sector.

The public sector also risks getting hijacked for political purposes, with projects and programmes done to repay political favours rather than for sound economic reasons. This behaviour directly leads to lower productivity and higher costs.

As outlined earlier[5], it's difficult to measure the performance of public organizations, which gets obfuscated. This makes it hard to compare output against input, making it easy for inputs to rise (i.e. cost increase) while not realising that outputs and performance have failed to keep up, resulting in poor cost control and over spends.

When the government takes over provision for a role, it tend to do it on a nationwide basis, in the process creating large monopolies offering the service, which then get unionised. As a consequence, salaries get set at national levels rather than varying them by local economic conditions, leading to the government unable to benefit from lower salary expectations in remote regions, and instead finding itself paying a higher national rate.

The government is a major employer; in the UK it employed 5.6 million people in

---

5   Section 24.1

2003, representing 20% of the workforce[6]. Politicians know that all these public sector employees are also voters, and fearful of losing votes, the government can be implicitly held to ransom by the public sector, and shy away from taking the correct steps due to their electoral implications.

Public sector jobs are more secure than private sector jobs, and applying the risk / reward ratio theory that people expect a higher reward for taking higher risks, one would expect to see public sector jobs paying less than private sector jobs. However in 2009 the UK median full-time public sector earning[7] was £539 per week whereas private sector earning was lower at £465 per week, this demonstrating the result of the structural issues discussed above which lead to poor cost control in the public sector and a waste of resources.

Another example of the poor cost control by the state is in its handling of pensions. In the UK there are almost no private companies still offering final salary pensions as it's simply too expensive, however final salary pensions are still the norm in the public sector. It's no wonder therefore that many of the public sector organizations have huge pensions liabilities. I'm not against pensions but it feels unfair that people working in the private sector are paying for conditions for state workers that the private sector workers themselves won't enjoy. If public sector pensions are to be higher, then they should be paid for by public employees retiring three or four years later than in the private sector.

As a couple of examples, while dealing with the NHS we came across a unit in Scotland processing information in a labour intensive way, needing to edit 300 files manually, while the same outcome could be achieved with a different setup and only needing to edit a single file. On discussing with the Director we were amazed to be informed that money wasn't an issue for the NHS, as they had plenty of money to spend and so they wouldn't be following up on our proposal.

Another example is that some UK Police forces have arrangements whereby if they have to take a phone call when off duty, they can charge for a complete hour, however as their accounting systems can only process in units of four hours, the officer got paid for four hours[8].

---

6   Public Sector Employment http://www.statistics.gov.uk/articles/nojournal/PSE_final.pdf
     http://www.statistics.gov.uk/cci/nugget.asp?id=1292

7   Median Earnings Public vs. Private Sector http://www.statistics.gov.uk/cci/nugget.asp?id=285

8   Police overtime for answering phone call
     http://www.telegraph.co.uk/news/newstopics/politics/lawandorder/7139525/Police-earn-100-overtime-for-answering-phone.html

24.5   State-Controlled Companies

State Controlled Companies are where the government is the majority owner of companies that compete in the marketplace for business alongside other companies that are fully in private ownership. With four of the top 25 companies in the Forbes Global list[9] being state-controlled, it's worth looking closer at this form of public sector organization.

As it's a company it has a balance sheet identifying sales, costs and profits and therefore unlike other public bodies its performance is visible and not obfuscated.

However being majority owned by the state, its directors are not free to make policy and strategy independently, instead they are subject to the whims of their political masters and decisions tend to be shaped and influenced by political concerns instead of being based purely on the economic criteria. This leads to sub-optimal decisions and outcomes.

State controlled companies are susceptible to the poor cost control influence of government bodies, and costs are likely to be higher. As they are owned by the state, they're insulated from the threat of a hostile takeover and so their management are likely to feel safer than their counterparts in other companies, with this safety translating into a reduced pressure to perform and less discipline.

State controlled companies are more susceptible to corruption, nepotism and rent seeking behaviour by public sector employees and politicians, using a network of patronage and influence. This further raises their costs of doing business.

Governments are going to have a large number of competing voices for their finance and will often make the decision based on political considerations. In this environment it's easy for state companies to get scarce resourced and forced to get by with inadequate investment, which could limit their ambitions and keep them treading water maintaining the status quo.

State companies are likely to be viewed with suspicion in other parts of the world where they would be seen as proxies for their parent government, with unclear motives. This means that people would be reluctant to allow their companies to be taken over by a state company from elsewhere. This resistance acts to limit the opportunities open to a state company and reduces its growth potential. An

9   Economist, Jan 23 2010, The growth of the State

example was the takeover by Dubai Ports of P&O, where Dubai Ports were obliged to sell the American ports that P&O had owned.

When companies expand and grow overseas, they promote knowledge transfer as their employees elsewhere get trained etc. With their international growth prospects curtailed to an extent, this means that state controlled companies are less likely to be in a position to transmit knowledge and expertise worldwide, thereby reducing the rate of knowledge transfer and growth.

To summarise, state controlled companies are more costly and open to corruption, have constrained and less flexible decision-making, have managements under reduced pressure to perform and lower international growth prospects. In short they are a bad deal and a poor use of citizens money.

Governments should therefore stop this ego trip and waste of their citizens' resources and look to privatise and set free their state controlled companies. The proceeds generated can be invested in improved national infrastructure; reduced taxes and sovereign wealth funds taking small minority stakes in publicly quoted companies.

The freed companies would perform much better on a global scale, perhaps even becoming new global champions, this combined with the benefits from investing the proceeds in infrastructure would mean far better value and a return on investment for the citizens of the country.

24.6   Could Public Sector co-operatives be the answer?

There has been talk of allowing public sector bodies the right to opt to become worker co-operatives who would manage themselves in the provision of the public service on behalf of the state. They would do the work under contract to the state that would monitor and ensure quality. The co-operative would be non-profit making but free to reinvest any surplus.

I feel these are a product of muddled thinking and a lack of political courage and ultimately will not give the desired result and only serve as distractions taking our eye off the real issues and solutions.

Giving away public property is tantamount to a crime

If the management of a private company wished to take over its assets and run it, they would need to raise finance from an investment bank or private equity firm and pay off the existing shareholders. The public owns public bodies, and simply giving it away to its employees would be reckless and giving away public property to a few lucky individuals who are already earning more than private sector counterparts[10]. Margaret Thatcher was (wrongly) criticized for selling the family silver, but following the co-operative policy would be giving away the family silver!

The government privatised British Telecom in three share sales raising £3.9 Billion in 1984, £5 Billion in 1991 and a further £5 Billion in 1993, generating a total of £14 Billion for the government[11]. Had we instead followed a "co-operative" route and chosen to convert BT into a workers' co-operative, then the public would have lost out on £14 Billion.

A great deal is made of market testing, rather than giving the assets to a co-operative, the assets and the opportunity to provide the service should be auctioned off and sold to the highest bidder, ensuring that the public get a fair price.

The only advantage to be gained by handing it over to the current employees is a political one as it allows the government in power to obfuscate the issue and conceal the fact that the management is being transferred into private ownership, the politicians hope being that privatisation with a zero price tag will not be regarded as a privatisation, however in the process, their lack of political courage losing the public large amounts of money that would otherwise be raised by the sale of the assets.

Failure to create a market
The factors that create good performance are the operation of a free market consisting of consumers who are presented with choice of supply and empowered to make their own purchase decisions and competition between suppliers where it's predicated that the inefficient ones will (and should) fail and go out of business making way for better performing suppliers.

Co-operatives by themselves don't create a free market and therefore cannot be a solution by themselves.

Not for Profit is No Recommendation
A great deal is made of the fact that co-operatives will be "not for profit", with

10   Median Earnings Public vs. Private Sector http://www.statistics.gov.uk/cci/nugget.asp?id=285
11   BT Privatisation History
      http://www.btplc.com/Thegroup/BTsHistory/Privatisationinfosheetissue2.pdf

the implicit common understanding that that fact somehow makes them virtuous. Once again this reflects muddled and populist thinking and a misunderstanding of profit.

It's extremely simple to become "not for profit" all one has to do is pay everybody inflated salaries and bonuses and become lazy and inefficient. Adopting these "virtues" should ensure the co-operative won't make any profits.

Benefits of co-operatives can be achieved in a far simpler way

There is merit in having decisions made closer to the action, rather than in some remote central government office. However transferring authority and decision making power could be done overnight, simply by changing the terms of reference between central government and the public organizations, and would not require the setting up of any co-operatives.

Inbuilt conflicts of interest

If a new disruptive technology or innovation comes out whose adoption would mean that 70% of the people in the co-operative could be made redundant, then would the co-operative seriously all put their hands up and vote in the new technology?

Need to recognize the real issue and not go off on tangents

Therefore co-operatives are unnecessary and a distraction as they take focus away from what is really needed – public service provision by private operators competing within a functioning market.

24.7 Organization of the Essential Public Sector

As a consequence of the earlier discussions, the general rule and bias should be for public services to be provided by the private sector. However where something is deemed strategic and of vital national interest and cannot sensibly be done by private organisations, then and only then should it be done by the state. Prime examples are the judiciary, police, local council and armed forces.

The issue then arises if it must be in the public sector, how should we organize it to minimise the distortion effects from being part of the public sector. The approach I'd propose is to try and make it as analogous to what happens in normal free markets.

Let's take each distortion in turn:

Performance is obfuscated and hard to measure – invent a "Satisfaction Currency"

The current approach of having numerous benchmarks is difficult because like the Observer effect in physics, the very act of measuring certain specified parameters alters what those parameters would be in the absence of the measurement regime. The alterations would be caused by the public body keen to get a good report.

That's why the market mechanism, where in effect every consumer of a service renders a judgement of the service by their purchase (or repeat purchase) decision is so powerful.

I think the important step is wherever possible to move the judgement away from bureaucracies measuring numerous manipulatable benchmarks, and let the consumers of the service make the decision of how good a service they got. Thus each time a service consumer interacts with or consumes a service from the public body, they need to be obliged to do a very quick satisfaction survey.

I would suggest inventing a currency of "Satisfaction Pounds" which doesn't actually have any monetary value. However each time a service is consumed by a citizen, they are obliged to anonymously choose how many of the Satisfaction Pounds for that service are to be given dependent on how satisfied they were. Then by comparing the actual satisfaction pounds received with the maximum possible satisfaction pounds would give the organization a rating of how satisfied their consumers were with their overall service. Crucially this will give a real time measurement as well.

The levels of Satisfaction Pound's earned by the organization would act to regulate and directly influence the salary levels received by the organization's employees. Low satisfaction levels would translate into reduced pay levels and higher satisfactions levels would lead to a bonus.

If the public body makes some major mistake and things go terribly wrong, then rather than being allowed to escape with apologies, they would need to be fined in satisfaction pounds, so that their overall satisfaction ratings would plummet, possibly taking them down from the top performing band to the bottom band, providing valuable feedback via their pay packets.

Attention would also need to be given to the inputs taken to generate that level of "satisfaction pounds" and another useful metric would be the satisfaction pounds divided by the cost of inputs.

As in a real market, this approach transfers responsibility for judgement to consumers, and also allows the public body to get timely month-by-month feedback on how they are performing in satisfying their customers and managing their costs.

The Make or Buy Decision

When it's accepted that something is a Government responsibility, it appears we short circuit the "make or buy" decision, implicitly opting for a "make" decision with the government taking onto itself the responsibility of "making" the service as well.

The default assumption needs to shift towards buying in the service in all instances, except those where there are overriding national security / strategic reasons to pursue the "make" approach and therefore where we're prepared to accept a lower efficiency and productivity as a price for retaining national security.

Internal Virtual Markets

The low innovation and growth in public organizations stem from them being secure and monopolistic providers with little competition. A good way of dealing with this is to break up the cosy monopoly and create internal markets in the provision of public services.

In creating the internal markets the large monolithic service providers needs to be broken up into various layers mapped onto the industry value chain, with competition and choice between the entities in each layer, and it being easy for consumers at each level to switch providers.

If feasible, ideally the internal market should operate within the same overlapping geographical region, with consumers in the region free to choose from one of a number of competing public sector bodies, each providing the same service. The competition between the public bodies will help drive innovation and growth. If due to its function it's hard to split and there can only be a single public sector body per region, then the bodies providing the service in other regions need to be treated as separate entities.

The various public sector providers of the same service should be classified into a high, medium and low performance band, and the pay budget should vary by band, with the high band getting say 20% more than the middle band, and the low band getting 20% less than the middle band. With this differentiation a public sector body in the top band would have 120% of the budget, whereas a body in the bottom band would have 80%. The increase in pay levels would allow public employees in the best performing bodies to get up to 50% more than their counterparts offering the same service in less well performing bodies.

By no longer treating everyone providing the same service as similar, it would wake up public sector bodies and force them to compete or face up to 50% less pay. This competition would drive innovation and growth.

If a particular public body is being mismanaged and continually in the bottom band for more than five years, then it would go into a "takeover pool" and a third of the takeover pool, chosen at random, should have their entire top management team face automatic dismissal and replacement by a new management team.

The satisfaction pounds currency would be a good way of separating the public bodies into the three different performance bands[12].

The inspiration for the above comes from trying to simulate the private sector, where one would expect well managed successful companies to be more profitable and pay their employees higher amounts than poorly managed less successful ones, and companies being continually mismanaged might face a hostile takeover and the removal of their entire board.

Creating internal markets and having differential pay as discussed above would also address the poor service, lack of cost control and error prone behaviour of public bodies by creating sanctions and feedback, and help stop being complacent and wasteful of resources.

As an example of the power of internal markets to achieve results, research done by the London School of Economics showed that there was an increase in productivity in the NHS in the early 1990s with the Conservative government's creation of an internal market in the NHS with GP fund-holders, and when the Labour government subsequently got rid of GP fund-holders this was accompanied by a sharp fall in productivity[13].

12   Although I mention three bands, if this is felt too coarse, it could easily be four or five bands instead, the key being to have a significant pay difference between the top and bottom performers
13   National Health Service – It isn't getting better yet
     http://www.economist.com/world/britain/displaystory.cfm?story_id=E1_TTRJQTR

24.8 Newton's Laws applied to the Dynamics of Public Sector Bodies

I have often mused that with a slight re-interpretation Newton's Laws of Motion[14] could be transformed to apply to public sector bodies.

Thinking it a tad harsh, I had not planned to include them even though they serve as useful shorthand to capture the essence of public sector bodies. However my view changed on hearing of the Kafkaesque announcement of the UK government's new body, created in response to the MPs' expenses scandal. The Independent Parliamentary Standards Authority (IPSA) being created with 80 staff, is to cost six times more[101] to set up than the amount MPs were ordered to repay. Although the body will undertake some additional duties as well, it seems bizarre to need 80 staff to monitor expenses of 646 MPs and to consider it right to spend so much more than the potential saving. A more efficient approach would have been to have the expenses rules redrafted to close loopholes and remove ambiguity and publish expenses online using aliases for anonymity and detailed annual inspections of a random selection. This example of gross overspend of public funds convinced me to include the Laws.

First Law
In the absence of a media expose, a public sector body will remain at its current headcount and budget irrespective of its value add.

Second Law
A public sector body undergoing a media expose will experience a pressure to change directly proportional to the media exposure and inversely proportion to its headcount.

Third Law
Whenever a public sector body is pressured to change, it will resist the change with an equal and opposite pressure and attempt to maintain the status quo.

Rationale for the Laws
Embedded in the first law are the points that it's hard to measure the output of public sector bodies, their clients have little power and often they are monopolies. Targets exist but they can be fudged and manipulated. As the body continues getting state funding, it can carry on regardless despite any inefficiencies or poor customer service.

14   Newton's Laws of Motion http://en.wikipedia.org/wiki/Newton's_laws_of_motion

The second law acknowledges that as the normal market regulators of profitability, competition and customer service don't apply to public sector bodies, it's only when the public sector body finds the media spotlight upon it that the heat gets turned up for it to change. It also makes the point that because of their size and inertia, large public bodies can absorb a fair bit of bad news without actually changing too much.

The third law encapsulates the point that in the absence of market disciplines, pressure for change usually needs to come from outside, whereas people at the top of the organization, having climbed the greasy pole are often wrapped up with self preservation and attempts to preserve the status quo and hard won privileges.

There will of course be exceptions and pockets of excellence in the public sector where outstanding management or idealists cluster and achieve good results. The point is to underscore the existence of structural factors that conspire to make public bodies sub-optimal compared to doing the same function in the private sector.

It's worth remembering that in its heyday, there were many companies in the Soviet Union whose outputs had a lower value than their inputs, and despite the fact they were destroying value they were deemed a success and getting the requisite tick in the box for meeting production targets.

> *Public servants say, always with the best of intentions, "What greater service we could render if only we had a little more money and a little more power." But the truth is that outside of its legitimate function, government does nothing as well or as economically as the private sector.*
>
> ~ *Ronald Reagan*

25. Sacred Public Sector Cows

25.1 The Inevitability of the Soviet Union

The preceding two chapters outlined how the private sector is structurally more efficient and innovative than the public sector. It was no surprise therefore that eventually even the Soviet Union, one of the richest countries in the world and endowed with immense potential slid downwards into "zastoi" or stagnation[1].

This was an inevitable consequence of backing a system that was structurally inefficient and sub-optimal, and led to a hollowing out of the state from within.

25.2 Gravity doesn't apply to us...

> *The only thing we learn from history is that we learn nothing from history.*
>
> ~ *Friedrich Hegel*

The previous two chapters might have appeared like pushing at an open door, however despite the larger than life example offered by the former Soviet Union of the dangers of following a public sector intensive path, we still find countries making "special cases" or reasons why their situation is different, or that particular sectors must be exempt. It's a bit like arguing that we accept gravity, but for these particular objects gravity no longer applies.

If it's a small portion of the economy, then the inefficiency can be tolerated however it remains an unnecessary and extravagant waste of resources.

As examples, I'll look at the Public Sector in India and the UK.

1   Education Forum Discussion, contribution by Mikhail Gorbachev
     http://educationforum.ipbhost.com/index.php?showtopic=907

25.3   The Indian tiger snared in its own net

India has a large number of public sector companies ranging from airlines, artificial limb manufacturing, power plant equipment, education consultancy, petrochemicals, aeronautics, insecticides, condoms, machine tools, watches, tractors, printing machinery to name just a few items[2].

What is puzzling is why the Indian Government should think it has any particular competence at running these companies. A quick look at some of their websites dispels that illusion, one a mining undertaking, bizarrely played out the melodies of greensleeves on its home page. All the factors discussed in the previous two chapters apply and it's immoral to be doing all these things when they could be better done in the private sector. In addition, were they in the private sector and unchained from the dead hand of government many of these might have leveraged their large home market to become world beating global players.

There are a lot of legitimate matters for the Indian Government to be looking at, such as building infrastructure and investing in human capital via education and health and removing stifling regulations. Running all these public companies is a complete distraction of government time and finances. It needs to learn and apply the lessons of the Soviet Union and not pretend that this time round gravity no longer exists.

It would do well to heed the online petition[3] by a number of Indian citizens to pursue its privatisation programme with boldness and set free the Indian tiger.

25.4   Sacred Public Sector Cows in the UK

In the decade from mid 1980s to mid 1990s, under Margaret Thatcher the UK privatised a large part of its bloated public sector, including telecommunications, gas, airlines, railways, water and electricity companies. The programme was successful with the UK being seen as a trail blazer and imitated by other countries around the world[4].

---

2   GOI Directory Public Sector Undertakings http://goidirectory.nic.in/psucentral.htm
3   Petition to Government of India to pursue privatisation with boldness
     http://www.nriol.com/petition/petition2.html
4   What We Can Learn from Margaret Thatcher
     http://www.heritage.org/Research/PoliticalPhilosophy/HL650.cfm

However the UK stopped short from privatising certain industries, it's almost as if these were "sacred cows" and untouchable. I don't understand this, if the private sector is structurally better at managing industry then why do we regard certain industries are special and somehow able to defy the laws that apply to all other sectors?

Ultimately I think it's down to muddled headed thinking and a lack of political courage after the "Iron lady" departed, however in this section I would like to explore these sacred cows in greater detail.

The herd of sacred cows contains Schooling, National Health Service (NHS), Royal Mail and the BBC. Were you to ever suggest to the man in the street that we might privatise the NHS or Schools, there would be an uproar with people thinking it morally wrong to profit from other people's ill health or from such a basic need as education.

With the government having to deal with the fallout from the Banking Crisis and high levels of debt, there is a greater imperative to improve efficiency and productivity and reduce government debt, further strengthening the case for privatisation, and instead of trying to balance the books by making savage cuts in public spending and services, privatising the herd of sacred cows would be a far better strategy, and in the long term a blessing in disguise

Food Retail

To illustrate the point, lets imagine that the Government controlled food retail and distribution so that all food was moved around and bought only in government shops. Then if one day we were to suggest that lets privatise food distribution the same misguided people would stand up and make the points that food is a "basic need" and one should not seek to profit from a commodity that's so essential for our survival. Others would worry that people would be priced into starvation.

However the private sector competition between the likes of Tesco, Sainsbury and Asda has relentlessly driven down the cost of food whilst improving quality and expanding choice for consumers. The companies have responded to consumer lifestyles and kept shops open when people want to shop resulting in shops being open 24 hours a day and over weekends, and have sourced foods from all corners of the world responding to our desire for choice.

Lets shut our eyes and imagine for a moment that the Government controlled food distribution, there would be targets for everything, shops would have strict opening hours shutting at 6:00 pm, there would be a much smaller choice of items with little innovation and things would be a lot more expensive. There would also be a huge emphasis on home-grown produce and all in all it would be a dismal "black and white" experience compared to the vibrant multi-coloured experience in today's private sector shops. Weekend opening on Sunday would be something you could only dream about.

Clearly the Government running our food distribution would be unacceptable because we can see the alternative. However we need to realise that in our schools and hospitals we're currently putting up with a black and white experience, because we're unable to envision the multicoloured service we'd get by moving these into the private sector. Over the next few section I'll explore how this might work.

25.5   Education

In schooling the minimum that needs to happen is to issue Vouchers to people that they are free to use at any school i.e. public or private. This would convert people from being entities going through the system to consumers of the service able to make choices. Having the vouchers useable at private schools would, overnight, bring extra competition into the sector.

Ideally though, schools should be privatised either individually or in groups with the government paying for people to study by giving vouchers. In case supply and demand got out of kilter in a particular area then market forces would pull in extra capacity or alternatively the government can act as a catalyst and encourage new schools to setup by offering incentives, thereby helping seed the market.

The voucher converts people from being mere consumers into customers, but it's an incomplete conversion, as the voucher would have a single value. It would be a rather odd market where all suppliers charged exactly the same. I envisage that privatised schools would charge varying amounts. If the school's rate is higher than the voucher value then the parent and state would each pay half of the additional cost. Where the school's rate is less than the voucher value then the parent would receive a cash amount of half the cost difference from the state, in effect both parties[5] sharing the saving equally. The purpose of this type of voucher, which I'm calling Flexible Shared Vouchers is that it incentivises the market to behave as

---

5   The parents and the government

markets should with varying prices and consumers getting the benefits of shopping around instead of having everything with a single price tag which would depress innovation and variety.

Having schools run privately would get rid of a large and costly education bureaucracy, as well as moderate the huge power currently wielded by Teaching Unions which acts as a constraint on reform.

Just as we have numerous hotel chains, with branches around the world, I see the same for schooling, with good schooling companies setting up around the world, in the process disseminating best practice in teaching and educational management worldwide and giving consumers what they want, whilst competing amongst each other for the best teachers and school heads etc. The ability to charge premiums on top of the basic voucher rate, and the strong competition between schools would drive up best practise and innovations in education as well as attract a higher calibre of entrant into the sector.

25.6   British Broadcasting Corporation (BBC)

I must confess at the outset I'm a fan of the BBC and like many others think it produces excellent programming output. However I recall being on an assignment out in Guyana and seeing CNN on the hotel TV and thinking at the time that the BBC Worldwide offerings didn't appear to be in the same league. Similarly News Corporation's Star TV is one of the major channels in India with ten specialist channels aimed at the Indian subcontinent but BBC Worldwide is only a token presence.

For sometime now I've felt that having the BBC shackled in the public sector has limited the scope of its ambitions and given an easy ride to the likes of News Corporation. For a nation with the creative skills that lead to the Beatles it feels entirely wrong that a major player in its creative industries has been neutered in such a way.

There has been talk of privatising BBC Worldwide[6], however I feel that's too timid, and the entire BBC should be privatised. This would free it up to become a global player in quality television. With the huge number of television channels, why

6   Call for sale of BBC Worldwide
     http://www.independent.co.uk/news/media/tv-radio/call-for-sale-of-bbc-worldwide-1877866.html

should we assume that audiovisual media is somehow different and needs a public sector company to provide it. If there is a valid reason for it, then surely the same rationale should apply for print media as well. However, if a government owned newspaper were to be suggested that would seem ridiculous. I think the only reason we put up with the BBC being in public ownership is as a historical legacy and it's something we're familiar with.

When people talk of privatising the BBC, the worry is that the BBC gets dumbed down, however that's negative thinking, and the upside is that the BBC will export its high quality television and radio programming skills around the world and bring a new quality option to media worldwide as well as being a huge boost to the creative industries worldwide.

I would not however stop the license fee, as the license fee is something that helps get high quality television programming with a minimum of advertising. We should continue collecting the license fee at the same level but make it available to all UK channels for preparing public sector broadcast (psb) programming for display in the UK. The BBC should not have a monopoly on deciding what's going to be of public interest and having this done competitively would improve the overall quality of psb programming. Channels (including the privatised BBC) would pay a royalty for displaying license fee funded programming outside of the UK, with this royalty going back to fund other psb programming.

Once it's in private hands, with its heritage and experience the BBC could tap global capital markets and expand worldwide, and we need to stop treating it like a sacred cow locked up in our backyard.

25.7   Royal Mail

When Margaret Thatcher's aide's raised privatisation of the Royal Mail, Mrs Thatcher replied that the Royal Mail was different, stamps had the Queen's image on them. The Hooper Report[7] pointed out that the Royal Mail was 40% less efficient than its competitors, whilst full time pay for Royal Mail employees was 20% higher than other postal workers.

Fifteen years ago the Dutch postal service KPN was sold by the state, and now as

---

7   Modernise or decline: Policies to maintain the universal postal service in the United Kingdom. http://www.berr.gov.uk/files/file49389.pdf

TNT it is a world-class company. It's instructive to compare its performance with that of the Royal Mail. The Royal Mail had double the labour cost, half the efficiency and a profit margin of 0 versus TNT's stellar margin of 14.8%.

2007	Labour cost as % of revenues	Walk Sorting Automation %	Walk Sequencing Automation %	Operating Profit Margin %
TNT (Netherlands)	27.9	95	85	14.8
Royal Mail	66.1	70	0	0.0

Figure 5: Comparison of Royal Mail and TNT
(figures from Hooper Report)

The bleak figures in figure 5 demonstrate the results of the arguments I've been making about public sector organizations. Had British politicians kept their nerve and privatised Royal Mail then it too might have been in the same league as TNT, with taxpayers avoiding losing their shirts!

When the part privatisation of Royal Mail was raised in 2009, then 140 Labour MPs opposed its privatisation, which makes me think that perhaps MPs need to undergo some form of economics examination before being judged fit to take a seat in Parliament, and their lack of economic judgement was a far greater sin than any member of parliament expenses overspend on duck-houses or moats that seemed to have so caught the imagination of the British Media and public.

The Royal Mail needs to be fully privatised allowing it to benefit from the automatic disciplines that would come with being part of a market along with greater access to finance.

It could be privatised as a single entity, however there's the danger of converting a public monopoly into a private one. My preference is for it to be split into three separate entities each receiving assets equally spread throughout the UK and each with responsibility for the whole of the UK. The aim being that they act as competing national postal companies and not regional monopolies. Each entity would issue their own stamps with people free to choose whose stamps to use, and I envisage there being a range of varying rates, service levels and terms[8] for different stamps dependent on the issuing entity. The entity whose stamp is on the letter would pay interconnect rates to its siblings if the letter is collected or delivered by one of its sibling entities. The interconnect rate would need to be regulated, and the entities would be free to choose not to use its siblings in an area and to expand their own delivery and collection centres.

25.8   Healthcare

As far as sacred cows go, the NHS[9] must probably be the largest and most sacred. The very thought of bringing in private enterprise would get treated as blasphemy by medical unions and public who've been taken in and unable to contemplate the thought rationally. Politicians therefore wisely but cowardly duck the issue and there's some justice in people getting the system they deserve.

I recall once taking my daughter to a private hospital in Delhi after an accident, and having to fill in a payment slip before the doctors would start any treatment. At the same time there was a young boy who had fallen from a roof, whose parents were being told the same by the doctors and one could see the obvious dilemma writ large on their faces[10]. At the time I was quite relieved to think that back home in the UK we had the NHS and this kind of dilemma would not arise.

I'm therefore completely in favour of the state ensuring provision of health care for its citizens and think how we treat our sick is a sign of our civilisation. However we've made an implicit assumption that provision of health care must also mean running the production units[11] that produce the care. There's absolutely no reason to make that assumption and we do so at our cost. The key thing is the quality of patient care, the ownership of the facilities is a mere technicality and is a case of what works best. Unfortunately the general public has been taken in that change of ownership implies an end of free treatment and medical unions have encouraged this misconception, leading to its discussion becoming a political taboo.

---

8   i.e. different terms and conditions
9   National Health Service
10   regretfully I did not step up as my thoughts were with my daughter but have wondered about their fate, there had also been talk of a state run hospital for them to go to.
11   i.e. hospitals

In the chapter on Public Sector, I outlined how various factors conspire to make public sector organisations sub-optimal and the lower performance should only be tolerated if there is some accompanying strategic national benefit. The comparison in figure 5 showed how the privatised Dutch post office knocked the socks off the Royal Mail.

There was an increase in productivity of around 11% in the NHS in the early 1990s with the Conservative's creation of an internal market with general practitioner (GP) fund-holders. When Labour reversed these changes, there was a corresponding fall in productivity[12] of 8%. These shifts show that there is nothing different or magical about health care, it too is subject to normal market dynamics and will react in the expected way.

It's puzzling that despite the strong example provided by the former Soviet Union of how centrally controlled and planned structures fail to deliver and are suboptimal, we still cling on to this outmoded approach in the management of the NHS. Future historians will have no option but to judge it as a caving in by the political classes. This wouldn't matter if it were a small organization, but with an annual budget expected to reach £110 Billion by 2011, it's a huge spend. There was a scandal over overstatement of MPs' expenses, but the real scandal is mismanagement of large budgets such as those in the NHS.

Were Tesco's were to shut at 5:30 pm on the basis that their staff needed a home life, and charged shoppers to use their car parks, there would be disbelief and uproar. Yet GPs' surgeries routinely shut at 5:30 and hospitals charge fortunes for parking and we simply accept it with a stiff upper lip.

In the chapter on Public Services, I spoke of the difficulty of measuring, that is a large part of the problem and it's hard for the public to get a handle of how good (or bad) the NHS actually is, and kind heartedly they give it the benefit of the doubt. If one looks at cancer survival rates, the five-year survival rate for prostate cancer in the US is 91.9%, in the UK[13] it is 51.1%. Put more starkly, if 100 people had prostrate cancer, then in the US there would still be 92 people alive five years later, however in the UK there would only be 51 people alive, i.e. the NHS would have failed 41 people who would have died. That kind of statistic is upsetting and underscores the need to change a flawed system and get politicians to summon their courage and look at better options.

12   National Health Service – It isn't getting better yet
     http://www.economist.com/world/britain/displaystory.cfm?story_id=E1_TTRJQTR
13   Huge gap in world cancer survival http://news.bbc.co.uk/1/hi/health/7510121.stm

Country	Per capita spending on health ($)	Doctors per 10,000 pop	Nurses and midwives per 10,000 pop	Hospital beds per 10,000 pop	Life expect. at birth	Avg Income Hospital Doctors (£000s)	Avg Income Primary Care Doctors (£000s)
United States	6719	26	94	31	78	135	97
United Kingdom	2815	23	128	39	80	83	82
Italy	2631	37	72	39	82	42	31
Germany	3465	34	80	83	80	40	61
France	3420	34	80	73	81	50	47

Figure 6. (Source: WHO / Guardian, HM Treasury)

Figure 6 is a comparison across Europe and US, showing that despite the US putting in twice the money, they only have 10% more doctors than the UK, and 20% less hospital beds, and a lower life expectancy. This should establish that it's not the amount of money that matters, it's how it's managed and organized that's key, and why it's so important that the subject is not a political no-go area.

Italy managed to have 38% more doctors despite spending 7% less than the NHS. France and Germany spent 23% more than in the UK but for that extra spend got 48% more doctors and 100% more hospital beds, whilst UK doctors earned twice the amount of their European counterparts. Comparatively, the NHS is not delivering value for money, an unsurprising conclusion given its suboptimal structure.

Furthermore the NHS has often let patients down, such as the case of the Mid Staffordshire NHS Trust where it was estimated that there were at least 400 more deaths than expected over a 3 year period, however despite this its ratings had gone up. For those still in denial and unconvinced of the suboptimal nature of public bodies, it's worth reflecting that all the public bodies that were charged with monitoring the trust singularly failed to pick up the problem with one even dismissing the concerns at one point, and it took the determined efforts of a private research group, Dr Foster, to flag the concerns that finally led to the exposition[14].

My prescription for the NHS would be to privatise the Secondary Care Sector i.e. hospitals into three parts each with national scope, creating strong local competitors throughout the country. The primary care layer should also be opened out to competition making it easier to setup and create new primary care service providers without needing prior permission from local health care bureaucracies other than meeting quality criteria.

The players in the primary care layer would need to be corporately distinct from those in the secondary care layer, to avoid any conflicts of interest between commissioning and provisioning of health care.

Patients would have vouchers, using the concept of Flexible Shared Vouchers that I outlined earlier[15], with voucher values set to the median value needed to pay for the treatment. In cases where the actual cost of treatment differed from the voucher value for the treatment, then patients would share any savings or extra costs with the government.

It may seem odd to prefer the various providers at the GP as well as Hospital levels to price differently for their services and have this somewhat odd sharing of benefit / extra cost between their price and the voucher value, but I see that as vital to encourage service differentiation, evolution and growth, by making each customer act as a micro level inspector weighing up alternative options. If everyone were forced to maintain the same price then we dilute the drivers for evolution through service innovation. Allowing people to charge more, gives scope to introduce new features, which then gradually get adopted by the other providers as they see their market share diminishing. Alternatively a provider could become a low cost producer and charge less than the voucher value, attracting extra custom – with both the patient and government gaining.

Once this is in place, I would expect GP surgeries to be open evenings and weekends, and the productivity, efficiency and use of capital to greatly increase perhaps with 24-hour shift working of major expensive equipment increasing their utilisation. The competition between the groups would drive down costs and increase efficiency with innovations in service and treatment therapies. The hospital groups created would grow over time to become world beating medical service providers with operations across the world rather than remaining cosseted in a single market. In

14   Hospital left patients 'sobbing and humiliated' http://news.bbc.co.uk/1/hi/health/8531441.stm
15   Section 25.5 on education

short once freed from the yoke of public ownership they would blossom and create extra value add for all concerned.

> *In Large states public education will always be mediocre, for the same reason that in large kitchens the cooking is usually bad*
> *~ Friedrich Nietzsche*

26. Global Warming

Everybody talks about the weather, but nobody does anything about it"

~ Charles Dudley Warner

26.1 Is Global Warming Real?

This may seem an odd question, but on typing "Is Global Warming" into a Google search box, the greatest number of search results starting with these words is for "Is Global Warming Real" with 30 million results, demonstrating that a large number of people are pondering over this.

Our tendency to generalise from isolated cases
One of the problems is that the climate is a hugely complex system, and one can always find special cases or local anomalies which differ from the global trend, which can be exploited to create media interest and sow seeds of doubt in people's minds. For example, we all know that smoking is bad for health, and increases the risk of cancer but equally most will have come across instances of active smokers living well into their nineties. The point is that each time you come across a smoker living into their nineties, no one would now seriously start questioning whether or not smoking is bad for your health. The same holds for climate change, just because there are occasional localised issues and factors that buck the trend, it should not detract from the main message, that on average at thousands of data points across the world there is evidence of global warming and climate change.

Our love for Conspiracy Theories
There will always be conspiracy theories surrounding any major event, for example people have questioned the Apollo moon landing, as well as who was responsible for the assassination of John F.Kennedy and the death of Princess Diana[1]. Given

---

1   Top 10 Conspiracy Theories http://listverse.com/2007/08/21/top-10-conspiracy-theories/

our penchant for conspiracy theories, it's hardly surprising that Global Warming would spawn its share of conspiracy theorists and disbelievers.

To err is human

In any large enterprise, you can be sure there will be some minor errors made, this being a consequence of our being human. Regardless of what is done to mitigate them they will appear. An example is in the construction of large software programmes, it's expected that bugs will appear and a stage in the development reserved for user and system testing. Similarly in the preparation of scientific papers the debugging process is peer review. It's not unheard of programmes having undiscovered bugs even after it has been through its test phase. Just because a few bugs are found, it doesn't stop the programme working.

Similarly in any large area of research such as that being conducted in Climate Change and Global Warming, it would be unusual if there were no small bugs or issues found, and they need to be seen in perspective and not taken as evidence of some sort of conspiracy.

A common sense approach

Imagine that there are five university students sharing a house, whilst they clean their own rooms, they've been unable to work out and enforce a system of cleaning the common areas of the house, with the consequence that the living room, kitchen and bathroom go without being cleaned. One day their lecturer walks in and is appalled at the disgraceful state of the common areas and queries it. If the students were to turn around and tell the lecturer that they didn't think that not cleaning the common areas would have an impact, almost everyone would shake their heads in disbelief at their foolishness and how they could contemplate saying something so obviously absurd.

Since the Industrial Revolution we've used coal, oil and gas which had laid buried for millions of years and generated energy by burning it and releasing the waste products into the atmosphere as carbon dioxide. We now release 27 billion tons of carbon dioxide, containing 7.3 billion tons of carbon, into the earth's atmosphere each year, and continue this year on year at an increasing rate[2].

How can we then rationally stand back po-faced and try and maintain that we can continue to release this much extra carbon dioxide into the atmosphere and that it

2   Global warming is real – Times Online
      http://www.timesonline.co.uk/tol/news/environment/article6931598.ece?token=null&offset=24&page=1

will have no impact on our climatic and biological systems? Anyone who tries to argue along these lines is behaving somewhat like those students in the earlier example and is equally absurd and flying in the face of common sense.

View of the Scientific Community

The Intergovernmental panel on climate change (IPCC) has 194 member countries and produced its Fourth Assessment Report, Climate Change 2007 with inputs from thousands of scientists worldwide. Their views on the causes of climate change are that it's extremely unlikely (under 5%) that the global pattern of warming can be explained without external causes, and that it is very unlikely that the causes are natural. Their view is that greenhouse gases are very likely (over 90%) to have caused the global warming observed over the last 50 years[3].

The IPCC view is that global warming is affecting many natural physical and biological systems, and there will be an increasing net annual cost as global temperatures rise[4].

The IPCC view has been supported by 32 national academies of science across the world as well as a large number of institutes and scientific societies[5], an example being the UK science community publicly expressing its utmost confidence in the IPCC Fourth Assessment Report[6]. The Nobel Foundation satisfied themselves with the quality of the IPCC work and awarded it the 2007 Nobel Peace Prize.

Other independent reviews such as that conducted by the UK Met Office looking at research published since the IPCC report has found evidence has strengthened for human influence on climate and a consistent picture of a warming world[7].

With the overwhelming majority of the world's scientific community supporting the Global Warming thesis, it would be foolhardy and reckless to simply write it off as some form of mass hysteria and conspiracy.

---

3   IPCC: Understanding and attributing climate change
     http://www.ipcc.ch/publications_and_data/ar4/wg1/en/ch9s9-es.html
     http://www.ipcc.ch/publications_and_data/ar4/wg1/en/tssts-6.html
4   IPCC: Impact, Adaption and Vulnerability
     http://www.ipcc.ch/publications_and_data/ar4/wg2/en/tssts-summary-of.html
5   Scientific opinion on climate change
     http://en.wikipedia.org/wiki/Scientific_opinion_on_climate_change
6   Statement from the UK science community
     http://www.metoffice.gov.uk/climatechange/news/latest/uk-science-statement.html
7   Climate change human link evidence stronger http://news.bbc.co.uk/1/hi/sci/tech/8550090.stm

The unequivocal answer therefore, to those 30 million queries on Google, is that Global Warming is real and taking place.

> *Our generation has inherited an incredibly beautiful world from our parents and they from their parents. It is in our hands whether our children and their children inherit the same world.*
> ~ *Richard Branson*

26.2   Global Warming Denial needs to be on the statute books

The arguments in the earlier section make a compelling case for global warming, so what puzzles me is why have we not yet taken it to heart and doing more to mitigate its effects.

Standard advise from insurance companies is to never admit liability and I suspect this is the storyline being subconsciously played out. Were we to admit that Global warming is real then we immediately have a dilemma – we need to either put up with guilt or will need to make serious changes to our life style. It's far easier to take an ostrich approach and latch onto fringe arguments as evidence of it being inconclusive and fabricating a moral green light to continue gorging a high-energy diet.

Although a firm believer in freedom of speech, just as there are laws against Holocaust denial in a number of European countries, I believe that all countries now need to create and put laws against Global Warming denial onto their statute books making it crystal clear that the phenomenon is real and hard for people to pursue a strategy of obfuscation and denial.

> *There is no debate among any statured scientists of what is happening. The only debate is the rate at which it is happening.*
> ~*James McCarthy, chair of the Advisory Committee on the Environment of the International Committee of Scientific Unions*

26.3   Global Warming is a problem of Success

Before doing too much hand wringing and descending into melancholy, it's worth remembering that Global Warming is a problem of success. As a race we've been hugely innovative and adaptable, creating large complex cities and all sorts of products and services across many sectors, and in that sense Global Warming is a by product of our inventiveness and success. Although it's clearly now a major issue and challenge, I'm confident that the same inventiveness that created the problem will come to our rescue and help find a solution, provided we address the issue seriously.

26.4   Our Global Warming Objective

Whenever taking on any undertaking, it's vital to set the correct objective. Carbon levels are currently at 430 parts per million (ppm) and rising at 2 ppm each year. The hope is that if world governments accept low emission targets, then we can stabilise Carbon levels between 450 and 550 ppm, which would mean a further one degree temperature rise[8].

Whilst 500 to 550 ppm may be achievable, if it still leads to further climate change issues, then just because it's an achievable target should not mean it becomes acceptable.

One can try and innovate by a process of incrementalism, but that sets a limit on what can be achieved, narrowing the horizon. To force a change of mindset, and the generation of solutions that can truly create step changes, it's necessary to set ourselves a target that cannot be achieved by mere incrementalism, and thereby force radical solutions into being.

On that basis, I think our target needs to be far more ambitious and we should seek to reverse the atmospheric Carbon build up and bring it down to a level of 400 ppm.

26.5   Political Stalemate

I spoke earlier[9] about the benefits that we would gain if we could somehow move over to a situation where we were politically organized as a single global country. This would allow us to work in unison as a single team with one agenda.

However our current arrangement of 193 separate countries, each with its own set

8   Stern Review: The Economics of Climate Change
     http://www.hm-treasury.gov.uk/d/CLOSED_SHORT_executive_summary.pdf
9   Chapter Three

of politicians, issues and agendas means we're simply not structured to work together efficiently on global issues, and trying to bring everyone together in a single binding agreement is a huge and time consuming undertaking.

The GATT talks on getting agreement on Global Trade took around fifty years before the World Trade Organization (WTO) was created and the talks are still continuing with the last round[10] on further trade liberalisation failing to reach agreement. This underlines the difficulties of getting multilateral agreements in place and therefore it was no surprise that the Cop15 Copenhagen Climate Conference in 2009 failed to reach agreement.

With Global Warming we don't have the luxury of time for long drawn out multilateral talks on working out a solution that is acceptable to all countries. It's also too important an issue to be simply left to each country to draw up its own plans.

This leads to a stalemate and it's vital to break this logjam through innovative and out of the box thinking.

> *I think it's crazy for us to play games with our children's future. We know what's happening to the climate, we have a highly predictable set of consequences if we continue to pour greenhouse gases into the atmosphere.*
> *~ Bill Clinton 42nd U.S. President, United Nations Climate Conference*

26.6   Carbon Capture and Storage and Oxygen Depletion

Carbon capture and storage (CCS) consists of taking carbon dioxide (CO_2) from large sources such as power stations and keeping it away from the atmosphere, typically by storing it underground in geological formations or depleted oil and gas reservoirs.

It is anticipated[11,12] that CCS could form 15% to 54% of our carbon mitigation effort until the year 2100.

---

10   Doha, 2008
11   Carbon Capture and Storage http://en.wikipedia.org/wiki/Carbon_capture_and_storage
12   Carbon Capture and Storage, Special Report, IPCC
      http://www.ipcc.ch/pdf/special-reports/srccs/srccs_chapter8.pdf

	Carbon	Oxygen
Coal	$85 - 91.5\%$	$2 - 5\%$
Crude Oil	$84 - 87\%$	$0.1 - 2\%$
Natural Gas	$65 - 80\%$	0%

Figure 7 (Sources[13,14])

As seen from figure 7, coal, oil and natural gas contain very little oxygen, and high amounts of carbon. When burnt as fuel, fresh oxygen from the atmosphere is taken up to form carbon dioxide as a by-product of combustion. When we subsequently capture and store carbon dioxide, we are in effect removing oxygen from the atmosphere and storing it.

Each 44 tons of CO_2 stored contains 14 tons of carbon and 32 tons of oxygen. Therefore by solving one climate issue, we would have embarked on a route to create another climate issue – a shortage of oxygen.

We may be able to live with the oxygen depletion initially, however over time as the depletion cumulatively builds up we would be creating a crisis for future generations.

With oxygen essential for life and needed in our bodies to create energy for us to function, going down a route that can affect the amount of oxygen in the atmosphere appears completely misguided[15,16].

13 Table 1-1, Nontechnical guide to petroleum geology, exploration, drilling and production By Norman J.Hyne
    http://books.google.co.uk/books?id=3A8YIW3uuX0C&pg=PA1&dq=chemical+composition+of+petroleum&cd=1#v=onepage&q=chemical%20composition%20of%20petroleum&f=false
14 Coal   http://en.wikipedia.org/wiki/Coal
15 O2 Dropping Faster than CO_2 Rising Implications for Climate Change Policies
    http://www.i-sis.org.uk/O2DroppingFasterThanCO2Rising.php
16 A more accurate term is geologic oxygen capture and storage
    http://socialenergyscriptorium.blogspot.com/2009/09/more-accurate-term-is-geologic-oxygen.html

26.7   Cap and Trade / Emission Trading and Carbon Offsets

Cap and Trade Systems / Emission Trading Systems (ETS) consist of setting a ceiling to the amount of emissions allowed in a particular sector. The firms in the sector are then given emission permits at free or low cost, then as the economy grows the firms would need to purchase additional emission permits from other companies. If a company becomes more carbon efficient then it won't need all its permits and can sell them on the market to others.

Carbon Offsets consist of a company sponsoring projects in developing countries to increase the carbon efficiency in the developing country. The idea being that by sponsoring the project in the developing country the carbon saved by that project offsets the carbon generated by the company's main activities.

Offset schemes appear logical in the sense that if you're creating CO_2 in the west, but then paying someone else in a cheaper part of the world to absorb the same amount of CO_2 then in theory you're carbon neutral.

ETS and Offsetting sound good in theory, and are better than doing nothing, however there are a number of fundamental issues with them, and on something as important as Global Warming, it's too high risk to put in place a flawed system.

Lets start by exploring some of the issues:

A Low Emission Traded Price is dishonest
When the Emission permit price (EPP) is less than the real cost of absorbing and removing carbon from the atmosphere then we're not being honest with ourselves.

Ultimately at some point in the future we will need to find a way of removing the excess carbon from the atmosphere and by not being responsible and picking up the full cost of our activities now, we're effectively stealing from future generations who will need to pick up the balance of the cleanup cost.

If the EPP were equal to the real cost of absorbing and removing carbon from the atmosphere then we would indeed be facing up to our responsibilities, and if emission trading is to continue, then we should set a price floor for the EPP equal to the real cost of mitigating the carbon, removing the implicit subsidy.

Imagine what would happen if the EPP were to go higher than the actual cost of removing carbon from the atmosphere. Firms would immediately protest at the warped logic of paying a greater amount for something when they can eliminate all traces of their activity for a smaller amount. In that sense Emission Trading is a one-way bet, only making sense if there's a subsidy to be had, and thereby avoiding the real cleanup cost.

In that sense Emission Trading really only exist as a form of pollution subsidy and avoidance of paying the real cost.

Firms should pay the actual clean up cost

When a company produces waste, it's normal for it to pay to have the waste removed from its premises and taken away for processing. This is accepted business practice at millions of places worldwide daily and is a straightforward concept of facing up to one's responsibility.

I fail to see why Greenhouse gases are treated different to any other waste product. The company producing the greenhouse gases should pay for producing and releasing them into the environment. The amount due needs to be the cost of mitigating the effect of the greenhouse gases released i.e. it needs to pay the actual cost of returning the environment to the exact state before the company performed its operations, in short so that the atmosphere after the company's operations can be returned to its initial state.

If the company doesn't wish to pay, then it has to find a way of capturing just the carbon out of the CO_2 and sequestering it and return the Oxygen back to the environment.

Why give anyone a License to pollute?

Giving firms emission permits at free or low cost is in effect handing out licenses to pollute. That's simply wrong headed thinking, why give anyone a license to pollute?

The policy should be if you wish to pollute then you need to accept responsibility and pay the cost for mitigating your operations or change your operations.

Emission Traded Price gives the wrong signals and is Dysfunctional

Having a price is good, and I'm not saying ETS systems are of no use, but they're distorting as they mask the real cost of mitigation and give out wrong signals, potentially leading firms to make good financial – but poor environmental decisions.

The Emission permits price (EPP) will vary with a number of factors. If there's a recession then demand for permits will drop and reduce the EPP. Then when a firm is looking to create a new plant, it can either buy the equipment to control its emissions but if the EPP is low, then it's better for it to conserve capital and forget about investing in new equipment and instead buy the permits at the artificially low EPP.

Emission Traded Prices can discourage mitigation effects

If the Emission permit price (EPP) doesn't reflect the actual cost of absorbing and removing carbon from the atmosphere then that can have a discouraging effect on the development of carbon sink technologies.

Firms developing carbon sink technologies would take their cue from the price of the emission permits, rightly thinking that if firms can buy cheaply priced permits then why would they invest in higher priced carbon mitigation technology.

This forms yet another reason for ensuring the Emission permit price should not be a traded price, but needs to be a fixed price set at the mid point cost of mitigating greenhouse gases and removing carbon from the atmosphere.

Offset Schemes create the wrong Mindset

Despite their apparent elegance, there are issues with Offset schemes such as whether the offset projects would have happened anyway without the offset and monitoring and verifying that the project actually delivers the planned reductions. It's no surprise major environmental groups are concerned about them and there is a huge shortage of quality gold standard schemes.

There are incentives for firms to exaggerate the results, and for collusion with suppliers, and therefore large opportunities for fraud, scams and dodgy accounting in an unregulated market[17].

The fraud and scams could in theory be rooted out by regulation and oversight but there's a subtler problem with Offsets – they absolve people and companies of "climate sin" creating the mindset "I've purchased offsets and so it's okay to

---

17   The Carbon Neutral Myth http://www.carbontradewatch.org/pubs/carbon_neutral_myth.pdf
Carbon Scam: Greenpeace report http://www.greenpeace.org/usa/news/carbon-scam
The inconvenient truth about the carbon offset industry
http://www.guardian.co.uk/environment/2007/jun/16/climatechange.climatechange
Carbon offsetting exposed as con http://www.foei.org/en/media/archive/2009/carbon-offsetting-exposed-as-con

continue with harmful activity." Although an inexact analogy, it has overtones of an obese person paying someone else to diet and jog on their behalf whilst they continue gorging on a high calorie diet.

This psychological absolution is somewhat wrong headed as we need to do the maximum everywhere, and just because we can do good at one location is no justification to continue doing harm elsewhere. The psychological absolution is a worrying aspect, as it removes the rationale and motivation for behaviour change.

Keep it Simple and just set a fixed set price based on the actual cost of mitigation

Drawing it all together, I think we should stop the Emission Trading Systems with their implicit pollution subsidy, as well as stopping the sale of Carbon Offsets with all of their complexities and instead opt for bringing it back to basics and keep it simple – if a company is emitting waste products into the atmosphere then it is obliged to pay the actual cost of mitigating the carbon and other green house gases that it's inserting into the atmosphere.

26.8   What if someone still disagrees with Global Warming?

Despite the many remaining uncertainties about the nature and the risks of the process (climate change), I believe that there is now sufficient evidence to support prudent precautionary action.
~Cor Herkströter, Senior Managing Director, Shell Oil

If despite the scientific advise and consensus, someone still disagrees with global warming and uses selective datasets to make their case, then should that create a controversy and affect our ability to charge for greenhouse gases (GHG)?

Lets say that someone is very sceptical and mistakenly thinks there is only a 5% chance of climate change being real. There then remains an argument that even if there's a low probability of it being real, we still need to act and take full precautions as it would be irresponsible to ignore the possibility that it turns out to be real i.e. a low probability is *not* a guarantee that it is not going to happen and therefore it still needs mitigating.

Apart from the risk approach there is another more direct way of looking at it. Most people would agree with the simple proposition that if someone leaves rubbish on the street, they are liable for it's clean up cost and would be expected to pay. Just because GHG happens to be colourless, odourless and can easily disperse, it still is a waste product that is being emitted and there remains a responsibility to pay for it's clean up cost. The point is that the atmosphere is being used as a sink for GHG and the producer needs to pay for this privilege regardless of whether or not they believe in global warming – if they don't wish to pay, then they should keep it bottled up on their own premises.

26.9   Charging for Greenhouse Gas (GHG) Emissions

So how much should we charge for emission of GHG? This will be something for the world community to evaluate and decide upon, taking into account targets for the allowable amount of carbon in the atmosphere and the cost of carbon mitigation.

It's worth noting that the cost of emission permits in Europe is $29 per ton of CO_2, and Bank of America[18] has anticipated a price of $20 to $40 per ton of CO_2. However those are permit prices and not necessarily related to the actual costs of mitigating carbon as pointed out earlier.

The IPCC Working Group III in their summary[19] for policy makers, came up with figures of 20 to 80 $/ton by 2030, and 30 to 155 $/ton by 2050 for achieving 550 ppm CO_2.

The Forestry Commission[20] commissioned an independent assessment to examine the potential of the UK's trees and woodlands to mitigate climate change. This estimated the cost was £41 per tonne of CO_2. To allow for the fact that we need to attempt to reverse the climate change effect and have been dumping GHG free of charge for decades, I would add 50% to that, and suggest a figure of £60 per tonne of GHG, i.e. $90 per tonne.

I favour taking a Purchase Power Parity approach in applying the £60 / tonne, thereby ensuring that the "climate change hardship" experienced around the world

18   Bank of America Puts a Price on Carbon
      http://blogs.wsj.com/environmentalcapital/2008/02/13/bank-of-america-puts-a-price-on-carbon/
19   IPCC Working Group III, Mitigation of Climate Change
      http://www.ipcc.ch/pdf/assessment-report/ar4/wg3/ar4-wg3-spm.pdf
20   Combating climate change, A role for UK Forests
      http://www.forestry.gov.uk/pdf/SynthesisUKAssessmentfinal.pdf/$FILE/SynthesisUKAssessmentfinal.pdf

was similar. This fits in with the fact that mitigation costs would vary around the world with differing labour and resource costs.

26.10 Splitting the Climate Change Prevention Costs – Approach Used

Imagine there are 10 families living on a street, of whom eight produce one bin of rubbish each week, and the remaining two produce four bins weekly. As two of the families produce as much rubbish as the remaining eight, most would agree that these two need to pay an additional amount to their council for waste disposal.

The principle has been further developed by the move towards charging for waste disposal by weighing rubbish bins, with the approach being experimented with in a number of European countries[21].

Lets try and apply a similar approach and principle to how we divide and share the costs of emitting GHG into the atmosphere.

Who Owns the Atmosphere?

The short answer is that all the inhabitants of our planet own the atmosphere, by that I mean its human inhabitants. Strictly speaking lower order animals too have a claim, however property rights don't really extend to animals.

There are two ways of dividing the costs, we can say that each country owns all the atmosphere above its territory, and therefore if a country is 4% of the earth's landmass then it also owns 4% of the earth's atmosphere.

Another route would be to take a more egalitarian approach, and say that all human beings are equal, and therefore each of us owns an equal share of our planet's atmosphere. If our global population is N, then each of us owns a $1/N^{th}$ share of the earth's atmosphere.

I prefer the more egalitarian approach, as it feels fairer.

---

21   Many councils 'bug' rubbish bins   http://news.bbc.co.uk/1/hi/uk/5404730.stm

Balancing Costs: Excess Emission Cost and Compensation Due

Balancing Costs is somewhat abstract and it'll be helpful to illustrate its meaning with an example. Lets assume there are only four people living on the planet, with two of the four people producing 10 units of CO_2 annually. The third produces 14 units, and the fourth 6 units, leading to a global average of 10 units.

Each of the four people owns a quarter of the atmosphere and lets assume that these four have no concept of the fact that gases disperse around the atmosphere, i.e. each thinks their atmosphere is uniquely theirs and isolated from that of the remaining three. At the end of the year, as the global average is 10 units per person, the additional 40 units emitted in the atmosphere lead to an extra 10 units per quarter of the atmosphere. From the perspective of the two people emitting 10 units, it's as if the 10 units they emitted remained in their quarter share of the atmosphere. The person who only emitted 6 units however now finds that there's an extra 4 units in their portion of the atmosphere – it's as if someone has come and fly tipped some waste into their atmosphere. The person who emitted 14 units finding that somehow 4 units has been miraculously mitigated for them.

The reality of course is that atmospheric dispersion causes the overall concentrations to level out, but the example above helps identify the two different types of costs.

The person emitting 14 units has sent 4 units into the atmosphere owned by the other person and so needs to pay them an Excess Emission cost equal to the cost of mitigating the four units of carbon. From the perspective of the recipient they're receiving compensation for allowing their atmosphere to be used.

The general principle is that if each of us is responsible for exactly the same amount of GHG then as we're emitting the same amount of GHG, we can say that our GHG are going exactly into our portion of the atmosphere and we don't owe anything to anyone else.

However if some people are emitting more GHG, then as the gases will disperse, they will be inserting GHG into atmosphere owned by other people, and therefore as they are making use of atmosphere owned by other people (to absorb their GHG) they need to pay compensation for this, so that the owners of that atmosphere can revert it to its original state.

Internal Usage Costs

The Balancing costs only deal with excess usage and compensation for people whose atmosphere has been used by others. There remains the cost of dealing with the emissions directly produced by each person, which remain in their "share" of the atmosphere. I'm naming this the Internal Usage costs, as it arises from their usage which remains internal to their share of the atmosphere. Thus the two people producing 10 units face an internal usage cost of 10 units each as their emissions remain in their share of the atmosphere. The person producing 14 units has an internal usage cost of 10 units and an Excess Emission cost of 4 units. Finally the person producing 6 units has an internal usage cost of 6 units and receives a Compensation income of 4 units.

26.11 Excess Emissions Cost and Compensation Due

Using the per capita emissions[22,23] of GHG by country and population levels, I've worked out the Excess Emission Costs and Compensation due on a per country basis with Figure 8 showing the countries owing more than $1Bn per annum. (Full list Appendix A)

The Excess Emission cost is the amount each country owes per annum to other countries to compensate them for emitting GHG into the others' share of the atmosphere.

---

22   List of countries by greenhouse gas emissions per capita
      http://en.wikipedia.org/wiki/List_of_countries_by_greenhouse_gas_emissions_per_capita
23   List of countries by population http://en.wikipedia.org/wiki/List_of_countries_by_population

Country	Population	CO_2 Per Capita	Total CO_2	Excess CO_2 Per Capita	Excess Cost Bn $	Excess Cost Per Capita $
USA	308,792,000	23.5	7,256,612,000	17.90	331.7	1074
Russia	141,927,297	13.7	1,944,403,969	8.10	69.0	486
Japan	127,430,000	10.5	1,338,015,000	4.90	37.5	294
Canada	34,020,000	22.6	768,852,000	17.00	34.7	1020
Germany	81,757,600	11.9	972,915,440	6.30	30.9	378
Australia	22,173,000	26.9	596,453,700	21.30	28.3	1276
United Kingdom	62,041,708	10.6	657,642,105	5.00	18.6	300
South Korea	49,773,145	11.4	567,413,853	5.80	17.3	348
Saudi Arabia	25,721,000	16.2	416,680,200	10.60	16.4	638
Italy	60,275,846	9.7	584,675,706	4.10	14.8	246
France	65,447,374	9	589,026,366	3.40	13.4	205
Ukraine	45,982,936	10.3	473,624,241	4.70	13.0	283
Spain	45,989,016	10.1	464,489,062	4.50	12.4	270
Iran	74,196,000	8.2	608,407,200	2.60	11.6	156
South Africa	49,320,500	9	443,884,500	3.40	10.1	205
Poland	38,163,895	9.8	374,006,171	4.20	9.6	252
United Arab Emirates	4,599,000	38.8	178,441,200	33.20	9.2	2000
Taiwan	23,119,772	11.8	272,813,310	6.20	8.6	372
Netherlands	16,593,900	13.8	228,995,820	8.20	8.2	494
Venezuela	28,683,000	10	286,830,000	4.40	7.6	265
Kazakhstan	15,776,492	12.7	200,361,448	7.10	6.7	425
Argentina	40,134,425	8.2	329,102,285	2.60	6.3	157
Kuwait	2,985,000	35	104,475,000	29.40	5.3	1776
Czech Republic	10,512,397	13.7	144,019,839	8.10	5.1	485
Belgium	10,827,519	13.2	142,923,251	7.60	4.9	453
Qatar	1,409,000	55.5	78,199,500	49.90	4.2	2981
Turkmenistan	5,110,000	18.9	96,579,000	13.30	4.1	802
Greece	11,306,183	11.5	130,021,105	5.90	4.0	354
New Zealand	4,358,700	18.8	81,943,560	13.20	3.5	803
Mexico	107,550,697	6.1	656,059,252	0.50	3.2	30
Ireland	4,459,300	16.7	74,470,310	11.10	3.0	673
Austria	8,372,930	11.5	96,288,695	5.90	3.0	358
Israel	7,509,000	11.5	86,353,500	5.90	2.7	360
Finland	5,356,700	13	69,637,100	7.40	2.4	448
Uzbekistan	27,488,000	6.9	189,667,200	1.30	2.1	76
Denmark	5,534,738	11.5	63,649,487	5.90	2.0	361
Singapore	4,987,600	11.3	56,359,880	5.70	1.7	341
Belarus	9,489,000	8.5	80,656,500	2.90	1.7	179
Hungary	10,013,628	8.3	83,113,112	2.70	1.6	160
Norway	4,860,900	11.2	54,442,080	5.60	1.6	329
Portugal	10,636,888	7.9	84,031,415	2.30	1.5	141
Bulgaria	7,576,751	8.6	65,160,059	3.00	1.4	185
Uruguay	3,361,000	12.7	42,684,700	7.10	1.4	417
Slovakia	5,421,937	9.3	50,424,014	3.70	1.2	221
Oman	2,845,000	12	34,140,000	6.40	1.1	387
Trinidad & Tobago	1,339,000	19.6	26,244,400	14.00	1.1	822
Mongolia	2,671,000	11.9	31,784,900	6.30	1.0	374
Libya	6,420,000	8.3	53,286,000	2.70	1.0	156
Sweden	9,340,682	7.4	69,121,047	1.80	1.0	107

Figure 8: Excess Emission Cost by Country[24]

24   CO_2 in Tonnes of CO_2c without land-use change, Year 2005. CO_2c is Equivalent carbon dioxide.

The table in figure 8 shows that the USA owes the most at $332 Bn per annum, followed by Russia at $69 Bn p.a., Japan at $38 Bn p.a., Germany at $31 Bn p.a., Australia at $28 Bn p.a. and the UK at $19Bn p.a.

Globally the amount owed for Excess Emission Cost works out to $789 Billion per annum.

The table in figure 9 shows the countries owed compensation for having their share of the atmosphere emitted into by other countries. India is due the largest compensation at $275 Bn annually[25], followed by Bangladesh and Pakistan at $45Bn p.a. and $41 Bn p.a.. Countries such as the Philippines are due $22 Bn p.a. and Kenya $13 Bn p.a..

Country	Population	CO_2 Per Capita	Total CO_2	Excess CO_2 Per Capita	Compensation Due Bn $	Compensation Due Per Capita $
India	1,177,761,000	1.7	2,002,193,700	-3.90	275.4	234
Bangladesh	162,221,000	0.9	145,998,900	-4.70	45.7	282
Pakistan	168,874,500	1.5	253,311,750	-4.10	41.5	246
Indonesia	231,369,500	2.7	624,697,650	-2.90	40.2	174
Nigeria	154,729,000	2.1	324,930,900	-3.50	32.5	210
Ethiopia	79,221,000	1	79,221,000	-4.60	21.8	275
Philippines	92,226,600	1.7	156,785,220	-3.90	21.6	234
Vietnam	85,789,573	2.1	180,158,103	-3.50	18	210
Congo, Dem. Rep.	66,020,000	1.6	105,632,000	-4.00	15.8	239
Tanzania	43,739,000	0.1	4,373,900	-5.50	14.4	329
Kenya	39,802,000	0.3	11,940,600	-5.30	12.6	317
Sudan	39,154,490	0.3	11,746,347	-5.30	12.4	317
Egypt	77,932,000	3	233,796,000	-2.60	12.1	155
Myanmar	50,020,000	2.2	110,044,000	-3.40	10.2	204
Afghanistan	28,150,000	0	0	-5.60	9.5	337
Uganda	32,710,000	1.1	35,981,000	-4.50	8.8	269
China	1,336,150,000	5.5	7,348,825,000	-0.10	7.8	6
Morocco	31,740,000	1.6	50,784,000	-4.00	7.6	239
Ghana	23,837,000	0.4	9,534,800	-5.20	7.4	310
Nepal	29,331,000	1.5	43,996,500	-4.10	7.2	245
Mozambique	20,226,296	0.1	2,022,630	-5.50	6.7	331
Yemen	23,580,000	0.9	21,222,000	-4.70	6.6	280
Côte d'Ivoire	21,075,000	0.4	8,430,000	-5.20	6.6	313
Madagascar	19,625,000	0.2	3,925,000	-5.40	6.4	326
Cameroon	19,522,000	0.4	7,808,800	-5.20	6.1	312

Figure 9: Compensation Due for absorbing other countries GHG[26]

25 Being of Indian ethnicity, it's somewhat embarrassing to have India top this list. I'm no longer a citizen of India, and this is just how the numbers worked out. Hopefully my earlier discussions will have demonstrated I have no time for nationalism.
26 CO_2 in Tonnes of CO_2e without land-use change, Year 2005.

Country	Population	CO$_2$ Per Capita	Total CO$_2$	Excess CO$_2$ Per Capita	Compensation Due Bn $	Compensation Due Per Capita $
Sri Lanka	20,238,000	0.7	14,166,600	-4.90	5.9	292
Burkina Faso	15,757,000	0.1	1,575,700	-5.50	5.2	330
Niger	15,290,000	0.1	1,529,000	-5.50	5	327
Malawi	15,263,000	0.1	1,526,300	-5.50	5	328
Mali	14,517,176	0	0	-5.60	4.9	338
Peru	29,132,013	2.8	81,569,636	-2.80	4.9	168
Angola	18,498,000	1.3	24,047,400	-4.30	4.8	259
Colombia	45,333,000	3.9	176,798,700	-1.70	4.6	101
Zambia	12,935,000	0.2	2,587,000	-5.40	4.2	325
Guatemala	14,027,000	0.9	12,624,300	-4.70	4	285
Chad	11,274,106	0	0	-5.60	3.8	337
Syria	21,906,000	2.7	59,146,200	-2.90	3.8	173
Cambodia	14,805,000	1.6	23,688,000	-4.00	3.6	243
Zimbabwe	12,523,000	0.8	10,018,400	-4.80	3.6	287
Rwanda	9,998,000	0.1	999,800	-5.50	3.3	330
Guinea	10,069,000	0.2	2,013,800	-5.40	3.3	328
Haiti	10,033,000	0.2	2,006,600	-5.40	3.2	319
Senegal	12,534,000	1.8	22,561,200	-3.80	2.9	231
Algeria	34,895,000	4.2	146,559,000	-1.40	2.9	83
Benin	8,935,000	0.3	2,680,500	-5.30	2.8	313
Burundi	8,303,000	0	0	-5.60	2.8	337
Brazil	192,559,000	5.4	1,039,818,600	-0.20	2.3	12
Cuba	11,204,000	2.2	24,648,800	-3.40	2.3	205
Dominican Republic	10,090,000	1.9	19,171,000	-3.70	2.2	218
Tunisia	10,432,500	2.3	23,994,750	-3.30	2.1	201
Tajikistan	6,952,000	0.5	3,476,000	-5.10	2.1	302
Togo	6,619,000	0.2	1,323,800	-5.40	2.1	317
Papua New Guinea	6,732,000	0.7	4,712,400	-4.90	2	297
Honduras	7,466,000	1.1	8,212,600	-4.50	2	268
Paraguay	6,349,000	0.6	3,809,400	-5.00	1.9	299
Ecuador	14,138,000	3.3	46,655,400	-2.30	1.9	134
Iraq	30,747,000	4.6	141,436,200	-1.00	1.8	59
Sierra Leone	5,696,000	0.2	1,139,200	-5.40	1.8	316
El Salvador	6,163,000	1	6,163,000	-4.60	1.7	276
Nicaragua	5,743,000	0.8	4,594,400	-4.80	1.7	296
Eritrea	5,073,000	0.1	507,300	-5.50	1.7	335
Central African Republic	4,422,000	0.1	442,200	-5.50	1.5	339
Kyrgyzstan	5,482,000	1.9	10,415,800	-3.70	1.2	219
Costa Rica	4,579,000	1.5	6,868,500	-4.10	1.1	240
Liberia	3,476,608	0.1	347,661	-5.50	1.1	316
Mauritania	3,291,000	0.6	1,974,600	-5.00	1	304

Figure 9: continued

(Full list appendix B)

During the period 2001 to 2007 Ethiopia received[27] slightly over $1 Bn annually in aid, however Figure 9 shows that the compensation owing to Ethiopia for using its share of atmosphere was $22Bn, and therefore it would be much better to forget about aid, and simply to pay Ethiopia for using and polluting its share of the earth's atmosphere.

The same is true for other countries, e.g. Kenya received around $0.8 Bn in aid but was actually due $12.6 Bn as compensation for polluting into its atmosphere.

I juxtapose these two figures because aid somehow implies an element of charity, and the expectation that recipient countries need to be grateful for what they are about to receive – but in reality as shown by the two examples above, these countries are actually owed huge amounts of monies for the usage being made of their natural resources – their share of the earth's atmosphere.

26.12 Internal Usage and Total Emission Costs

The Excess Emission Cost and Compensation are transfer costs dealing with producing more than the global average amounts of GHG and making use of other countries atmosphere as pollution sinks. There remains the issue of dealing with the countries emissions that remain in their own share of the atmosphere, i.e. the Internal Usage Emissions described earlier[28].

Figure 10 presents the complete picture, showing the Balancing Excess / Compensation and the Internal Usage costs, leading to a Total Cost per country. It shows the USA topping the list and needing to spend $ 767 Bn per annum, followed by China at $433 Bn p.a., Russia $186Bn p.a., Japan $118 Bn p.a., Germany at $89 Bn p.a. and the UK at $58 Bn p.a.

It also shows that although India needs to spend $120 Bn p.a. on mitigating its Internal Usage carbon, it is due a compensation of $275 Bn p.a. and therefore emerges with a net compensation due of $155 Bn p.a.

---

27   Foreign Development Aid: How much is Ethopia Getting?
     http://www.ezega.com/news/NewsDetails.aspx?Page=news&NewsID=1776

28   Section 26.10.

Country	Population	CO$_2$ Per Capita	Total CO$_2$	Excess CO$_2$ Per Capita	Excess Cost Bn $	Compensation Due Bn $	Own CO$_2$ Cost Bn $	Total Owed Bn $	Total Owed Per Capita $
China	1,336,150,000	5.5	7,348,825,000	-0.10	0	7.8	440.9	433.1	324
India	1,177,761,000	1.7	2,002,193,700	-3.90	0	275.4	120.1	-155.3	-132
USA	308,792,000	23.5	7,256,612,000	17.90	331.7	0	435.4	767.1	2484
Indonesia	231,369,500	2.7	624,697,650	-2.90	0	40.2	37.5	-2.7	-12
Brazil	192,559,000	5.4	1,039,818,600	-0.20	0	2.3	62.4	60.1	312
Pakistan	168,874,500	1.5	253,311,750	-4.10	0	41.5	15.2	-26.3	-156
Bangladesh	162,221,000	0.9	145,998,900	-4.70	0	45.7	8.8	-36.9	-228
Nigeria	154,729,000	2.1	324,930,900	-3.50	0	32.5	19.5	-13.0	-84
Russia	141,927,297	13.7	1,944,403,969	8.10	69.0	0	116.7	185.7	1308
Japan	127,430,000	10.5	1,338,015,000	4.90	37.5	0	80.3	117.8	924
Mexico	107,550,697	6.1	656,059,252	0.50	3.2	0	39.4	42.6	396
Philippines	92,226,600	1.7	156,785,220	-3.90	0	21.6	9.4	-12.2	-132
Vietnam	85,789,573	2.1	180,158,103	-3.50	0	18.0	10.8	-7.2	-84
Germany	81,757,600	11.9	972,915,440	6.30	30.9	0	58.4	89.3	1092
Ethiopia	79,221,000	1	79,221,000	-4.60	0	21.8	4.8	-17.0	-215
Egypt	77,932,000	3	233,796,000	-2.60	0	12.1	14.0	1.9	25
Iran	74,196,000	8.2	608,407,200	2.60	11.6	0	36.5	48.1	648
Turkey	72,561,312	5.5	399,087,216	-0.10	0	0.4	23.9	23.5	324
Congo, Dem. Rep.	66,020,000	1.6	105,632,000	-4.00	0	15.8	6.3	-9.5	-143
France	65,447,374	9	589,026,366	3.40	13.4	0	35.3	48.7	745
Thailand	63,389,730	5.6	354,982,488	0.00	0	0.0	21.3	21.3	336
United Kingdom	62,041,708	10.6	657,642,105	5.00	18.6	0	39.5	58.1	936
Italy	60,275,846	9.7	584,675,706	4.10	14.8	0	35.1	49.9	828

Figure 10: Total Costs [29]

29   CO$_2$ in Tonnes of CO$_2$e without land-use change, Year 2005

Myanmar	50,020,000	2.2	110,044,000	-3.40	0	10.2	6.6	-3.6	-72
South Korea	49,773,145	11.4	567,413,853	5.80	17.3	0	34.0	51.3	1032
South Africa	49,320,500	9	443,884,500	3.40	10.1	0	26.6	36.7	745
Spain	45,989,016	10.1	464,489,062	4.50	12.4	0	27.9	40.3	876
Ukraine	45,982,936	10.3	473,624,241	4.70	13.0	0	28.4	41.4	901
Colombia	45,333,000	3.9	176,798,700	-1.70	0	4.6	10.6	6.0	133
Tanzania	43,739,000	0.1	4,373,900	-5.50	0	14.4	0.3	-14.1	-323
Argentina	40,134,425	8.2	329,102,285	2.60	6.3	0	19.7	26.0	649
Kenya	39,802,000	0.3	11,940,600	-5.30	0	12.6	0.7	-11.9	-299
Sudan	39,154,490	0.3	11,746,347	-5.30	0	12.4	0.7	-11.7	-299
Poland	38,163,895	9.8	374,006,171	4.20	9.6	0	22.4	32.0	840
Algeria	34,895,000	4.2	146,559,000	-1.40	0	2.9	8.8	5.9	169
Canada	34,020,000	22.6	768,852,000	17.00	34.7	0	46.1	80.8	2376
Uganda	32,710,000	1.1	35,981,000	-4.50	0	8.8	2.2	-6.6	-203
Morocco	31,740,000	1.6	50,784,000	-4.00	0	7.6	3.0	-4.6	-143
Iraq	30,747,000	4.6	141,436,200	-1.00	0	1.8	8.5	6.7	217
Nepal	29,331,000	1.5	43,996,500	-4.10	0	7.2	2.6	-4.6	-155
Peru	29,132,013	2.8	81,569,636	-2.80	0	4.9	4.9	0.0	0
Venezuela	28,683,000	10	286,830,000	4.40	7.6	0	17.2	24.8	865
Malaysia	28,306,700	5.7	161,348,190	0.10	0.2	0	9.7	9.9	349
Afghanistan	28,150,000	0	0	-5.60	0	9.5	0.0	-9.5	-337
Uzbekistan	27,488,000	6.9	189,667,200	1.30	2.1	0	11.4	13.5	490
Saudi Arabia	25,721,000	16.2	416,680,200	10.60	16.4	0	25.0	41.4	1610
North Korea	24,051,706	5	120,258,530	-0.60	0	0.9	7.2	6.3	263
Ghana	23,837,000	0.4	9,534,800	-5.20	0	7.4	0.6	-6.8	-286
Yemen	23,580,000	0.9	21,222,000	-4.70	0	6.6	1.3	-5.3	-226
Taiwan	23,119,772	11.8	272,813,310	6.20	8.6	0	16.4	25.0	1080
Australia	22,173,000	26.9	596,453,700	21.30	28.3	0	35.8	64.1	2890
Syria	21,906,000	2.7	59,146,200	-2.90	0	3.8	3.5	-0.3	-11
Romania	21,466,174	6.1	130,943,661	0.50	0.6	0	7.9	8.5	394

Country	Population	CO$_2$ Per Capita	Total CO$_2$	Excess CO$_2$ Per Capita	Excess Cost Bn $	Compensation Due Bn $	Own CO$_2$ Cost Bn $	Total Owed Bn $	Total Owed Per Capita $
Côte d'Ivoire	21,075,000	0.4	8,430,000	-5.20	0	6.6	0.5	-6.1	-289
Sri Lanka	20,238,000	0.7	14,166,600	-4.90	0	5.9	0.8	-5.1	-250
Mozambique	20,226,296	0.1	2,022,630	-5.50	0	6.7	0.1	-6.6	-325
Madagascar	19,625,000	0.2	3,925,000	-5.40	0	6.4	0.2	-6.2	-314
Cameroon	19,522,000	0.4	7,808,800	-5.20	0	6.1	0.5	-5.6	-288
Angola	18,498,000	1.3	24,047,400	-4.30	0	4.8	1.4	-3.4	-181
Chile	17,040,000	5.1	86,904,000	-0.50	0	0.5	5.2	4.7	277
Netherlands	16,593,900	13.8	228,995,820	8.20	8.2	0	13.7	21.9	1322
Kazakhstan	15,776,492	12.7	200,361,448	7.10	6.7	0	12.0	18.7	1187
Burkina Faso	15,757,000	0.1	1,575,700	-5.50	0	5.2	0.1	-5.1	-324
Niger	15,290,000	0.1	1,529,000	-5.50	0	5.0	0.1	-4.9	-321
Malawi	15,263,300	0.1	1,526,300	-5.50	0	5.0	0.1	-4.9	-322
Cambodia	14,805,000	1.6	23,688,000	-4.00	0	3.6	1.4	-2.2	-147
Mali	14,517,176	0	0	-5.60	0	4.9	0.0	-4.9	-338
Ecuador	14,138,000	3.3	46,655,400	-2.30	0	1.9	2.8	0.9	64
Guatemala	14,027,000	0.9	12,624,300	-4.70	0	4.0	0.8	-3.2	-231

(Full list appendix C)

26.13 Climate and Atmosphere Stabilisation Executive (CASE)

It's quite futile to try and reach an overarching multilateral agreement on Global Warming, by the time the politicians got one in place, we'd probably all be toast. Even if by some miracle, one were in place, there would be the thorny issue of monitoring and enforcement.

The Global Warming issue has arisen because as outlined earlier[30], the key weakness is that no single country owns the atmosphere and consequently it's a bit of a free for all, for releasing effluents such as greenhouse gases into the atmosphere.

As the problem has arisen because no one owns the atmosphere, the solution should be to create a new entity, the Climate and Atmosphere Stabilisation Executive (CASE), which will "own" the atmosphere. In a formal sense CASE will have legal title to the earth's atmosphere i.e. be its rightful owner.

In effect what's happening is that all the 193 countries agree to cede sovereignty of their atmosphere to CASE, which would be tasked with managing and stabilisation of the worldwide climate and atmosphere. An analogy is the way the Bank of England was given independence from political control and freed to set its own monetary policy without political interference, and tasked with meeting an inflation target.

CASE would be managed in a similar style as the Bank of England, free of all political control, it would be tasked with putting in place the global policies and practices to ensure climate stabilisation and report monthly on its efforts, along with releasing public minutes of its meetings.

Therefore all the set of 193 countries need to do is one single task – agree the creation of CASE, ceding it the rights to the atmosphere in all territories and setting CASE the objective of managing global greenhouse gas concentrations.

CASE would be tasked with behaving in a fair even-handed way ensuring no country had an advantage or disadvantage. In effect the world community would have removed the political sting and outsourced / delegated management of the atmosphere to CASE and from that point onwards it becomes CASE's job to formulate and execute policies and plans to ensure climate stabilisation.

---

30   Section 3.9

CASE Targets

There would be a steering group with a representative from each country and this would set the targets for CASE to meet. Representatives would have voting rights broadly[31] proportional to their country's population. Once the representatives have been agreed, the targets would become whatever the steering group arrives at by majority vote.

The day-to-day work of CASE and actual formulation and execution of policy would be carried out by a board of directors supported by a management team. The directors would have formal review meetings with the steering group, similar to a group of shareholders meeting their board.

CASE Income

As CASE is the owner of the atmosphere, if a country is not Carbon neutral and wishes to emit greenhouse gases into the atmosphere, then that emission must be by agreement and license from CASE.

CASE would charge for this facility using consistent, transparent and fair rules. However the rate would be entirely at the discretion of the CASE board, and CASE could vary the rate from country to country within certain bands (e.g. plus / minus 25%) and use that discretion to encourage countries to move along a particular direction.

There is a fundamental principle, that the "owner" can charge for usage and so CASE would have the right to set its tariffs in order to ensure that overall greenhouse gases concentrations keep to the target levels.

The Excess Emission, Compensation and Internal Usage costs worked out in the last two sections would be payable to CASE. Where a country is a low emitter of carbon and is due a compensation payment, then as CASE would have received the compensation payment, I envisage CASE spending half the compensation in the country itself and spending the other half globally in its efforts to mitigate carbon as there may be more effective projects elsewhere.

CASE Policies

CASE would draft and put together a consistent set of policies on how to account

---

31   Ideally the voting rights need to follow the approach outlined in Section 14.3, with adjustments made for factors such as democracy, level of enterprise and human rights.

for emissions, ensuring that worldwide the same consistent approach is being used and closing any loopholes.

CASE Operations

CASE would not be a mere rule drafting body, it will initiate and execute actions i.e. be an executive body.

It would have a strong cash income gained from countries paying to release greenhouse gases into the atmosphere, and would use this to fund numerous projects and initiatives worldwide as part of its job to stabilise weather systems. I say fund as I don't see CASE itself doing the projects, it would put its projects out to competitive tender to be carried out by private companies.

CASE projects would range from direct operations to absorb and reduce greenhouse gases such as planting new forests, to research and development of new approaches, as well as supporting alternative options such as wind-powered ships by giving development grants.

Having CASE in existence doesn't mean countries have nothing further to do, CASE would put together best practice guides for countries and incentivise countries to follow these practices.

CASE Access

CASE operatives would need to have global Visa's giving them unrestricted access to all countries, and the freedom to install monitoring equipment wherever they feel fit, and CASE would have operations in every country.

26.14 CAT – Carbon Added Tax

With countries needing to pay for their carbon emissions, I see the responsibility being pushed back to the producers of carbon emissions and the emergence of a Carbon Added Tax (CAT). Each product or service purchased would have CAT included in its price, and each firm in the supply chain would add an incremental CAT element to its product / services proportional to the additional carbon that it's emitting.

When the price tag of an item is displayed the CAT element will also need to be clearly shown as a separate element. As CAT is a tax, there is no need to charge VAT on it, this being another reason for it being separately displayed.

The monies raised by the CAT would be paid to CASE or an equivalent body charged with managing global carbon mitigation.

The CAT would apply to any product or service associated with generating carbon emissions, and its scope would range from large carbon generating sectors such as energy generation, aviation, commercial and public transport, to fuel for personal transport, clothing, manufactured products and food.

Foods that have been shipped around the world would have their carbon emission element included in their sale price and highlighted separately as well. Meat too would have a CAT element reflecting the amount of carbon dioxide emissions released by the animal during its lifetime.

Provided the CAT is initiated by countries around the world in a common timeframe, it will not lead to any competitive issues since it'll be a bit like the tide, everyone's boat rising by the same amount. By having the cost of carbon measured using Purchase Power Parity it will tend to keep cost ratios constant between countries.

The impact of CAT would be to increase costs to consumers therefore it's not going to be popular with all. But what it does is stop our current dishonest behaviour where we're being irresponsible and not paying the full cost of our consumption.

26.15 Financing the CAT

The cost of mitigating all the Carbon Dioxide released is $2,267 Bn per annum, and works out to $336 per person on the planet (appendix C). The annual costs per person are $2,484 in the US, $1,308 in Russia and $936 in the UK (figure 10).

These are large costs and will be difficult for people to accept. Therefore it's important to work out a way of managing budgets and financing the additional CAT cost.

Adopting the WDO

Earlier on in Section 15.5, I wrote about the World Defence Organization and calculated there would be a $1,300 Bn peace dividend annually by reorganizing our defence systems and creating the WDO. The savings from the WDO represent 58% of the annual amount required for mitigating CO_2 globally.

By implementing the WDO we could use the $1,300 Bn that no longer needs to be spent, to reduce taxes and put money back into people's wallets, helping offset 58% of the new CAT costs, and therefore taking the bite out of the new cost.

There's something appropriate about this as we would be swopping spending on defence against each other, with spending for the common defence of the planet.

Reducing Public Sector

After the WDO savings have been taken out, there still remains $967 Bn to be found annually and this can be found from restructuring public sector enterprises.

In the chapter on Public Sector[32], I covered how the state was poor at cost control, and by its own admission the UK public sector median income was 16% higher than that in the private sector. I highlighted[33] the difference between the state owned Royal Mail with its profit margin of 0 and the privatised TNT with its margin of 14.8%.

Privatisation of the remaining sacred cows in the public sector would reduce government spending, and with the privatised entities being more productive, overall costs in the economy would decrease.

The savings in monies currently being overspent in the public sector could be used to further reduce the overall tax burden, making the new CAT affordable.

26.16 Carbon Balance Sheet

In the UK all limited companies are required to file statutory accounts detailing their profit and loss and balance sheet annually with the authorities[34]. With carbon emissions being a major issue, the statutory reporting needs to be extended, and all companies over a certain size need to be required to lodge a Carbon Impact and Use Balance sheet annually along with their annual financial statements, reporting on their carbon emissions and activities taken to reduce their footprint.

The Carbon Balance sheet would show year on year comparisons, and facilitate comparison across firms in the same sector.

32   Section 24.4
33   Section 25.7
34   Companies House

26.17 Carbon Action Programme

Getting a scheme such as CAT in place will be difficult due to the various vested interests ranging from producer lobbies to consumer groups. One doesn't envy the politicians either caught in the middle of all this.

De Gaulle once remarked he had come to the conclusion that "Politics is too serious a matter to be left to the Politicians", and this is a case in point. I think it be helpful for concerned people around the world to get involved in a peaceful way, in the process making it easier for politicians to act.

The kind of thing I had in mind is a Carbon Action Programme (CAP) in which concerned people around the world display their concern, and in a peaceful and non-violent way put pressure for moving to a carbon pricing economy.

The CAP could take many forms ranging from global petitions to voluntary temporary boycotts of all goods and services produced by a country that's perceived to be blocking progress towards a climate change settlement e.g. if a particular country is perceived to be stubborn and blocking change then maybe an organization such as the CAP could promote a one month global boycott of its products and services, and help encourage them to behave more responsibly. Initially of course the CAP would try softer tactics such as petitions but if they fail then moving to sterner measures.

The CAP should ideally be organized and run by environmental bodies, however my fear is that over the years they may have got somewhat institutionalised and less radical. Perhaps they were young tigers once, but now their claws seem to have got blunt and teeth wobbly. If the existing environmental bodies are unable to rise to the challenge then maybe new more radical ones need to come into being to fill the gap.

26.18 Transport Policy and Reducing Car Usage

As mentioned earlier in Section 23.7 the UK government privatised its rail network by awarding franchises to different companies but created local monopolies on routes, leading to high rail fares. These high fares lead to more people using their cars.

This illustrates how Transport Policy is a key area for focus in the battle against

Global Warming, and governments need to ensure that Transport Markets are operating competitively and benefitting from competition between operators.

A Futuristic but Pragmatic Approach towards reducing car usage

A leading intellectual appeared on radio recently and expressed the view that Global Warming was now inevitable as there was no way the genie could be put back into the bottle. His view was that even if we wanted to, we could not find a way to do without our cars, as we're so dependent on them for our way of life. I think that's a bit pessimistic as we're quite an innovative race and able to come up with options, and as an example have outlined one possible approach to overcome that "inevitability".

One way we could reduce our dependence on cars is to say that any car driving with spare seats is obliged to give lifts to anyone else who requires it. Anyone wanting a lift need simply wait at a traffic light, and get onto the next car passing that has a spare seat. The same approach could work on motorways too, with people changing cars at toll points or service stations.

There would need to be some form of security credentials exchanged and payments setup. Prior to getting into a car the potential passenger would text the registration number of the car to a central location, which would log the car, time and location of the starting point. For security the central server would send a reply text to the driver and passenger each containing the other's photo so that each can verify the other is who they claim to be and eliminate the possibility of a stolen car or mobile. Once the person gets off they would each send a text to the central server, which then works out the distance and credits the driver's account for having given the lift and debits the passengers account for the journey. To ensure fair play the central server would acknowledge to each of the parties that the other party has ended the journey. There would be other safeguards such as a female need only give lifts to other females.

There would be exclusions for people who feel strongly against such a system, and they would need to pay punitive opt out fees. For the people taking part in the scheme, the added income from giving lifts would help pay for the cost of the additional carbon added tax (CAT) discussed earlier.

Although this system is somewhat futuristic, with the safeguards mentioned it would be able to work with today's technology. The scheme would at a stroke convert *every* private car into a public transport vehicle and greatly bring down the numbers of cars needed on our roads.

26.19 A Gift from China

Before moving off the topic of Global Warming, it's worth mentioning an inadvertent gift from China.

China adopted a one child policy in 1979 to limit its population growth. Although a temporary measure it's continued for over 25 years. The policy is an infringement of their basic human rights. Article 26 of the Universal Declaration of Human Rights states that parents have the right to choose the kind of education to be given to their "children" – the plural form used shows that it was never envisaged parents would be limited to one child.

The one child policy has resulted in China's population being approximately 22% lower than it would have otherwise been, this representing 300 million fewer inhabitants[35]. This shortfall in China's population is equal to the entire US population, and will have lead to a reduced carbon footprint for China. Although not condoning the policy in any way, nonetheless we all owe a big thank you to the Chinese people who have given the world additional breathing space in dealing with the global warming issue.

> *We find ourselves, one way or another, in the midst of a large-scale experiment to change the chemical construction of the stratosphere, even though we have no clear idea of what the biological or meteorological consequences may be.*
>
> ~ *F. Sherwood Rowland*

26.20 Extension of the CASE concept to the Oceans – OSE

The world's oceans have faced a similar problem as the environment, of not belonging to any single nation and therefore getting overused. Countries have sovereignty over their coastal waters, however if they abuse that sovereignty and pollute their waters, that pollution will eventually diffuse outwards into the wider global water systems causing problems for others.

Whilst there are international agreements governing fishing, it may be an idea to use something similar to the CASE approach to manage the worlds oceans, giving

---

35   China's One Child Policy   http://geography.about.com/od/populationgeography/a/onechild.htm

responsibility and ceding sovereignty of "owning the oceans" to a new body, the Oceans and Seas Executive (OSE) which would have its own dedicated resources to police and manage the worlds oceans and seas from a pollution and fish stock perspective.

In case resources are found in the ocean such as new oil fields or other minerals, rather than it becoming a free for all for the adjoining countries to claim and argue their stake, ownership of the resource would automatically flow to OSE which would have responsibility for regulating and licensing their use, employing the proceeds to improve global water stocks and mitigate the impacts of pollution.

If countries fail to manage their coastal waters then the OSE would have the legal right to take them to task and impose fines and action plans to reverse any damage.

Section 4:

Spirituality

27. God

It is incomprehensible that God should exist, and it is incomprehensible that he should not exist.

~ Blaise Pascal

27.1 Does God Exist?

The question of god is one of the great mysteries of life. Numerous civilisations in the past have created elaborate religions and gods, and yet each new generation feels the need to ask the same fundamental questions of how we got here and whether god exists.

A recent television programme[1] which had members of five faiths in discussion, put them the question of how did they know that god exists. Their consensus response was that it required an act of faith. However that appears a circular argument i.e. you have faith because you have faith, and feels an avoidance of the issue.

As human beings we are mortal and will die at some point. One thought is whether our belief in god is a way of helping us deal with death. If there were no god, then there would be no afterlife either and our existence in this world would be similar to that of a wave in a pond created by a stone being thrown in. The small circular wave starts out with a splash and spreads, growing until it reaches the perimeter and fades away with little memory of ever having existed. That's a frightening thought, and I wonder whether in our desire to escape from death and its stark message that this is all there is and after this there's nothing, we've created an elaborate concept of god and religion, thereby fabricating some meaning to life and our existence and making death easier to handle by casting it as a portal to another existence.

---

1   Revelations: How Do You Know God Exists?
     http://www.telegraph.co.uk/culture/tvandradio/6030148/Revelations-How-Do-You-Know-God-Exists-TV-Review.html

One of the reasons given as proof of god's existence is that how could something as complex as our human body be created without some external intelligent creator working behind the scenes. However it's been shown that evolution and natural selection are sufficient to explain how we developed over 3.8 billion years from simple cells to modern day humans[2]. Although natural selection is a slow process, the small incremental changes that give a species an evolutionary advantage get incorporated, accumulating and building on each other and given sufficient time, result in huge changes.

If theories such as Chaos Theory[3] can explain how given sufficient time a swirl of dust can convert into intelligent life, then that pushes the question further back, how and where did these swirls of dust come from, i.e. if there were no god then how do we explain all the planets and where did they arise from. Science once again has an answer to this – the Big Bang Theory with our universe coming into existence around 13.7 billion years ago as a singularity[4].

It's accepted scientific wisdom that the universe started with the Big Bang 13.7 billion years ago, and that is when time began. However this creates a host of further questions: If all the material was in a black hole of infinite density (called a singularity) then where did this singularity arise from and where did all the material in it come from? How long had it stayed in this zero time state, and what happened to trigger the singularity to start expanding into the universe i.e. what made the cohesive gravitational force flip into a repulsion / expansion force?

These are all unanswered questions. Even if we did get an answer to them, and we find that some agent caused the big bang, all that does is push the questions and uncertainty back a further step, raising a new question that where and how did the new agent come about. The process is like peeling an onion, every time we answer one question, our answer uncovers another layer and we're faced with the issue of explaining the existence of new layer. This recursive process, looping back on itself to keep posing the same question, would continue indefinitely until we arrive at something whose existence needs no explanation – a contradiction as it's illogical to expect something to be responsible for its own existence.

An example of this recursive process is seen in the ancient civilisations of Greece,

2   Timeline of Evolution http://en.wikipedia.org/wiki/Timeline_of_evolution
3   The Secret Life of Chaos http://furnacetv.com/programmes/secret-life-of-chaos
4   The Big Bang Theory http://www.big-bang-theory.com/
     http://nasascience.nasa.gov/astrophysics/what-powered-the-big-bang

Egypt and the Aztecs all of which had a Sun God, however as our knowledge of the universe grew, the Sun became a planet and our ignorance shifted to a new horizon with uncertainty over how the big bang was set up.

If one tries to break out of the recursive process, we end up having to rely on circular logic, which arises of necessity when one tries to explain the existence of a system from within the system itself without recourse to an external agent.

An example of this circular logic is physics theories such as M-Theory, which purport to be able to account for the existence of the Universe without requiring any divine intervention[5]. According to this theory[6] because there is a law such as Gravity, the universe can and will create itself from nothing. However matter exists only within the context of the universe, and prior to the universe coming into existence there would not have been any matter and as Gravity is the law dealing with the interaction between matter, in the absence of matter, Gravity would have been a somewhat meaningless concept[7]. Gravity could only come into being once matter, and therefore the universe, were in existence, and in that sense gravity is dependent on there being a universe. Therefore the reasoning that the Universe came into being because of the Law of Gravity appears circular logic.

Faced with something that due to its recursive nature, we can never expect to explain logically then the only way we can arrive at an answer is by looking outside of logic. Therefore God as a label for the original creator of the universe and whose existence requires no explanation, is as good an explanation as any other, and can be the only final word.

27.2   Is there Life after Death?

Religion is the human response to being alive and having to die.
~ Forrest Church

Over the years we have always believed in life after death. The ancient Egyptians made elaborate preparations for it by stocking their pyramids with items that would

---

5   Has Stephen Hawking ended the God debate?
    http://www.telegraph.co.uk/news/newstopics/religion/7979211/Has-Stephen-Hawking-ended-the-God-debate.html
6   Stephen Hawking: God did not create Universe   http://www.bbc.co.uk/news/uk-11161493
7   As the subject of its focus, mass or matter, was non-existent at the time, there would be no meaning to a law dealing with something that did not itself exist

be needed in the afterlife. The Chinese too did the same as evidenced by the large terracotta army that was there to guard the first emperor. More recently there has been a market in psychics and mediums helping people make "contact" with departed relatives. Major religions too hold out support for the idea of the afterlife with some promising their followers additional rewards in heaven if they die while fighting for their faith.

So the question is: Is this all true, or is it wishful thinking and manipulation by religions to incentivise us to behave in ways that suit them?

Before we can answer this, we need to be clear about what makes us "us". If we lose a limb we don't regard ourselves as having died, so our limbs don't uniquely define us. The bit that we can't lose without losing our identity is our brain, and so the "us" resides in our brain. This leads to the question which bit of the brain defines us? Many parts of the brain are there to control various functions of the body e.g. sight, breathing, balance, controlling muscles and as these happen at the subconscious level, therefore they don't uniquely define us either. Ultimately the only parts of our brain that could uniquely define us are the cells that hold the current thought being processed and our memory. If our brains had evolved without a memory then we would be left with a brain that lived only in the "now", and we'd have no sense of our past life or events and would be living in a perpetual now state almost like a biological automaton. So the important piece of the jigsaw that gives us our identity and makes us uniquely "us" is our memory, and in that sense, boiling it down to its essence, we're like a collection of memories attached to a thought processing biological machine.

It's helpful to introduce some new vocabulary. In software, objects in a computer's memory can be persisted to permanent store such as a computer hard drive or a database with this process called serialization as the object gets serialised into a string of computer data able to be stored as characters in a file and transmitted. The reverse happens when we want the object back and we need to read data from the file and deserialize it or rehydrate the object i.e. bring the object back to life using data from the file, so that it's exactly identical to the object in the computer's memory prior it's being serialized.

Therefore if we're to be awakened and brought back to life after death in some "heaven", it would be necessary for us to be reattached to our collection of memories. However our memories are stored in biological memory in the cells of our brain and therefore somehow all our memories would have had to be serialized and transmitted to the afterlife where they gets deserialized and reattached to us. Only then could we be reconstituted to "live" in the afterlife. So how do all these terabytes of data get transmitted? Where and by what physical mechanism does the data transfer take place? In the computer world elaborate electronic instrumentation is needed to ensure the secure transfer of data. The data is broken into small chunks called packets so that if transmission errors occur then only faulty packets needs retransmission. Special values called checksums are included with each packet to allow the receiving end to detect data loss, and a protocol or language developed to allow communicating computers to request retransmission when data loss is detected. Transferring the many terabytes of biological memory would require the equivalent of this type of sophistication to be somehow replicated in the cell structures of our brain to ensure correct data transfer and therefore I simply don't see our brains as having developed the sophisticated capabilities to support transfer of our biological memories.

Human beings are mammals and have evolved, but we share the same basic brain anatomy as well as common genes with other mammals such as chimpanzees and dogs[8,9,10]. Having a common evolution one would expect that whatever happens to us also occurs to other mammals. Therefore if our memories get transferred to an afterlife then our shared evolution and brain structure would suggest the same should happen to other mammalian memories. The thought that when a dog dies, its memories get transferred to an afterlife seems rather bizarre and unlikely, and so by extension the same can be said of our own memories being transferred. This together with the previous point about our brains lacking instrumentation to support data transfer, lead to my view that sadly our memories are lost when our brain cells die.

Religions talk of the spirit or soul[11] persisting, for example Hindu's believe the spirit persists and gets reincarnated as different animals in the cycle of life and death, with the human form being an opportunity for the spirit to escape the cycle of life and death depending on the behaviour or karma.

I don't have a view on the persistence of the spirit, as it's hard to prove either way, however I don't think it's relevant, and the focus on the spirit feels a bit of a red herring. Even if our spirit persists, our collection of memories is what uniquely defines us and with our memory collection gone, then a spirit on its own,

8   Animal Consciousness http://plato.stanford.edu/entries/consciousness-animal/
9   Human Brain Structure http://www.news-medical.net/health/Human-Brain-Structure.aspx
10   Dogs, Humans Share many Genes, Researchers Find
     http://articles.latimes.com/2003/sep/26/science/sci-dog26
     http://news.bbc.co.uk/1/hi/sci/tech/4106163.stm
11   I use the terms soul and spirit interchangeably

unattached to our memories is not really us, and the real "us" has gone and we are no more. Even if it did exist our soul would be somewhat like a spiritual skeleton, and just as our physical skeleton persisting after our death doesn't imply our continued physical existence, the same can be inferred of our spiritual skeleton.

28 Religion

Religion is to do right. It is to love, it is to serve, it is to think, it is to be humble.

~ Ralph Waldo Emerson

28.1 Is Religion Beneficial?

It's a big question and on reflection the answer not that obvious. Before trying to get at an answer lets enumerate some of the benefits and disbenefits.

Benefits of Religion - Moral Code and Behaviour
Most religions have a moral code and specify do's and don'ts and ways of living. Thus they help societies behave more responsibly and be more orderly.

Sometimes they provide an explanation and make it easier for people to come to terms with their position in life – for example the Hindu's belief in reincarnation and "karma" allows them to rationalise that someone enjoying good fortune deserved it due to their good deeds and karma earned in an earlier existence, and this belief system allows them to avoid getting bitter and frustrated with their present state thinking that perhaps they don't deserve more because of misdeeds in an earlier existence. In this case it directly helps social harmony and a reduction of tension.

In some sense religion pacifies people and makes them more orderly and tolerant. It was with this in mind that Karl Marx referred to religion as being the "opium of the masses". The moral code and way of living promoted by religion inculcates a lot of discipline in people, which helps create a more stable and orderly society, with people willing to work within society's rules.

Stress Reduction and Long Term Health
As we go through life, it's a certainty that regardless of our situation we will face difficulties and challenges, and dealing with these likely to cause stress and anxiety.

If we have a strong faith and belief in god then that allows us to share our problems with god and seek her[1] support. This means that despite our circumstances we no longer feel alone and the saying "a problem shared is a problem halved" works in this context and will reduce the attendant stress and anxiety and provide some comfort. Stress acts as a kind of internal friction, absorbing energy and internal resources, rendering us less able to deal and cope with the situation, and it's somewhat analogous to a rabbit becoming immobile on seeing the headlamps of an approaching car. With the reduction in stress we're less likely to become overwhelmed by the situation, and there's a greater probability that we're going to come up with creative solutions to deal with the situation.

This has benefits even if the issue we're facing is ill health. Our belief in god and faith means that after praying we internally feel that we have this powerful force able to intervene and help us, and this acts as a form of placebo[2] helping us deal with pain by producing natural painkillers and reducing stress.

In a sense therefore, religion and faith act as a kind of cushioning absorbing the impact of knocks and blows as we go through life and reducing their impact and stress upon us. Stress ages the immune system[3] and the long-term reduction in stress from our "faith cushion" ought to help us to remain healthy for longer. This line of reasoning would imply a correlation between religion and health and on searching the literature a link certainly appears to exist[4].

Illusion of Control over the Uncontrollable

There are many things in life outside of our control yet we're hugely dependent upon them. For example, a farmer waiting for the rains to come is going to get increasingly stressed out during a period of drought, as his entire livelihood and possibly even his and his family's existence might depend on it.

In such circumstances waiting around passively and hoping, is going to lead to considerable frustration and stress. However by having faith and religion and performing some religious rites and ceremonies the farmer is able to feel they are

---

1   As a break with the implicitly sexist convention of referring to god in a masculine gender, I shall be using the feminine gender when referring to god.

2   Placebo Effect http://www.abc.net.au/science/news/health/HealthRepublish_1468236.htm
     http://www.ukskeptics.com/explanation.php?dir=articles/explanations&article=placebo_effect.php

3   Stress ages immune system http://news.bbc.co.uk/1/hi/health/3034410.stm

4   The Link between Religion and Health http://www.sciencedaily.com/releases/1997/11/971101093808.htm
     http://www.ovid.com/site/catalog/Book/3179.jsp?top=2&mid=3&bottom=7&subsection=11

not merely sitting idly by letting events take their course, but are taking proactive action, and wresting some control back over the situation.

One of the basic causes of stress is when people think the situation is outside their control, and in the example above, by feeling they've taken some action and got some "control" back, the farmer would gain hope and reduce stress levels.

Even if the perceived control is illusory, the feeling of control, along with the hope and reduced stress are real for the farmer, and beneficial as a source of temporary relief.

Mental Relaxation through Prayer and Meditation

When people pray they often end up chanting the same mantra or bit of prayer repeatedly. As the words they're vocalising are well known to them, this chant can be done with little or no mental effort. The prayer diverts them from their everyday problems and issues and it's a bit like putting their brain into a free wheeling or "do nothing" state where no demands are being made of it, no decisions to be taken etc.

It's a bit like shifting the brain into neutral and giving it a complete break from everyday concerns, and can be quite relaxing, with the person feeling refreshed and invigorated after the prayer session.

Scientists have found that during prayer and meditation changes take place within the brain, with intense activity taking place in the brain's parietal lobe circuits[5], whilst at the same time the frontal and temporal lobe circuits which track time and create self awareness become disengaged, and the limbic system with responsibility for tagging events as emotional gets activated. These changes all come together to create a meaningful and relaxing episode.

As the benefits come from shifting one's brain into neutral, they ought to be accessible by atheists as well and are not exclusive to people of faith. However having faith probably makes it easier to meditate and more likely for the ritual to become part of a regular routine, and in that sense faith leads people to adopt a healthier lifestyle.

Promotes a Sense of Community, Kinship and Belonging

Religions create many opportunities for shared experiences amongst their followers

---

5   Can Prayer Heal? http://www.medicinenet.com/script/main/art.asp?articlekey=50874

ranging from regularly coming together for prayer, celebrating the same festivals, having similar significant life events and rites of passage to a common dress code and sharing value systems and beliefs.

All of these promote a strong sense of identity and community between followers of a religion, with individuals no longer feeling themselves to be alone, but instead as part of a large caring family. As human beings we're social animals and with the fragmentation in society caused by increased mobility and industrialisation and the rise of the nuclear family, we have inbuilt yearnings for a lost tribal existence. The sense of community and belonging provided by religion helps satisfy our desire for community and tribe.

Disbenefits of Religion – Opportunity Cost

> *Men never do evil so completely and cheerfully as when they do it from religious conviction.*
>
> *~ Blaise Pascal:*

Practising a religion can take up a lot of time and valuable resources. Many religions require followers to pray a prescribed number of times daily, reducing the time available for other activities.

Religions may also require followers to learn by rote religious texts as part of their education thereby reducing the mental effort and time available for other more general academic studies.

Aggregated over the population as a whole, at a macro level that leads to a significant amount of time, which could have been spent on other potentially more productive pursuits, and therefore religion has an opportunity cost[6].

Divisions between communities
Religion creates a strong sense of community amongst its followers with a lot of social interaction and mixing. However the flip side is links with people outside the religion become relatively weaker and in that sense a natural consequence of religion is it tends to divide communities.

---

6   Opportunity cost in the sense that it's taking away the opportunity to do other things.

These divisions are susceptible to manipulation by people for their own personal motives such as the seeking of political power.

Over the years religious divisions have led to wars such as the Crusades, the splitting of communities such as the Catholics and Protestants in Northern Ireland, the many lives lost in riots in India between Hindus and Muslims, and it was also a factor in the conflict in Kosovo, to name just a few.

Ego, Arrogance and Fascism

When people believe and follow a faith, they can get so wrapped up that they accept every aspect of the belief, giving it their blind obedience. In some sense they become like "religious zombies" with their will not being their own, but dictated from outside via their choice of religious pulpit. Along with that comes an ego and arrogance that only they have the one "true vision" and armed in the certainty their actions are blessed by their god, in their minds they can do no wrong. This type of mindset is scary because it's the kind of thinking that can lead to intolerance, conflict and wars.

Holds Back Social Development

When religions were formed few thousand years ago, at the time of their creation their founders would have imported and derived their practises from society's custom and practises prevalent at the time. People tend to resist step changes and to derive their religion's practises from those current at the time would have been a reasonable thing to do in order to assure their acceptance.

However once the customs and practises had been "baked into" the religion, then it became harder to change them, as change was no longer just up to society, but religious leaders too held the key.

Although society could move forward at a particular pace, there's no reason to expect religious law to keep up and every likelihood of them diverging especially with society being more responsive to people whereas religion tended towards an autocracy. Thus as society branched off, religion clung to its roots and the past, creating a parallel way of doing things.

This divergence between civil society and religion is in effect a case of religion holding back social development, leading to tensions and confusion as people get caught in the gap in-between the two. The main effect being that by holding onto practises baked into it in an earlier era religion is somewhat inflexible and acts as a drag on social development.

Formalises Prejudices

Religious texts will usually put things in general terms leaving room for interpretation. However if people in certain sects or branches of a religion wish to promote a particular behaviour, then rather than being open and in a democratic way seek to have society accept or reject the behaviour on its merits, there's a tendency to reinterpret religious guidelines and bend them to make out the desired behaviour is an essential part of the religion. By labelling it a religious requirement, they neatly sidestep having to justify or defend the behaviour, in effect making it "non-negotiable" as an edict or mandatory requirement of the religion.

In reality though it's a case of prejudices getting formalised and enshrined as religious requirements.

To be fair, this particular point is not a flaw inherent in religion, it stems from the way that practitioners choose to interpret the text, however its worth noting that religions can become hiding places for prejudices masquerading as religious requirements.

Is Religion Beneficial?

Lets return to the question asked at the beginning of this section: "Is Religion Beneficial?"

Clearly there are pros and cons and the answer not obvious. In posing the question, we need to differentiate between god and religion, with religion being a practise or method of praying to god, and it's the practise that we're seeking to judge.

Having an orderly and stable group with defined moral codes, low stress and a strong sense of community would all have been factors giving early humans an evolutionary advantage over groups that lacked these, and therefore I believe religion has been beneficial in the past and there may have been an evolutionary bias in favour of religious groups.

However as we become more successful as a species and spread geographically across the planet, the religions' areas of influence collide and the disbenefits come into play especially the divisive aspects of religion and holding back of social progress, and although hard to admit, I feel the disbenefits now tip the scales.

This creates an imperative to attempt to find ways of reducing the divisive aspects of religion.

28.2　Religion and Soul Share

At times Religions behave as if they're in competition with other religions for "soul share" i.e. their share of the religion market. This behaviour evidenced by the missionary and proselytizing work done around the globe.

Why would a religion wish to grow and get more followers? One reason might be they're genuinely convinced their religion offers the only path to salvation and people who aren't following this path are somehow damned. With this mindset they feel that by converting others into their faith, they're saving or redeeming their soul, and thereby doing a good deed. I'm willing to accept this as plausible but feel it's ultimately misguided.

An alternative reason could be ego and self-image, with the people heading the religion wishing to be part of a successful growing faith body, and the fact that others are attracted to their religion validates them and their belief. A larger number of followers means greater relevance, influence and vitality whereas if their following decreases then that spells decline and irrelevance, reducing the significance of their life's work. There's also a desire to pass on their "heritage" and not to be the generation that allowed the religion to become irrelevant.

The desire to grow has led to some unexpected and inappropriate behaviour. When Catholic priests were found guilty of child sex abuse in Ireland and other parts of Europe, then in the past this tended to be covered up[7]. In effect the religion was acting as a business might, to protect its brand image, and hold onto its market share.

Seeking to convert people from one faith to another strikes me as hugely egotistical, as there's an implicit judgement that one faith is somehow better or superior to the other faith. However what gets missed is that encoded into a faith are a lot of cultural values and by changing faith people risk losing part of their cultural heritage and identity. I therefore frown at any attempts to proactively seek to convert people, however if people voluntarily wish to change their faith then I don't see any issues.

28.3　Does any one religion exclusively have the True God, and can one religion be the only path to salvation?

As part of their doctrine, some religions tell their followers that they alone are the

---

7　Pope Benedict apologises for Irish priests' sex abuse http://news.bbc.co.uk/1/hi/8577740.stm

true path to salvation and other paths and gods are false. Their followers duly primed adopt the same position. In this section I'd like to explore whether there is any truth in this.

A view from the past

In the past all major civilisations had their own religions and creation myths. The Egyptians built massive pyramids for the burial of their kings together with numerous items for the afterlife. The Chinese had similar ideas with the First Emperor of China, Qin Shi Huang having a Terracotta Army of over 8000 life size soldiers[8]. The Aztec's believed in the afterlife with ceremonial temples called Teocalli and offering sacrifices to their gods. The Greeks had their mythology and gods with an afterlife consisting of Hades – an underworld, Tartarus – a place of torment, and Elysium – a pleasant place.

At the time of these civilisations, people in these societies believed their particular religion to be completely true and would look upon any doubter as someone who had something wrong with them and view them with suspicion. Yet today we look back and see their religions as myths.

What's to say that our contemporary religions are not the same as the "myths" of these previous civilisations, and our behaviour in staunchly defending whatever faith we have signed up to, exactly the same as someone in these long gone civilisations defending their own faith?

We can of course say that we're somehow different or that our religion is different etc, but my point is that in the previous civilisations they too would have taken exactly the same line and defended their beliefs in much the same way.

I wonder whether a few thousand years from now, people might look back and view us in much the way as we view these past civilisations and similarly discount our contemporary faiths as myths of our time.

An experiment on the origin of faith

Lets conduct a thought experiment – assume a woman gives birth to five sons, however due to personal circumstances she's only able to look after one of her sons and puts the remaining four up for adoption, with the condition that they'll all meet on their 21st birthday and until then they will not be told that they're adopted.

---

8   Terracotta Army http://en.wikipedia.org/wiki/Terracotta_Army

Lets assume that the lady herself is a staunch atheist, but it so happens that each of the four sons are adopted by a Catholic, a Muslim, a Hindu and a Buddhist family respectively, with each family being staunch believers in their faith.

When the five brothers meet on their 21st birthday, before being told they're brothers, each of the young men is asked about their faith. At that point we'll find each will strongly profess belief in their own particular faith. The Christian will only be willing to countenance Jesus, the Muslim will be unable to hear of anything other than Allah, the Hindu likewise will profess his complete belief in Shiva, the Buddhist will talk of Buddhist principles and the Atheist will maintain that there is no god.

Still without revealing that they're brothers, if we ask them to agree on a common faith view, they will be unable to comply, each believing the religion they were brought up in to be the only correct one.

It's a hypothetical experiment, and would be immoral to deliberately set up, however most people would agree that we would get the outcome suggested.

In reality therefore our faith is a result of what we've been taught and brought up with from infancy, and is part of our internal "mental DNA" forming our world view. Subsequently when someone questions it, it pulls at our roots.

Therefore the particular religion we follow is somewhat random in the sense that it's not usually chosen by us, and in reality it's a birth family lottery and depends on which family you happen to get born into as to which particular faith (or none) that you get indoctrinated into.

Different Religions cannot have unique gods

Lets conduct another thought experiment – imagine that our planet had three very high impenetrable mountain range stretching from one pole to the other. The three ranges divide the planet into three segments[9], each completely cut off from the other. Lets assume that each segment is populated by humans as there were passes that had been open in the past but were subsequently sealed off by glaciers.

The people in each segment would develop their own unique religion and gods, and we'd end up with three religions and three different gods. The religions and gods

---

9   visualise it as following the segments of an orange

would differ as the people had parted company tens of thousands of years ago when the mountain passes closed.

If we now said that instead of three mountain ranges we had an extra mountain range, then the planet would be divided into four segments, and we'd end up with four religions and four gods. We could continue this line of reasoning and for each new mountain range we'd end up with one extra religion and one extra god, e.g. with 20 mountain ranges we'd have twenty religions and twenty gods.

Clearly the number of actual gods in the universe is not going to vary with how many mountain ranges we have on the planet, and yet we will have created a new religion and god for each new mountain range.

The only way of resolving this is that each new god of a new religion must be mapped onto the same set of existing universal gods.

Theorem proving that no religion can be the only path to salvation

To prove this we need to start with a postulate or truism about God i.e. something that we can accept as self-evident without the need for proof, and which is always true. I propose the following as a postulate: "God will not sequentially behave in an irrational manner, that is to say God will not repeatedly make the same mistake."

Lets say that there are 4 religions A,B,C and D and lets assume that Religion A offers the only path to salvation.

We'll now try and test whether that assumption can be correct.

As religions A offers the only path, then followers of B,C and D despite praying and following their religion diligently will be unable to attain salvation. The followers of B,C and D will generally be of that religion because they were born into families practising B,C or D, therefore it is not the fault of the individuals that they were indoctrinated into B,C or D.

In effect the individuals themselves had very little chance as they simply went along with what their families and those around told them. Therefore it feels wrong to penalise them and deny them salvation for something that they had very little hand in and which was not of their making, and it would be irrational of God to do so. If every person following B, C or D is denied salvation because they hadn't followed

A, then in effect God would be sequentially behaving in an irrational manner – which we have already postulated that God would not do.

Therefore our assumption that "Religion A offers the only path to salvation" cannot be true, because were it true it would lead to a contradiction[10] of our postulate

Hence no religion can claim to offer the only path to salvation.

28.4 How did Religions start and spread?

> *Those who say religion has nothing to do with politics do not know what religion is.*
>
> ~ *Mohandas K. Gandhi*

The major religions in the world are well established and their continued existence beyond doubt. However how did they actually start and what processes and stages did they go through in gaining popularity. It's important as it has bearings on our present relationship with religion.

Scenarios for the Founders of a Religion
All religions need to have a founder and I see a few scenarios of how the founders arose.

Conscious Decision

Imagine you're a deeply spiritual person and you've been preaching on spiritual matters but find you're not getting your message through with people not taking you seriously and you're in danger of becoming sidelined. However if you wrap your message within the cloak of a religion and present it as a new religion then that gives it added gravitas and the prospect of being taken seriously.

Alternatively you could be successfully getting your message through but suspect that after you pass away your message and teachings will wither with little to show for it. In this circumstance it would be quite tempting to create a new religion and give continuity and permanence to your teachings.

Another option is that you're a follower of a deeply religious person, and after your

---

10 It would imply that our postulate was incorrect - however by definition our postulate must always be true – therefore the assumption itself must be incorrect.

mentor passes away you find yourself at a bit of a loose end, and if you do nothing then you risk losing all that you've been working on, and therefore decide the natural thing to do is to write up your mentor's sermons and create a new religion to give permanence to their thoughts, and meaning to the time you've spent following your mentor.

The key point in this category is that religions are founded or created as a conscious decision taken by someone.

Drug Induced Religious Experience

There are a number of naturally occurring psychedelic plants[11,12]. Some of the effects caused by psilocybin mushrooms are changes to the audio, visual and tactile senses with strange light phenomena such as auras or halos around light sources and other beings, increased visual acuity and surfaces that appear to ripple and shimmer.

It quite possible that someone deeply religious, who's gone to a remote location to contemplate on god and creation, happens to eat one of these naturally occurring psychedelic plants and puts the resulting hallucination down to a religious experience and that God had been communicating with them. They may end up feeling special and that they had been marked out for an exclusive link or relationship with god e.g. as a messenger from god.

Double blind tests done by Johns Hopkins University into the spiritual effects of psilocybin mushrooms found that a third of the participants reported it as the single most spiritually significant moment of their lives.

Our religious person could then come back and state truthfully with full conviction that they had had a vision and God had communicated with them. As they had been in "communication" with god, they would have felt chosen in some way for some task, and hence felt it right to set up their own religion to communicate and spread what god had told them.

Actual Religious Experience

A third possibility is that the founder of the religion had a genuine religious experience and God or an angel did indeed reveal themselves to the founder.

---

11   Psilocybin mushrooms http://en.wikipedia.org/wiki/Psilocybin_mushrooms
12   List of psychedelic plants mushrooms http://en.wikipedia.org/wiki/Psilocybin_mushrooms

Establishing Credentials

If someone wants to set up a new religion, they can't simply write up the doctrine and practises and start preaching, they need to establish their right to create a new religion, in a sense they need to demonstrate their credentials.

For founders coming via either of the religious experience routes (drug induced and actual), it's straightforward enough, they'll simply point to their religious experience as establishing that they were singled out for this task.

If the founder comes via the Conscious Decision route, they can't say they "decided" to setup a new religion, as then it would be seen as just another lecture and their opinion. They would benefit by saying they had a religious experience and "communicated" with god. Saying this gives them credibility and is risk free as nobody can prove their story was fabricated. It has the added benefit of placing their doctrine above criticism as the founder can point out that it came via their communication with god. Therefore feigning a religious experience would be rational and they could ease their conscience by reasoning the ends justified the means.

Spreading the word and gaining market share

I've used the word "market share" because that's exactly what the founders would have had to do, they would have had to "sell" their newly created religion to the religion's early adopters.

The founders could choose to follow a direct sales approach and spread the word to small groups at a time. This would work but clearly would take time to spread.

A second more interesting approach is to approach a ruler of a small state and convince them to convert. If the ruler were weak or facing problems managing their subjects, they may have calculated that the new religion would help bring discipline and order into their kingdom as their subjects would now also be reporting into a higher order. Therefore regardless of whether they themselves believed in it, they might jump at the chance of promoting the new religion. The increased discipline and order would make the state more manageable and consequently successful and in that sense religion has evolutionary advantages not just for humans but for states as well.

Over time other states may seek to copy the successful state's "management philosophy" and adopt the religion. In addition the successful state would grow more powerful due to the competitive edge from its religion induced discipline, and might take over other less well managed and chaotic states, spreading the religion in turn.

I believe that the second approach was the more dominant one as politics and religion used and benefited from each other[13], and is evidenced by a number of states even today having close links with particular religions.

Relative likelihoods of the different approaches to formation of religions
I'd outlined three different scenarios on how the founders of a religion may arise, lets try and look at their relative likelihoods.

From general observation, in most spheres of human life it appears that God's preferred approach is to let people get on with things and not to make direct interventions or appearances. From a consistency viewpoint one would expect this hands off approach to continue even when it came to religious matters, and therefore for the founders of a religion to arise as a result of direct religious communication with God seems less likely.

Furthermore, it's mostly been men who have communicated with God whereas one might have expected God to be gender neutral when choosing whom she would communicate with. The fact that men were dominant in society in the earlier days makes me wonder whether the male bias is due it being a conscious decision by male founders, with the absence of female founders due to women lacking the confidence to found a new religion.

In arriving at a decision, it's also worth considering that just because millions of people believe a particular religious narrative that by itself doesn't make it true – in the past millions of people in ancient Egypt believed in gods such as Osiris, which we now regard as myths of a bygone era.

As we're not going to be able to arrive at a definitive view of the origination of any particular religion, this leads to the question: "does it actually matter"? The answer depends on whether the religion is interpreted flexibly and its practices allowed to vary to fit in with societal changes. If it is interpreted flexibly, then the exact origination doesn't really matter, however if the origination belief fosters inflexibility then it does matter.

28.5 A Unified Model of God and Religion

There is only one religion, though there are a hundred versions of it.
~ *George Bernard Shaw*

---

13   The desire of rulers to harness the power of religion for their own ends is also demonstrated by many
      ancient rulers claiming ancestry from the gods.

Although religions have developed separately there is more in common between them than many followers may realise, and in this section I'd like to pull together our diverse concepts of religion and god into a single unified model of god and religion.

In order to do so we'll benefit from some terminology and concepts used in software development where designers routinely model complex situations, and I'll give a brief introduction to these prior to using them to develop the model.

Software Design Primer

There are a lot of detailed software design concepts in this short primer, and it normally takes software students a whole semester to get to grips with these[14].

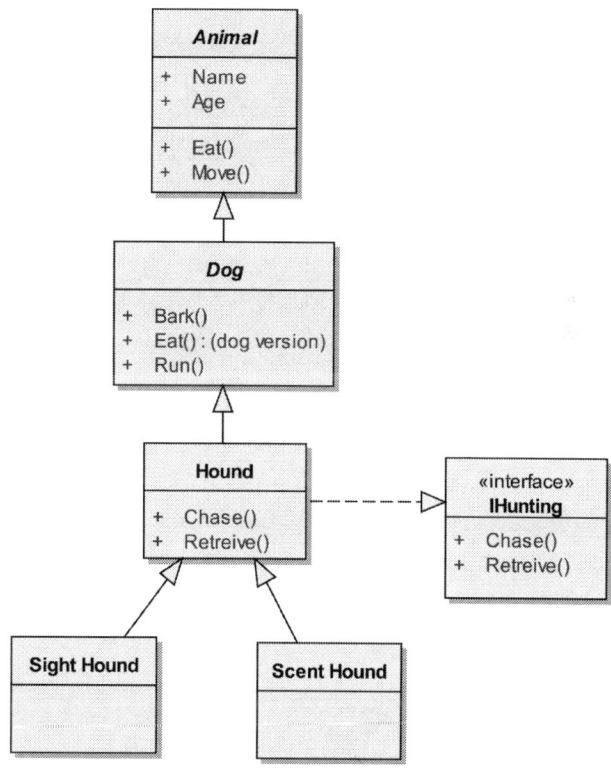

Diagram 1: Animal Model

14   Its a lot to take in therefore, and may benefit from reading twice, following along with the diagram will help

Classes are the workhorses in software design and represent the type of an entity in the model. Classes are used to model real world entities giving them properties and behaviours e.g. an Animal class could have properties for "Name" and "Age" and behaviours of "eat" and "move" (see diagram 1). A Class can extend another class, this process known as inheritance, with the Child Class inheriting from its Parent Class. In our Animal model, we could have a "Dog" class, which derives from our Animal class, the arrow in the diagram signifying this relationship.

The child class will inherit all the properties and behaviours in its parent class, but will normally add additional properties and behaviours of its own. For example our Dog class could have extra behaviours for "bark" and "run" in addition to the behaviours inherited from its parent i.e. the Animal class. The child class could keep the behaviours it inherits from its parent unchanged, or choose to override and manifest the behaviour in a different way, e.g. a dog could eat in the same way as the general animal, or it could be implemented in a different way more suitable for a dog. When a child class modifies the behaviour inherited from its parent this is known as overriding. In a similar fashion, child classes can override inherited properties.

An interface is a way of clumping together a group of behaviours, and classes are said to "implement" an interface when the class has all the behaviours defined in the interface. For example we could have a Hunting interface called IHunting that has chase and retrieve behaviours. Thus we could define a Hound class that inherits from Dog but also implements the IHunting interface, meaning it has the chase and retrieve behaviours. We could further specialise it by defining Sight Hound and Scent Hound classes which extend the parent Hound class (diagram 1).

When we're looking at an object of a more specialised class, we can also treat it as an object of a higher level, more general class, this process known as casting. For example a Sight Hound could also be treated as a Hound, a Dog or an Animal[15].

An abstract class is a class that is abstract in the sense that you would never see an object which is solely the abstract class type in real life, but would only find some derivative of the abstract class. An abstract class is useful as it pulls together common properties and methods. An example will help, in our example Animal and Dog are abstract classes as we won't find anything that's just an animal or dog, but we'd always have specialised types e.g. a Sight Hound. However the specialised type can also be regarded as being of the base abstract type, i.e. we can cast and treat a Sight Hound as a Dog or as an Animal. Thus if we have two Sight Hounds

---

15   A Sight Hound is merely a particular type of Hound, and similarly a Hound is a particular type of Dog etc

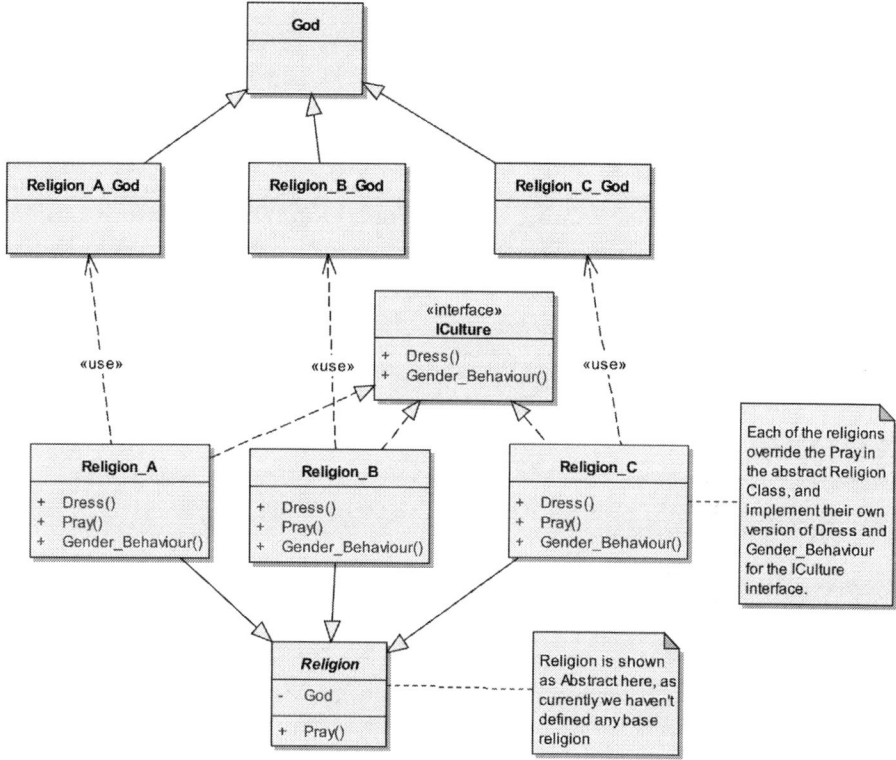

Diagram 2: Unified God and Religion Model

and three Scent Hounds in a room, casting them into the abstract dog or animal classes, we can simply say that we have five Dogs or five Animals in the room.

Unified God and Religion Model

The Unified God and Religion Model shows[16] an Abstract Religion from which all other religions are derived. This Religion is abstract because as a global community we have not defined this religion and it doesn't as such exist. However it can exist in an abstract sense to hold the common properties and behaviours of the real religions, called A,B and C in the model. Thus the abstract base religion has a god property and a pray behaviour.

All our real religions can be seen as being derived from a common base abstract religion. In the model all the religions override the Pray behaviour meaning that each of the religions implement their own praying methods and rituals.

16 at the bottom of Diagram 2

The religions inherit the God property from the abstract base religion, and each religion sets this property to its own version of God, however from the model it's seen that each of the three versions of God are derived from a single common God. This ties in with the earlier discussion[17] where I'd shown that different religions cannot have unique gods.

There's a cultural interface ICulture which defines cultural traditions such as dress and inter gender behaviour. Each of the religions implements this interface and has its own culturally driven behaviours.

Applying the concept of casting, each of our three religions can be cast back to the base abstract religion, and from that perspective followers of Religion A, Religion B and Religion C can all be said to be followers of the same abstract base religion, the only difference being that the pray behaviours in the religions have been implemented differently.

Similarly even though they're praying to different gods, as all the gods are derived from a common god, each of the god's they're praying to can be cast back to the same common God and one can say that in reality the three religions are all praying to the same god.

Thus the Unified Model[18] leads to a single abstract base religion and a single god, which then get defined and labelled differently to suit different cultural and historic traditions and preferences.

By-products of the Unified God and Religion Model

Dual Religion Followers

A by-product of the Unified Model is that someone can belong to Religion A and Religion B simultaneously with no conflict, because under the hood, the Religion A god is the same as the Religion B god, and both the religions themselves are just specialised implementations of the same common abstract base religion.

Makes Religion Conversions Obsolete

As all religions derive from a common abstract base religion, and gods from a

---

17   Section 28.4
18   Unified God and Religion Model; (shortened for brevity)

common god, this removes the motivator for religion conversions and makes them unnecessary and obsolete.

In any case, even if people liked the practices in a different religion, there would still be no need to convert as they could simply take up dual religions as mentioned in the previous point.

The Need to Define a New Common Base Religion – Darism

In the current model the common base religion is abstract and therefore we can't have a religion that is only the common base religion, we always have to have a more specialised religion that derives from the base religion. The common base religion only exists in the sense that a more specialised religion can be cast back to the common abstract base religion.

Dealing with abstract notions is sometimes awkward, and it would be helpful if we could create a new real religion that represents this common base abstract religion.

This would mean that everyone following a more specialised religion (i.e. Religion A, B, C etc) would automatically be a follower of the new base religion, however people could be followers of the new base religion, without needing to follow any of its more specialised derivations (i.e. Religion A, B, C etc).

I'd propose the name Darism[19] for the new common base religion, in recognition of the cross religion efforts of Dara Shikoh, the eldest son of the Mughal Emperor of India, Shah Jahan. Dara was defeated by his brother Aurangzeb in a struggle for the Mughal throne and put to death in 1659. Dara spent a lot of effort in seeking common ground between Islam and Hinduism and translated 50 Upanishads from Sanskrit into Persian, and in a speculative hypothesis stated the work referred to in the Qur'an as "Kitab al-maknun" or "hidden book" was the Hindu Upanishads. He had also been invited to lay the foundation stone of the Golden Temple in Amritsar by the Sikhs[20].

In terms of defining Darism as the universal world religion, the route would be for a council of world religious leaders to come together and agree the core essentials of the new religion and define the common ground in terms of properties and

---

19 Darism is merely my suggestion for a name, however the actual choice should be decided by a wider more democratic process and debate.

20 Dara Shikoh http://en.wikipedia.org/wiki/Dara_Shikoh

behaviours (or practises) which are then inherited and extended i.e. overridden in each of their faith's more specialised implementations of Darism.

28.6   What's more important Religion or Behaviour?

From the unified model perspective introduced above, as all religions can be seen as derived from a common base religion, our specific religion does not matter when looking at the question of religion vs. behaviour.

When looking at this, it needs acknowledging that behaviour is often influenced by people's religious beliefs and so there's no neat demarcation.

Viewed dispassionately it's not our religion that counts because Religion in a sense is a kind of internalised conceptual framework, what really counts is the way that we behave towards and treat other people.

If somebody claims to be highly religious, but in their behaviour they go about causing pain and suffering to others, then in the final analysis they would be less godly than someone who follows no religion but instinctively behaves well and respects the rights and feelings of others.

Although not denying the value of religion, I think behaviour always trumps religion, and the way we behave towards each other is of far greater importance than any specific religion.

28.7   Universal Declaration of Religious Belief

Religion ought to be pure, untainted and noble, yet has somehow ended up getting sullied and finding itself on opposite sides in conflicts between people. Communities tend to follow the same religion and struggles between communities for resources can get transposed into a religious struggle. Politicians too get tempted to harvest cheap votes by playing the religion card.

It's time we found a way to prevent religion being hijacked by special interest groups and I see the need for the leaders of all the major faiths to come together and adopt and proclaim a Universal Declaration of Religious Belief. This would be a religious equivalent to the Universal Declaration of Human Rights adopted by the UN in 1948.

The Universal Declaration of Religious Beliefs would formulate and reaffirm certain basic truths about the major religions and provide unified religious leadership, and help prevent religions being co-opted by special interest groups.

I've outlined below a draft of what I believe should be amongst the key statements.

Draft Outline of Universal Declaration of Religious Belief

Article 1
The God(s) of all religions are derived from and manifestations of a single universal god.

Article 2
All religions offer the same chance of salvation, with no religion having any better or worse prospects of salvation than any other religion.

Article 3
All religions can be viewed as having derived from a single common abstract world religion (Darism), and are specialised versions of this common universal religion modified for culture, tradition and practise.

Article 4
As all religions are derivations from a common base, it is acceptable for people to follow two or more religions simultaneously.

Article 5
As a consequence of Articles 1 to 4, there is nothing to be gained by someone converting from one religion to another, and therefore all religions agree not to proselytise.

Article 6
All religions will be open to new followers joining them, and will not require new followers to renounce their earlier faith.

Article 7
Agreement that it is a beneficial task to create and define the common abstract world religion (Darism) and work towards making it into a real faith.

Article 8
Agreement that human life is sacred and anyone who wilfully takes another person's

life will be automatically excommunicated by all religions with the following exceptions:

(a) Where the person acted in direct self-defence, and inaction would have meant their own life would have been in imminent danger.

(b) Where the person is in the armed forces and is fighting in a defensive war sanctioned and approved by the United Nations.

(c) Where the person killed had committed a serious crime and was sentenced to death by the formal legal authorities of the country following a full judicial trial and appeal.

Article 9
Agreement that no religion will impose any condition or requirement as mandatory if by so doing it compromises the individual's fundamental human rights defined in the Universal Declaration of Human Rights.

29. Culture and Religious Practices

The history of woman is the history of the continued and universal oppression of one sex by the other. The emancipation of woman is her restoration to equal rights and privileges with man.

~ Tennesse Claflin

Religions imported the cultural practices prevalent at the time of their creation, and as society has tried to move on, by clinging to their practices so as not to lose their perceived heritage, religions have acted as an anchor slowing down social development and becoming a home for prejudices.

The issue of cultural and religious practice's becoming blurred is a generic one, and faced by most religions and societies as they grow up and mature. Just as people differ in timing of going through adolescence and reaching maturity, the same may be said of religions and societies. I'm convinced that we will all reach maturity, eventually, however some societies and religions still have the painful growing up process with its attendant tantrums to get through.

In this chapter, I'd like to explore some of these cultural and religious practices, where we need to transition from adolescence to maturity, as well as illustrate that they're generic issues.

29.1 Treatment of Women is a Determinant of Level of Civilisation

In early societies women had less civil rights and privileges and increased restrictions on their freedoms relative to men, who had clearly cast these early societies to their own advantage. Societies have changed hugely over the last two thousand years and we've steadily become more civilised.

As we've become more civilised, societies have become more egalitarian and fairer with the status of women increasing as a consequence. The industrial and information technology revolutions have reduced the importance of physical strength and further helped women to progress.

Therefore it's valid to use the status of women and their treatment as a proxy or measure of how civilised and progressive we are as a society.

On that basis, we can only be considered to be fully civilised when there is full gender equality. Full Gender Equality means:

- Equal participation in politics with half of all politicians being female
- All laws are gender neutral
- Identical rights for male's and female's
- Any condition that applies to female's must identically apply to male's[1]

Using data from the Global Gender Gap 2008[2], no country as yet can be considered to have reached a fully civilised state. The Nordic countries of Finland, Norway, Iceland and Sweden are the furthest ahead with the highest political empowerment scores of a female to male ratio of 0.5, translating into women having a 33% representation[3].

However even advanced western countries such as UK and US have political empowerment levels of only 0.28 and 0.14 showing despite popular myths they have considerable territory to cross before becoming fully civilised by this yardstick (to be fully civilised the empowerment ratio would need to be 1.00, i.e. one female for one male)

At the bottom end, countries such as Iran, Yemen and Saudi Arabia have less than 2% female representation.

Thus as a global community, we're all moving forward along the path to civilisation, with some further ahead than others, but that should be no excuse even for countries in the lead to rest on their laurels.

This may appear an impossible target, however that's an illusion as there are no fundamental laws of physics standing in our way! With the right will it could be

---

1   The only exception being leave for pregnancy
2   The Global Gender Gap Report http://www.weforum.org/pdf/gendergap/report2008.pdf
3   0.5 is the female to male ratio, i.e. 1 female for every 2 male politicians, or a 1 in 3 representation overall, i.e. 33%

achieved overnight by simply mandating that each district that elects candidates to regional and national political assemblies must always elect two candidates – one male and one female.

29.2   Impact of Women having a Lower Status

The true role of government must be to help each individual maximise their potential, and by allowing women to have a lower status, the government itself is by definition failing in its core role.

If women have a lower status, or have restrictions placed upon them and what they can do, then that must affect their morale and motivation and will have a number of repercussions.

Reduced prosperity of the state and global community

Imagine if in a football team, one side decides to puts lead weights into the shoes of half of its players, restricting their ability to move freely and slowing them down. Clearly that team is going to be left behind and drift to the bottom of the league tables.

In exactly the same way, any restrictions on women, functions similarly and is an own goal. Women will be less able and motivated to play their full share in the development of the country and the economy will suffer overall and be suboptimal.

It's not just the particular state or country that misses out, by shortening horizons for women, we lose out as a global community on female scientists and future Nobel prize winners who might have pushed back the frontiers of science.

Impact on the next generation

Parents play a hugely important role in the development of their children, helping to encourage and motivate them as well as ensuring they explore all their options and maximise their potential. It's important that both parents are able to take independent views as and when needed and able to hold their own in robust discussion, ensuring that options and ideas get fully explored.

If the mother is in a country where women have a lower status and subject to restrictions, then they're going to feel un-empowered and with their own confidence affected and horizons limited, it'll be harder for them to play an informed and proactive role in helping develop their children.

On aggregate the likely impact will be a systemic bias towards reduced development and personal growth of children, with less breadth of outlook and interests leading to a lower level of creativity[4] and innovation. These reduced development outcomes get multiplied over successive generations with a compounding effect, placing the country on a lower development path.

29.3   The Word of God Trap

An Illustration of the Command Persistence Assumption

Imagine you're on a naval charting exercise and visiting remote islands in the Pacific and come upon an island where you find the inhabitants are performing military patrols around the island dressed in old World War II US navy uniforms. After speaking to them you find they're descendants of a US naval mission who were guarding the island but then lost radio contact, and the ship carrying their commanding officers who had dropped them there had been sunk and no-one at head quarters knew that this group had disembarked on this particular island and therefore the assumption being they'd gone down with the ship.

As the group never heard again from their next in line, they continued diligently carrying out their orders to patrol and guard the island, and in time their children continued with the same duties, inheriting the duty from their parents.

This illustrates the Command Persistence Assumption, in which a command is assumed to persist, and the people carrying it out continue the task in perpetuity, delegating it to each successive generation.

Its obvious absurdity can be seen from the example given above where many decades after peace had broken out, the descendants of the original unit were still faithfully guarding their tiny atoll in the Pacific.

The Word of God as a classic instance of Command Persistence

I believe religion suffers from a similar issue. When religions started, there was some communication between God and the founder / creators of the religion, leading to the religion and its practises and rituals being defined. As mentioned earlier, these

---

4   As an illustration of the proposed relationship between female empowerment and creativity, the Nordic countries of Finland, Norway, Iceland and Sweden which had the highest levels of political empowerment of women, were in the top eleven in a ranking of countries by number of patents per capita http://www.nationmaster.com/graph/eco_pat_gra_percap-economy-patents-granted-per-capita

practices would have taken their inspiration and inherited / derived from the commonly accepted practises of the day.

Successive generations of priests would see the practises and rituals as sacrosanct and as the "word or command of god" and so be loath to alter these in any way, i.e. they're locked into a "Command Persistence" behavioural model, narrowly interpreting their role as gatekeepers and preventing the religion from progressing.

However as society inevitably progresses and changes, these changes rub against and cause friction with religion's practises and rituals leading to tensions and conflict within society.

We should not deny God the right to change

We often change our mind on all sorts of topics and see it as completely normal. So why should we deny God this opportunity? Surely just because she[5] said something few thousands of years ago to the creators of a religion, that was then, and as times have changed and new technologies and administrative systems and procedures brought into place and societies have matured, why should we for one moment assume that God would stick inflexibly to her earlier commandments? Surely an intelligent god would adapt her recommendations to us taking our current situation into account.

Therefore admonishment of the religious establishment of the need to stick inflexibly to a few thousand-year-old messages from god is flawed.

Restarting the Communication with God

All religions need to set up and formalise a channel for communication with God and get updates directly from god via this channel, asking her advise on how to deal with new issues and whether she still wants us to keep to older practises and rituals or whether those practises have outlived their shelf lives and as a society we've outgrown them and so they can be considered obsolete.

One way of doing this is for each religion to nominate nine people who would have access to the ports of communication with God and every year to communicate with God and get her views on all and any aspect of religion taking into account developments during the year. It would be up to these nine people to take questions and matters bubbling up from their juniors and to collectively put them to God and

---

5   I'm continuing my convention mentioned previously of referring to God using a feminine   gender
     to redress the implicitly biased convention of using the male gender.

agree between themselves how to interpret her response. The grassroots members of each faith would vote for and select the nine people into the roles on a five-year tenure.

That would then allow each religion to progressively move forward year on year and not be locked into practises that God only meant for us to follow in the circumstances and environment prevalent a few thousand years ago.

29.4   Caste

Hinduism divided society into broad groupings called Varnas. These groupings formed the basis of the Caste System[6]. Caste was a determinant of the type of work that a person was expected to do, and their relative status in society. Caste also influenced a person's dietary habits and their interactions with other castes.

There are four main caste groups the Brahmins, Kshatryas, Vaishyas and Shudras, with thousands of sub-caste's mapped onto the four main caste groups. Figure 11 shows the occupations and status levels for each caste.

Caste	Occupation	Status
Brahmins	Priests, Teachers	Highest
Kshatrya	Warriors / Rulers	Second Highest
Vaishyas	Traders, Farmers, Merchants, Artisans	Third
Shudras	Labourers	Fourth

Figure 11: Caste, Occupations and Status

Indian society has a complex concept of purity and pollution, but a broad simplification is that high castes pursuing more rarified professions are more pure and as one goes to lower caste's they become impure and polluted.

Approximately 20 % of Hindus are without a Varna, and therefore outside of the caste system, becoming in effect "outcastes" with a status lower than that of the

---

6   Caste System http://www.friesian.com/caste.htm,
     http://www.indianchild.com/caste_system_in_india.htm, http://www.english.emory.edu/Bahri/caste.html

Shudras. These outcastes were regarded as "untouchable" because they traditionally did work such as sweeping, cleaning and night soil collecting, which were seen as making them polluted or impure. Mahatma Gandhi named them Harijans or children of god, however this was seen as patronising, and more recently they have become known as Dalits deriving from the a word meaning oppressed / suppressed.

Current Situation on Caste[7]

The Constitution of India outlawed discrimination based on caste in 1950, however ideas of caste and relative status are rooted deep in people's psyche and akin to racism are hard to eradicate. Sixty years later, despite affirmative action programmes by the government, discrimination based on caste is still an issue affecting 150 million Dalits in India[8,9].

Dalits find it hard to escape from their traditional roles as higher castes refuse to purchase or associate with them. Discrimination is widespread and present at home, at school, in the workplace and in access to the police and judiciary. The issue was acknowledged by India's Prime Minister Dr Manmohan Singh who called it a "blot on humanity".

Ruling Group Power and Status Preservation through Discrimination

There appears a common theme running through societies – the group having power and status seeks to preserve it by altering and redefining the rules of the game to deny other groups access or make it harder for them to take their share. As the current power holders it's easier for them to make the changes to preserve the status quo.

Although unethical and not in the national interest, it may be seen as rational behaviour by the ruling group, as it disadvantages the other groups, and makes it easier for the ruling group and their descendants to hold onto and consolidate power and maximise their share of resources.

It's one of the main motives behind racism and anti-immigration sentiments and there is an element of it in caste discrimination too as it enables higher caste's to keep certain roles their exclusive preserve, limiting competition from other groups.

---

7   Current here means 2010
8   Caste System still Blighting India
     http://www.telegraph.co.uk/news/uknews/1542669/Caste-system-still-blighting-India.html
     http://www.washington-report.org/backissues/0791/9107019.htm
9   Caste System in India an International Issue
     http://www.telegraph.co.uk/news/worldnews/asia/india/7597109/Caste-discrimination-against-Indias-untouchables-is-an-international-issue.html

Job Status and Dignity

One of the implicit beliefs in the Caste system is that the type of work one does, types the person's status and worth in society, and that if they're doing a job that involves dealing with dirt then that dirt somehow gets internalised and the person becomes impure.

Although the caste system has extrapolated the belief to an extreme, there's still a lurking sentiment and acceptance in broader society with most people inclined to agree that one's job determines status and pecking order in society.

In reality things are never cut and dry, a lot depends on one's starting point defined by the country one's born into, the family's wealth and kind of upbringing they can afford to give you. Individual efforts and aptitude are of course important, however so is luck. Therefore the actual job one ends up in is not entirely due to our own efforts, and it's questionable to give people credit for something when so much depended on factors outside of their control.

Furthermore, as outlined by the discussion in Box 1 (below), if one is creative in the interpretation, quite different professions can be seen as having similar outcomes, and trying to assign varying status levels to different professions is like attempting to make one link in a chain more important than the other links.

I was giving a lift to the teenage children of family friends of ours. They were all planning to go to medical school and looking forward to careers as doctors and surgeons and excitedly comparing notes on the merits of different universities. After a while I mentioned it could be argued a doctor should have the same status as a sweeper. I asked them what they felt about this and whether they agreed.

After some hesitation, out of deference, they replied it was correct that we should give respect to every job. Accepting this as valid, I responded that it could still be argued that in some way both these professions may be seen as having a similar impact. They were unable to work this out, and asked me to expand.

I replied that if you are suffering from an infection then a doctor would diagnose and prescribe medication to fix it, ridding you of the infection and restoring you to health. However a sweeper by keeping the place clean ensures that the germs that might infect you are eliminated before they get a chance to come near you, and therefore, similar to the doctor, helps keep you free of infections and in good health.

Box 1: A discussion on relative job status

I think therefore we need to break the link between job type and status, and regard all jobs with equal dignity, each playing a unique role in the value chain of society.

Eliminating Caste Discrimination

Despite discrimination based on caste having been outlawed sixty years ago, and the presence of a strong affirmative action programme, caste based discrimination is still a daily reality for 150 million people in India[10]. Clearly something additional is needed to alter the status quo, and I've outlined some possible courses of action to fix this blot on society.

Streamlined Reporting of Caste Based Incidents

Caste based crimes are further complicated by the complicity of people in the constabulary who often sympathise with the perpetrators and delay or refuse to record caste based incidents, preying on the knowledge that the disadvantaged individuals don't fully appreciate their rights or have alternative recourse to enforcing them.

It would be useful to have a nationwide free-phone number backed up with a call centre for the reporting of caste based crimes. The number would be promoted widely and allow circumvention of biased local level constabulary.

Fast Track Judicial System for Caste Crimes

Currently the average length of a trial in India is 15 years[11], whilst being a serious issue that affects everyone, it also means that perpetrators of caste based crimes have 15 years or more of impunity, and the struggle and time implications of people who're already disadvantaged and resource poor leads to the inevitability of making legal recourse hard to contemplate apart from the most extreme cases.

This mindset allows low to medium level infringements to continue unabated. What is needed is for the judicial system to branch and create a new parallel fast track specialised judicial system to exclusively handle caste based crimes, with a process that allows a binding decision within a maximum of six months from first filing.

---

10   India: Humanity, Equality, Destiny?
      http://www.newstatesman.com/human-rights/2010/01/caste-discrimination-india
11   India introduces plea bargaining http://news.bbc.co.uk/1/hi/world/south_asia/5149338.stm

Village Level Programme for Adopting Caste Equality Charter

A Charter of Caste Equality needs to be drafted which outlines the principles of Caste Equality. Village's should be incentivised to publicly adopt the Charter by the Government putting Charter Villages onto a fast track development path with additional incentives to follow over a 10 year period provided they remain true to the Charter with minimal infringements.

The initial adoption of the charter by the village needs to be marked as a major event, almost akin to a wedding as there's the coming together of different social groups. Just as in an Indian marriage there's a Milni[12] ceremony, similarly the Charter Adoption event needs to be choreographed and have a Milni ceremony where people at all levels from the different caste's take part[13] in the Milni. As food tends to be one of the issues in Caste separation, the food at the event should be jointly prepared and consumed by members of all caste's.

The Caste Charter document needs to be signed publicly at the event by selected members of all the castes' and a copy of the main page put on public display.

Draft Charter of Caste Equality

1. People of all castes are equal in dignity, rights, respect and purity.
2. All professions and jobs are worthy of respect and have equal status and dignity.
3. Just as a priest will help purify our soul, people doing a job such as sweeping purify our environment and both are of equal importance and dignity.
4. Discrimination based on caste is illegal and a criminal offense.

Developing a full set of clauses is outside the scope of this book, however the above are some of the key elements. Additional clauses need to be imported from the Universal Declaration of Human Rights, and the Charter should also stress gender equality.

Caste Equality Day

To underline the principles of Caste Equality, there should be a Caste Equality day when the politicians at state and central government level, meet and reaffirm the

---

12   Milni is hindi for Meeting or Coming together
13   At a marriage, during Milni, corresponding relatives (uncles to uncles, sisters to sisters etc) of both sides meet, embrace and place garlands of flowers on each other.

Charter, and take part in a meal that's been prepared by Dalits[14]. The day should coincide with Mahatma Gandhi's birthday as this is already a public holiday, and by sharing food prepared by Dalits the politicians would be emulating Mahatma Gandhi who used to do this to convince people that all castes were equal.

29.5   Burqa

As illustrated by the conversation in Box 2 below, I've been perplexed over the wearing of the Burqa for quite some time, and shall explore the issues in this section.

Thirty years back, shortly after graduating, I was changing flights at Moscow airport and had a seven hour wait in the transit lounge. With time on my hands, I got talking with a young muslim man in his late teens, who was there with his family.

As we had time, and reasoning that we weren't likely to see each other again as we were heading different ways, with the naivety of youth I asked my new found friend the reason for muslim women wearing the burqa. He pondered a while and said he would enquire from his parents and went off to consult them.

He returned shortly with a smile and informed me the reason was when men saw women in normal clothes, they may get physically attracted to the women which could lead to impure thoughts in their minds. I listened intently and then said "So really it's to protect and prevent the men from having such thoughts". My friend nodded, appearing relieved that I had understood the rationale.

I remained quiet for a further moment reflecting on this, and then asked "But how about the women, couldn't they also feel physical attraction for men, and therefore they too may get these kind of thoughts, don't the women also need to be protected?".

My friend remained silent, the beginnings of a frown starting to appear on his brow. I continued as if thinking out aloud, "So perhaps men too should wear the burqa?". By now the frown was fully developed, but he remained silent as he pondered the logic.

Sensing the opportunity, I continued, "However wouldn't it be more practical to dispense with the robes, and simply wear very dark sun glasses? They would act to reduce visibility and the chance of impure thoughts. Both men and women would wear the glasses."

My friend muttered that he would consult with his parents and get back to me, and that was the last I saw of him.

Box 2: Conversation in Moscow Airport

14   Dalit's refers to people outside the Caste System, earlier known as Harijans and Untouchables.

Is wearing of Burqa a Religious or a Cultural Requirement?

I've been puzzled when Muslim women have asserted they need to wear the Burqa in order to practise Hijab as required by their religion. If that were true, then how does that account for the fact that there are many Muslim women who don't practise Hijab and wear neither the burqa nor the headscarf.

It's hard to get exact numbers as statistics are not collected, but women practising Hijab are in an overall minority, with their percentage varying by region. It's quite high (60 – 70%) in the Middle East with some countries at 99%, but then very low (3 – 5%) in South Asia and at a moderate level (30%) in the Far East[15]. The mode of Hijab varies from a simple headscarf covering the hair, to the full cloaking provided by the Burqa being relatively uncommon.

The religious texts refer to the need for "modesty"[16] and using outer covering to conceal their "charms". Therefore there is no specific requirement, and it's a matter of interpreting the meanings of modesty, outer garments and charm.

Outer coverings might be interpreted as ones normal outer garments (e.g. a suit or sweater worn over a blouse is outer relative to the blouse). Modesty and charm too will vary depending on context and region.

The moment things become open to interpretation, they become susceptible to allowing prejudices and biases to be redefined as religious requirements, and allow what is in reality a cultural preference to be cast as a religious requirement, thereby putting it outside the scope of reform.

The fact that many Muslim women don't feel the need to wear the Burqa or practise Hijab must imply the existence of a large informal practical consensus that it's not a firm religious requirement.

Impact on Society

Imagine someone waved a magic wand and overnight society changed and all people – male and female were obliged to wear a cloak covering their face and body. What kind of world would that be? Self evidently it would be a grim and austere place, with all liveliness and spontaneity sucked out due to reduced chances for

---

15   What percent Muslim women wear Hijab?
      http://ask.metafilter.com/60321/What-percent-Muslim-women-wear-hijab
16   Hijab (Wikipedia) http://en.wikipedia.org/wiki/Hijab   http://en.wikipedia.org/wiki/Burqa

communication. The only people whose faces you would see would be your friends and family.

Lets give that extreme scenario a score of 100 on a newly defined Grimness scale. Now lets say that the cloaking rule only applies to women, and instantly we become able to see half the people. Accordingly there would be a drop in the Grimness value to say 50.

However with all women still fully cloaked, the world would still appear fairly grim and as if someone had painted all the butterflies black.

If the cloaking rule was further changed so that only 10% of the women had to be cloaked. Then clearly the Grimness value would drop further[17], from 50 to a level of 5.

This example illustrates that the decision to cloak doesn't just impact the individuals concerned, but impacts and pulls down energy levels in the entire society.

Restricted Communication and Domain

Body language experts say that in getting our message across only 7% of our communication is from our choice of words, 38% is from our vocal style (pitch, speed, volume, tone) and 55% is visual and down to our body language and eye contact[18].

By preventing visual communication, wearing a burqa shuts down over half of our personal communication channels, and is a severe restriction of communication.

Furthermore, by restricting visual communication, the burqa stops spontaneity and casual conversation and therefore also acts to restrict the domain of personal contacts of the wearer, in effect ensuring they mix socially only within a select group of known people.

However restriction of communication and contact is form of punishment given to people sent to prison, and one can appreciate the point made by President Sarkozy of France who when talking about the burqa referred to women as prisoners behind a screen[19].

---

17 10% of 50
18 Body Language: A key to success in the workplace http://finance.yahoo.com/career-work/article/102425/Body_Language:_A_Key_to_Success_in_the_Workplace
   http://www.bodylanguageexpert.co.uk/communication-what-percentage-body-language.html
19 Sarkozy on Burka http://www.timesonline.co.uk/tol/news/world/europe/article6557252.ece
   http://news.bbc.co.uk/1/hi/8112821.stm

Prevention of Freedom of Expression

The clothes we wear are an important part of our self-expression. They allow us to signify whether we're quiet and conservative, or flamboyant and outgoing. Choosing classic styles versus the latest trends also allows us to demonstrate our personality and preferences.

Once someone is cloaked it makes them anonymous and prevents this form of self-expression, and in that sense it's a form of prevention of freedom of speech.

Health Impact

Vitamin D deficiency has been mentioned sometimes as a possible side effect of wearing the burqa. Although theoretically plausible, I'm somewhat sceptical because we only require a few minutes to half an hour[20] for the body to synthesize the required amount[21] of Vitamin D.

I am concerned however that wearing a burqa will lead to increased stress because the wearer is less able to communicate freely with people around them and are likely to feel somewhat isolated especially with the impaired peripheral vision. The ensuing stress may cause illness by affecting the immune system[22].

Someone wearing a burqa is less in the public eye and I suspect that the anonymity combined with the stress and concealment of their body shape is likely to predispose a burqa wearer towards becoming overweight[22]. Being overweight has well documented health risks.

Practising the Hijab by wearing Headscarves

Many women practise the Hijab by wearing headscarves, which either cover just the hair or also cover the neck.

Our hairstyle, its length and colour are all forms of self-expression and although much less repressive than the burqa, the headscarf too is a form of denial of self-expression.

---

20   The amount of time varies with skin pigmentation and time of day / strength of sun
21   Time in the sun, how much is needed for Vitamin D
      http://health.usnews.com/health-news/family-health/articles/2008/06/23/time-in-the-sun-how-much-is-needed-for-vitamin-d.html
22   Stress ages immune system   http://news.bbc.co.uk/1/hi/health/3034410.stm
23   This is only a supposition based on the logic as I have not been able to locate any specific research

The headscarf also serves as an implicit physical reminder to women of their position and role in society and its expectations, and in that sense may be viewed as having a somewhat coercive role.

Denial of fundamental rights to women

The restrictions and lack of freedom imposed by the burqa constitute a denial of fundamental rights to women and are part of a wider denial of equal rights to women. Some may argue that it preserves the dignity of women, but that's a disingenuous line of reasoning: there is no dignity in having your rights curtailed.

It's no coincidence to find nine of the bottom ten countries in the list of countries by female political empowerment[24] are countries where the burqa is actively practised.

This denial of fundamental rights is entirely consistent with the subtext of the Cairo Declaration of Human Rights in Islam (CDHRI), which sets out general guidance for the member states of the Organisation of the Islamic Conference[25]: the CDHRI has been criticized for not endorsing equality between men and women and by omission asserting the superiority of men.

29.6   Female Circumcision

Female Circumcision or Female Genital Mutilation (FGM) as it's more commonly known, is a deeply rooted cultural tradition in many parts of Africa and practised by both Christian and Muslim communities. Although it's a cultural tradition there is a blur, with some communities believing their faith requires it, this particularly true of Muslims[26], and a staggering 137 million women in 28 African countries have been mutilated[27].

The benefits ascribed to FGM vary by community but range from a purifying ritual, a female rites of passage, a guarantor of female chastity, boosting female fertility and enhancing male sexual pleasure.

FGM has a number of health risks: infections and risks from the procedure, chronic

24   The Global Gender Gap Report p13, http://www.weforum.org/pdf/gendergap/report2008.pdf
25   Cairo Declaration on Human Rights in Islam
      http://en.wikipedia.org/wiki/Cairo_Declaration_on_Human_Rights_in_Islam
26   The controversy of Female Genital Mutilation
      http://www.irinnews.org/IndepthMain.aspx?IndepthId=15&ReportId=62462
27   Female Genital Mutilation
      http://www.economist.com/world/middle-east/displaystory.cfm?story_id=E1_TRVJGG

urinary infections, cysts, complications during childbirth, chronic incontinence and the possibility of infections that can lead to infertility. It also makes sex painful and reduces a woman's sexual desire.

FGM has been outlawed in a number of African countries, but with a majority of people supporting the practise, governments fearing a backlash have not dared to enforce the law and the practise still has widespread support.

It's somewhat strange that women who as a group suffer the practise, still support and promote it and is a testament to the coercive power of culture, tradition and social pressure. If society views girls without FGM to be impure, not fully grown up and less fertile, and male's refuse to marry them then that too creates a powerful incentive for families to acquiesce and go along with FGM.

What I find particularly disturbing about FGM is its repression and control of female sexuality for male gratification, and is an example of the familiar theme of female subjugation.

Eliminating FGM

Outlawing FGM may appear a solution, but risks driving the practise underground and pushing people into the arms of unscrupulous practitioners. The real solution is to change the hearts and minds of the people and to embark upon co-ordinated cultural change programmes, and a campaign should be considered even where the practise has been outlawed.

I've outlined below some of the elements that a programme could incorporate[28]:

Female Circumcision Obsolescence Charter

A charter needs to be drawn up, the central theme of which is that FGM is a thing of the past and is now obsolete as all of its benefits can be attained through other means: modern feminine hygiene products mean that purity and cleanliness are no longer an issue; fertility can be tackled through IVF procedures; the sex industry produces a wide range of items for sexual enhancement.

The Charter should also point out that modern medicine has exposed that FGM had many self-defeating risks, and clarify that it is not a religious requirement.

---

28 It's worth noting that as it's dealing with culture change, the overall structure contains some of the same elements as dealing with Caste in India

Village / Town Charter Adoption Programme

A programme should be run to give additional development grant and aid to villages and towns, which officially adopt the FGM Obsolescence Charter. The aid would be some kind of new facility e.g. a school, hospital or clinic etc. The Charter Adoption process should be marked with a public ceremony where the village / town's leaders all publicly sign the charter.

To avoid a relapse into the bad old ways, rather than being a one off, there needs to be a stream of additional development aid over a sustained time period for remaining a charter village / town, with an annual ceremony marking the charter adoption.

Cultural Artifacts / Product Placement

A wide range of cultural artifacts should be encouraged, including the use of partial subsidy, to help make the point and get the message across subliminally. The artifacts could consist of a mix of pop songs, plays and films that incorporate the message into a sub-plot, in effect a kind of product placement. Other options are to stage popular media events such as the Live Aid Concerts in Africa cast as an Anti FGM Concert to help raise funds for anti-FGM initiatives.

Education and Advertising Campaigns

Ultimately stopping FGM is about educating people on the issues and risks and that there are other options, and clarifying that it is not a religious requirement. A series of education programmes should be put together to get the message across, and roll these out as campaigns over the various regions. The campaigns could include public discussion forums as well as radio and television advertising and be supported by thought leaders, medical specialists and religious leaders.

29.7   Honour Killings

Cruelly misnamed, "Honour Killings" refers to the murder of women by male relatives as punishment for bringing dishonour onto the family by her actions. UN sources estimate around 5,000 such murders occur annually[29].

---

29   Impunity for domestic violence, 'honour killings' cannot continue – UN official
  http://www.un.org/apps/news/story.asp?NewsID=33971&Cr=violence+against+women&Cr1
  http://www.alertnet.org/thenews/newsdesk/IRIN/6f6d5166f24330a0e8edcb79796ca5cc.htm
  http://en.wikipedia.org/wiki/Honor_killing

The action being punished is broad ranging and depends on whatever is seen as "bringing dishonour" in the mind of the male relatives and community. This can include having an affair, dating or falling in love with someone seen as inappropriate, getting pregnant outside marriage, dressing in a revealing manner and in one case even chatting to a male on a social networking site. Perversely girls who've been raped instead of being treated sympathetically as victims can get seen as guilty of having brought dishonour and become a target of honour killing.

Experts say that some Honour Killings might have other motives such as to cover up incest and for inheritance reasons.

The practise is concentrated in the Middle East and in countries in the West with large Middle Eastern immigrant communities, and is yet another example of the denial of fundamental rights to women in this region that was discussed earlier[30]. It's a cultural practise and not sanctioned by religion, however people falsely believe their religion condones it.

The ability of men to escape lightly after honour killings acts as an unspoken threat against women and creates a coercive environment forcing women to stay within and conform to narrowly prescribed roles.

The over-importance of honour

I struggle to understand why the concept of honour has become that important, people are taking themselves far too seriously. In 100 years everyone here today will no longer be here, so in a 100 years does it actually matter if some bigoted individuals who'll have long perished with no trace, have carried some concept or judgement in their head about a particular dishonour? In the broad scheme of things it's completely irrelevant.

The Honour Killers Mindset

Honour Killers clearly feel that they have the right, even duty, to carry out the killing. Implicitly embedded in that feeling, is the strand of thought that they have some kind of "ownership" right over the woman, and flowing from that the right to do the killing. This is hugely disconcerting and treating women as chattel is ancient thinking and it's almost as if people have stayed isolated in a vacuum in poverty stricken backwaters, resulting in them not developing, and still waiting for enlightenment.

30   Section 29.5

The Irony of Honour Killings

The *real* dishonour in an Honour Killing, is the taking of the victim's life, with no trial or due process, and on the basis of bigoted thinking rooted on questionable and outdated morals.

It's sadly ironic therefore that the murderers committed the murder to "protect" the honour of their family, but in their action to remove what they perceived as dishonour, instead in the eyes of the entire thinking world, they have brought huge dishonour onto themselves, their family and society.

Soft laws shielding the perpetrators

A number of countries in the Middle East have soft laws that allow leniency to people guilty of Honour Killings: for example despite voting for the UN Universal Declaration of Human Rights, Syria allows judges to have discretionary powers to waive or reduce the sentence for Honour crimes[31].

Having laws that allow leniency for Honour Killings is perverse, implicitly sending out the message that women have less rights. It also ignores the fact that the victims had no chance of any defence or trial, and sanctifies mob rule.

A helpful role model is provided by Turkey, which has updated its legal system to ensure people who commit Honour Killings, as well as those who plan them, are treated severely. It also gets state employed Imams to declare Honour Killings sinful in weekly sermons. However Turkey still has Honour Killings, showing that laws although necessary, are not sufficient by themselves and more has to be done to alter the national psyche.

Different Development Paths

It's easy to cast societies that offer support for and tolerate Honour Killings as being wrong headed and intrinsically immoral with lopsided values.

However if one looks back a few hundred years then even in currently advanced societies such as the UK, women were treated particularly harshly with devices such as the Scold's Bridle and Ducking Stool being used to punish women for scolding or nagging (Box 3).

---

31 Honour Killings in Syria and Turkey
    http://www.economist.com/world/middle-east/displaystory.cfm?story_id=E1_TQDQVNRQ

During the Tudor times in England, under the Whipping Act of 1530 men and women could be whipped simply on the grounds of being a vagrant, and mothers were whipped for having illegitimate children.

Women had a particularly hard time and it was an offence to scold or nag. The punishment consisted of placing a Brank or scold's bridle over a woman's head. The scold's bridle had an iron bit that fitted into her mouth and prevented her from talking. This punishment was later replaced by the ducking stool, which came in use between early 1600s to early 1800s. The woman was strapped to a chair on the end of wooden beam and ducked in a pond or river so as to "cool her immoderate heat". In some instances the ducking was over done and resulted in the woman dying.

At the beginning of the nineteenth century, there were around 220 offences that carried the death penalty and people could be hanged for stealing anything of the value of five shillings or more. In 1801 a 13 year old boy was hanged for stealing a spoon, and in 1807 a girl aged just seven was hanged.

Box 3: Punishment during 1500 – 1750[32]

In that context therefore, it appears that "growing up" or enlightenment is a stage that all societies have to go through, and with that perspective societies that tolerate Honour Killings are simply lagging in development and are yet to find and go through their period of enlightenment, which will happen in due course.

Reducing and Eliminating Honour Killings

The Turkish experience shows that despite changes in the law and Imams stressing that Honour Killing is a sin, there is still support for honour related crimes. Eliminating honour killings will require sustained co-ordinated action, and I've outlined some key elements:

Rename Honour Killings

Names and Labels matter and by ascribing a noble aspiration to the killing, the

---

32   Christopher Hibbert: The Roots of Evil; A Social History of Crime and Punishment; published 1963.
Lord Phillips, Lord Chief Justice of England and Wales, High Sheriff's Law Lecture, Oxford
http://www.judiciary.gov.uk/docs/speeches/lcj10102006.pdf
Old Time Punishments http://www.lordverulam.org/old_time_punishments.html

term Honour Killing is portrayed as something separate and distinct from other killings. There is no Honour in Honour Killings – only dishonour in the cold blooded taking of life, and Honour Killings should be renamed for what they are – Male Supremist Murders.

Redraft Soft Laws

Soft laws enshrining leniency towards Honour killers in the legal system, need to be redrafted to treat these killers the same as any other category of murderers.

I discussed[33] modulating the voting rights of a country in the UN General Assembly using the country's performance on a number of factors, including their performance on Human Rights and Gender Equality. Accordingly countries having these kind of unjust soft laws would be penalised by lower voting rights at the UN, hopefully encouraging them to rectify the anomalies.

Repositioning the Religious Context of Honour Killings

Religious leaders need to follow Turkey's example of declaring Honour Killing a sin, however there is a need to go beyond that and stress that the real dishonour is the cold blooded murder and taking of life which far outweighs any perceived social dishonour from the victim's behaviour.

Religious leaders need to assert that Honour killers will be considered to have excommunicated themselves by their actions. As Honour killers don't act in a vacuum, the excommunication should also apply anyone who encouraged or instigated the honour killing.

Cultural Change and a Gender Equality Charter

Reframing of laws and religious direction are necessary but not sufficient in themselves.

The real solution is for these societies to be man enough to admit they have failed to renew themselves and to embark upon cultural change, through which their people adopt and internalise a new value system giving women full equality in all respects. One way of doing this is for them to proclaim a new Gender Equality Charter giving full and equal rights to women.

---

33   Section 14.3

Although raised in the context of Honour Killings, the Gender Equality Charter would be useful in many other countries as well.

Worldwide polling shows that there would be popular support for such an initiative with eight out of every ten people in favour[34], and so it comes down to leaders being bold enough to take the initiative and claim their role in history[35].

29.8   State Sponsored Religious Schools[36]

In the olden days, religions used to be repositories for learning, with monasteries and priests acting as guardians of knowledge and playing a vital role in passing knowledge down the generations. It was natural therefore for religions to take the lead in education and the setting up of schools.

As countries evolved, it created an issue of what happens to the schools being run by the religious orders. The solution varies with the history of each country. In country's such as France, which had a revolution creating the opportunity to rethink their society, there is no formal teaching or place for religion in state schools. However in the UK, which arguably has had a gentler transition creating the space to hold onto traditions, in 2004 there were almost 7,000 state maintained faith schools, making up 36% of primary and 17% of secondary schools[37].

Although it may not seem apparent at first glance, the large amount of education being provided by religious orders is a cultural practice that we've inherited. It's easy to point at deficiencies created by other country's cultural practices such as gender inequality and be smug in the satisfaction that we're past that stage, however the difficulty of cultural change comes home when we look at the way we ourselves tread water when dealing with issues such as faith schools.

Faith Schools cause divisions in society
Different religions developed and grew to prominence in different parts of the

34   Poll on Equal rights for women
http://www.worldpublicopinion.org/pipa/articles/btjusticehuman_rightsra/453.php?lb=bthr&pnt=453&nid=&id=&gclid=CIXEs-7yoaECFYts4wodpUTNyA
35   and follow in the inspired footsteps of Kemal Ataturk who instigated a step change in Woman's rights in Turkey
36   In this section I shall focus on the faith school sector in the UK, however the discussion is generic and will apply to faith schools worldwide.
37   Office of National Statistics: Religion http://www.statistics.gov.uk/cci/nugget.asp?id=963

world, with each geographical region tending to be fairly homogeneous in terms of faith. Religious conversions through territorial conquests did change this somewhat, but it remains broadly true that there is a close correlation between a person's religion and their geographical origin or ethnicity.

Having faith schools with the ability when oversubscribed to make their admission decisions using faith based criteria, boils down to an admission decision being made on race, with religion acting as a proxy for race due to the close correlation between the two.

If there were a schools admission policy based on race, there would be uproar, however from the above, a similar outcome is being achieved with religion acting to obfuscate the issue[38].

Therefore faith schools create a form of apartheid by stealth within the education system, ironically sponsored by state and taxpayer money.

Are there any Educational Benefits from faith schooling

At the risk of stating the obvious, the primary role of schools is to educate students. However the rules of mathematics, physics, chemistry, biology or English grammar etc., have no dependence on religion, and therefore religion as such has no relevance or value add in the curriculum and teaching of these subjects. Therefore I see no educational benefit from having a faith school.

It may be argued that a faith school is better placed to instil discipline, however I feel that comes down to good management skills and procedures which are not the exclusive domain of any religion.

The benefits from faith schooling

Having stood the test of time, clearly there must be some benefits from faith schooling.

In the UK, the number of people describing themselves as non-religious has grown from 31% to 43% between 1983 and 2008, and church attendances have been steadily falling[39]. Faced with the continuous decline, faith schooling offers the

---

38 I had wanted our daughters to study in an excellent local Church of England school but was denied on the grounds that they needed to give priority to candidates from their faith.

39 Religion and Belief: Some surveys andd statistics
    http://www.humanism.org.uk/campaigns/religion-and-belief-surveys-statistics

church something of a trump card to bolster their attendances with the carrot of school admission.

Faith schools insulate students from mixing with students from other faiths and backgrounds, and this may be perceived a benefit by parents who're keen to ensure their children follow their own faith unquestioningly, without having to confront any divergent opinion.

Due to the relationship between faith and ethnicity, another group of parents may prefer faith schools for the racial segregation opportunity it potentially offers.

These benefits are questionable, as the Church ought to be able to engage with believers without the need for incentives, and parents preferring segregation are missing the broader picture of social harmony.

Faith Schools and the Unified Model of God and Religion

I proposed[40] a unified model of God and Religion, outlining how all religions could be viewed as having derived from a single common base religion. With that construct, as all religions can be cast back to the single base religion, the concept of discriminating admission based on religion would become redundant[41].

The difficulty faced by political reformers

One has to be sympathetic to the plight of politicians, whilst they may privately acknowledge some of the issues discussed, to implement them as policy, risks losing a lot of votes and failure to be re-elected.

This implicitly highlights the problems of having a party based system discussed earlier[42], where politicians make decisions based on the survival of the party rather than on the nobler desire to do what's right for the country.

Referendum on Faith Schools

With politicians rendered impotent due to their vested political calculations, the fairest way of dealing with the issues created by faith schools is a national debate and referendum on the subject.

---

40   Section 28.5
41   This overlooks atheists, who would not belong to the common base religion.
42   Chapter 10

29.9 Polygyny – One Man, Multiple Wives

The practice of Polygyny[43] in which a man is allowed to have a number of wives at the same time is supported by a number of religions and societies.

This is an example of how religions incorporated practices prevalent at the time of their formation and once baked into the religion the practices have been shielded from the winds of social change and remained part of the doctrine. As a consequence, a practice that may have been appropriate a few thousand years ago remains part of the present doctrine of some religions and societies.

Polygyny is intrinsically unfair to women. The man can play one woman against another and create a divide and rule regime in order to get things his way. He also has the possibility of withholding intimacy to further ensure he gets the upper hand in the relationship.

The negligible take up of Polyandry in which a woman has multiple husbands[44], is further evidence that Polygamous relationships give the single gender spouse greater power in the relationship. The low take up of Polyandry being attributed to the male ego finding it difficult to contemplate taking a lower position in the relationship.

There is an argument that if consenting adults enter such relationships willingly then where's the harm and why should anyone intervene; however the same argument could be used to justify exploitative work relationships and the reason minimum standards on pay and working time have developed over the years. It also ignores the reality that a lower status role may only seem acceptable to women facing reduced career choices due to structural discrimination in the education system and workplace arising from the prevalent cultural mindset.

The human sex ratio at birth is 105 boys to 100 girls[45, 46] and this gives a clue as to what nature's views are on the matter. The fact there is rough parity between the

---

44 Non-anthropologists often erroneously refer to this as Polygamy, however Polygamy includes Polyandry where a woman is married to a number of husbands at the same time.

45 Cultural Anthropology p.216: an applied perspective, Gary Ferraro. Published by: Thomson Wadsworth.

46 CIA World Factbook
https://www.cia.gov/library/publications/the-world-factbook/fields/2018.html?countryName=&countryCode=&regionCode=%C2%AA

47 Ratio of males to females http://en.wikipedia.org/wiki/Sex_ratio

two genders at birth shows that in the grand scheme of things humans are meant to pair up on a one to one ratio. For the religious minded, clearly God intended for us to marry on an equal i.e. one to one ratio, and had she any other ratio in mind then she would have ensured that the human sex ratio reflected her alternative plan. Following that line of reasoning, one can assert that Polygyny is contrary to god's wishes.

Apart from the theological question, the sex ratio creates a more pragmatic issue, if every man in a community practising Polygyny wanted to marry two wives, then where would all the extra women come from? With the birth ratio being 1.05 males for every female, the community itself will be unable to provide the extra women, and the practise may create an incentive to attract women from outside the community to convert and enter the community. This ongoing need creates a force for instability that may in time lead to friction and tensions between communities.

Polygyny may have been valid few thousand years earlier, but in today's highly codified world with the rule of law, civil society, knowledge working and education, the concept is an anachronism and communities need to stop the sacrifice of female equality on the alter of male ego and libido and disallow Polygyny as being fundamentally disrespectful to women and in breach of the laws of nature[48].

29.10 Changing and Extending Religion

Religions and societies need to take a lesson from life and nature, where organisms evolve over time, adapting to new circumstances, developing new genes and behaviour and discarding ones that have outlived their usefulness. In the absence of evolution, the world would not be the place it is today.

Religions need to stop acting as dinosaurs, clinging to ancient doctrines, and as outlined earlier[49], find ways of continuous renewal and reinterpretation of their doctrine to suit changing contexts. Doing this would reduce tensions and increase its relevance. This is already happening in many cases but needs a lot more impetus.

An example of a change in religion and tradition is the practice of Sati in India, under which the wife was expected to jump into the funeral pyre of her husband.

---

48   Not everyone will be swayed by the gender equality argument, and hence it's worth considering that as it is not supported by the human sex ratio, Polygyny runs counter to the Laws of Nature and by inference for the religious, God's wishes.

49   Section 29.3

The British Government banned Sati in 1829. However it took major social reforms by Indian leaders to actually stop the practise[50]. This demonstrating that to change religious practices and traditions requires a change of law, as well as campaigns by social leaders to change peoples thinking and getting them to internalise new value systems.

As a parent, the nature and content of our instructions and dialogue with our children changes continuously as they grow up from a baby through childhood, teenage years and eventually reaching adulthood. The same can be said for the dialogue between god and us, and we would expect her message and dialogue to change as we mature as a society.

Extending the scope of the Kosher and Halal concepts

It's tempting to conjecture what such a new dialogue might bring in terms of extensions to our religions. The Kosher and Halal concepts have a universal appeal, as they are concerned that when we consume things, the consumption be done in such a way as to minimise the impact and suffering of others.

With Global Warming putting our planet's eco-systems under pressure and likely to cause major changes and suffering if unchecked, it would be good to see these two concepts expanded to include the environmental impact of our consumption. This could lead to particular cars with excessive fuel consumption being deemed not to be Halal[51], or it be declared non Kosher to fly more than a particular number of miles per annum.

---

50   The tradition of Sati in India   http://www.kamat.com/kalranga/hindu/sati.htm
51   Both these examples are of course made up to illustrate how this might work.

30. Happiness

Happiness is when what you think, what you say, and what you do are in harmony.

~ *Mohandas K. Gandhi*

The United States Declaration of Independence states "Life, Liberty and the pursuit of Happiness" are fundamental rights. The founding fathers of the United States clearly put Happiness alongside Life and Liberty in terms of importance.

So what exactly is happiness? It's a state of mind forming the context or backdrop within which our brain and thoughts are functioning. If we're unhappy, it's as if we're operating in a black and white world, with melancholy music playing in the background and we're somewhat self absorbed and introspective and less aware of the nuances and subtle delights of the world around us, as if we're viewing the world in a lower fidelity. On the other hand when we're happy, it's as if we're in a full colour world with the sounds of a fun fair in the background and we're more outward looking and responsive to the external world, sensitive to and picking up any tiny changes and cues in our environment.

At the risk of stating the obvious, clearly being happy is a far more pleasurable and satisfactory state, leading to an enhanced experience of life.

It's worth looking at the distinction between happiness, pleasure and long term satisfaction; pleasure is a fleeting feeling of enjoyment for example when you taste something completely new; however I see happiness synonymous[1] with long term satisfaction, as I don't see how you can maintain a continuous state of happiness without also being satisfied.

30.1 Evolutionary Advantage

Being happy makes people optimistic and likely to give themselves the benefit of

---

1   I will however mostly be using the term happiness.

the doubt, leading to greater confidence. They're less introspective and consequently more externally focussed resulting in a greater sensitivity to what's happening around them.

In the early days of human development these strengths would have led to a man becoming a better hunter and more able to provide, in turn leading to them attracting better and healthier mates.

These are likely[2] to make people who were happy more likely to breed and in greater numbers, leading to an evolutionary bias towards happiness.

30.2   Feedback Loop

Happiness may also be viewed as a feedback variable in a natural control system designed to help us meet our basic needs.

If we're unable to satisfy our needs, this leads to a gap between where we are and where we would like to be. This gap creates unhappiness and stress, which in turn act as a driver to motivate us to do something about it; in effect acting as a feedback control signal which gets amplified and acts upon us to alter our behaviour.

When our needs are being met and we're happy with where we are, then there would be no feedback signal going back to motivate us to alter our behaviour and we remain in a satisfied state.

Paradoxically it may have been easier to be happy a few hundred years ago, as our needs were more basic. In today's age of mass marketing and product placement, it's easy for our needs to get ratcheted up leading to a continual state of unhappiness and striving to succeed.

The control model leads to the observation that one of the factors that will determine our happiness is the level of our needs, and one route to happiness is to question our needs and determine how real and essential they really are. For example someone may feel they must have the latest gizmo but fifty years earlier the item wouldn't have existed and people would have been perfectly happy without it.

---

2   I say likely, because this is a line of reasoning I'm following, rather than a proven fact.

30.3 Health

When we're happy we're in quite a benign mood, and satisfied that our needs are being met, we experience low stress levels. Furthermore the rather calm and relaxed mood we're in means we're able to handle life's knocks gracefully, taking them in our stride without getting too worked up or pressured by events.

Stress has an impact on our health[3] and by lowering stress levels and placing us in harmony with our environment, one would intuitively expect Happiness to have a positive impact on health.

Researchers have indeed found happier people to have a greater protection against heart disease, stroke and type II diabetes, and there is the possibility of a link between happiness and longevity[4].

Specifically, happiness has been found to correlate with low levels of the stress hormone Cortisol, high levels of which are linked to hypertension and type II diabetes; and people who said they were happy had lower levels of a blood protein fibrinogen, high concentrations of which can imply future disease[5].

Therefore happiness isn't something merely there for pleasure or self-gratification, it's a key emotion of well being, with a profound impact on our physical and mental health and therefore as we ourselves have an active part to play in determining our level of happiness, it's important to learn how to nurture and manage it.

30.4 Hierarchy of Needs

Babies have a simple behavioural model, when a baby has a need that's not being met they signal this to their parents by crying. As we grow up and develop socially, this early model remains however the crying is replaced by an internal sense of dissatisfaction and unhappiness, which might be viewed as a kind of repressed crying.

---

3 Stress ages immune system http://news.bbc.co.uk/1/hi/health/3034410.stm

4 The health benefits of happiness
http://news.bbc.co.uk/1/hi/programmes/happiness_formula/4924180.stm

5 Happiness helps people stay healthy http://www.newscientist.com/article/dn7282-happiness-helps-people-stay-healthy.html

In his widely accepted Theory of Human Motivation[6,7], Maslow categorized our needs into five broad hierarchical groups (figure 12).

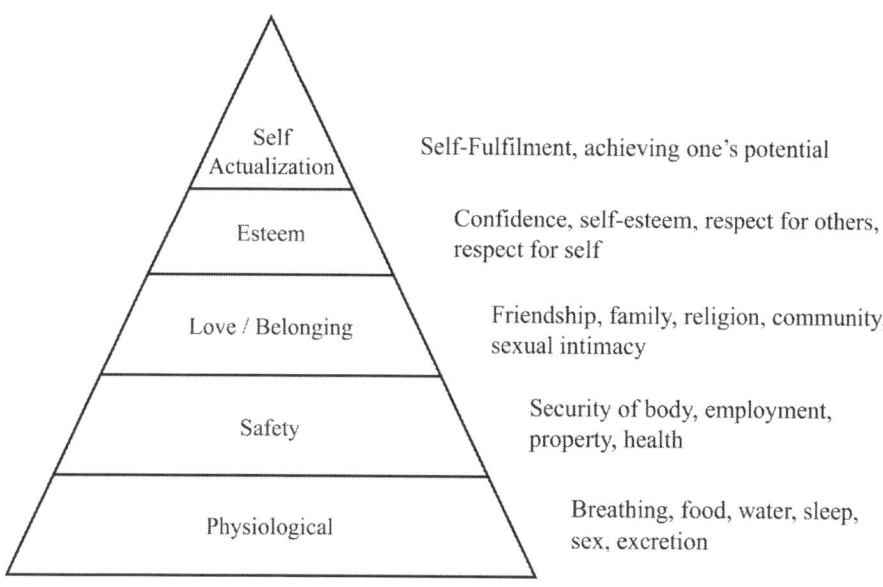

Figure 12: Maslow's hierarchy of needs

The hierarchical aspect of the needs groupings comes from the belief that until a lower level need is met and the appetite for it sated, the higher order needs are not considered and remain outside the individual's attention span.

Thus we would initially seek to meet our Physiological needs such as food, water, sleep and until these are met our Safety needs are of less importance and over the horizon. However once we've met our basic physiological needs then we'll focus on our need for Safety, and it's only when our Safety needs are fulfilled that we turn to Love / Belonging and want to make friendships and relationships.

Once all our lower order needs are met, then we're able to self-actualise ourselves, and to try and achieve all that we're capable of, attaining our full potential.

6   A Theory of Human Motivation, Maslow (1943) http://psychclassics.yorku.ca/Maslow/motivation.htm
7   Maslow's hierarchy of needs http://en.wikipedia.org/wiki/Maslow's_hierarchy_of_needs

Behaviour of other people
Apart from the low level Physiological needs and the high level Self Actualization, it's worth noting that the three core groups of needs in the middle depend upon the behaviour of people around us.

Our self-esteem and confidence is influenced by how those around us react towards us. Love and Belonging is clearly dependent on the behaviour of those around us. Safety too has some dependence on how people around us behave; for example people living on a large housing estate can get very worked up and insecure when groups of local teenagers engage in anti-social activities such as stealing and joy-riding cars and other acts of neighbourhood vandalism.

Religion
The enduring appeal of religion can be understood through the lens of the needs hierarchy.

Religion addresses our need for security by getting god "on side" – not just in this life but also, for believers, in the next life. The religion's community acts as an extended family, meeting the need for belonging. Finally there's a sense of self esteem created by being seen to be religious and motivated by what's perceived as higher or nobler ideals.

Self-Actualisation
In his original paper[8] Maslow postulated that a healthy person was someone who was primarily motivated by a desire to self-actualize themselves, i.e. to maximize their potential and achieve what they're capable of.

By substituting happiness for health, we can extend that to say people are only intrinsically happy when the four lower level of needs have been met and their primary motivation in life is self-actualization. Until we reach that state we still have unfulfilled lower order needs.

Self-actualization is a never-ending process, as it loops back upon itself. As we achieve and reach new milestones, our capabilities and potential increases, and therefore so does our self-actualization targets. In parallel, satisfaction with any particular self-actualization achievement tends to fade over time, stopping the temptation to rest on our laurels and motivating the search for new ways of self-actualisation.

8   A Theory of Human Motivation, Maslow (1943) http://psychclassics.yorku.ca/Maslow/motivation.htm

Therefore self-actualization is akin to continuous development and life long personal growth and achievement and would be expected to continue up to and beyond our retirement.

30.5   Expectations and Outcome

Expectations

The hierarchy of needs explains how our needs change, moving from one set to another, finally ending up at self-actualization. However what determines the point at which an individual is going to feel sated with a particular need? We're all different and clearly this will vary across people. Therefore whilst one person may be content with a certain level of security and turn their attention towards Love / Belonging, in the same situation another may continue with activities to increase their sense of security.

Our experiences, cultural and personal values and upbringing combine in our subconscious with our ego and ambition to determine our appetite for each of the need groups. In that sense, by implicitly setting the targets, we ourselves become an important input factor in determining our eventual happiness (figure 13).

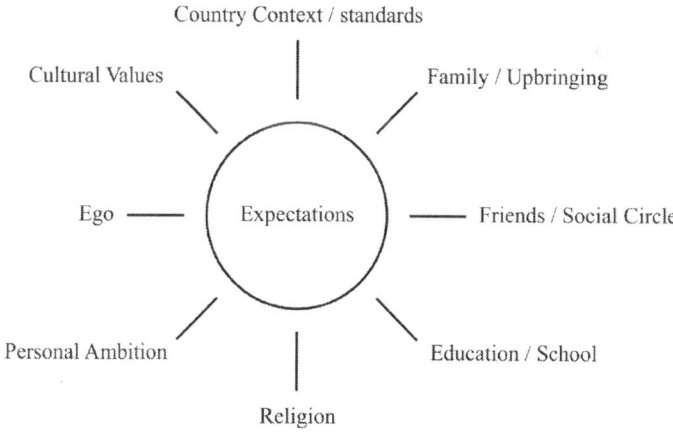

Figure 13: Build-up of Expectations

A corollary is that a sure and relatively cost free route to happiness is to work on the demand side of the equation and seek to be explicit about our expectations and to challenge them and see if they really need to be set at their current levels.

Outcome
A common fallacy is the implicit assumption that the outcome of any endeavour is deterministic and under our control. The reality is that outcome is a complex function with many input parameters only some of which are under our control.

Case study – Joe's Pizza Parlour

Joe's been working for the last twenty years, but had always dreamt of having his own business. Joe does a lot of research and finds a location along a main road that's ideal for a pizza parlour and takes out a large mortgage on his house to set up a pizza franchise, leaving his steady job to run the new business.

The new business does great initially and Joe's pleased that he's made the right decision. However two other large national pizza chains had also spotted that this area had a shortage of pizza parlours, and both had been working in parallel to set up their own restaurants. Therefore within eight weeks there were two other pizza parlours, and it so happened that each was a quarter of a mile on either side of Joe's pizza parlour.

The net result was that passing traffic from each direction was more likely to pull into one of the two rival chains and Joe's pizza parlour was starved of clientele. Three months later Joe's pizza parlour was running at a monthly loss, and six months downstream Joe had to close the business, making a hefty loss.

Case Study – Alternate Ending

On seeing Joe's Pizza Parlour open, the two rival fast food chains decided to shelve their plans for their outlets and focus on other locations.

Joe's Pizza Parlour went on to be a great success and after a few years there was a chain of Joe's Pizza Parlours across the state.

The Case study on Joe's Pizza shows how there is only a tenuous link between the action and the ultimate outcome, which could swing either way depending on actions and decisions taken in the wider environment outside of Joe's control.

Figure 14: Outcome dependencies

The diagram in Figure 14 shows how Outcome is dependent on many factors, with our personal input / effort being just one of them. We can of course try and de-risk the situation by taking out insurance, define strongly worded contracts, backup plans etc, which will all help up to a point, however it doesn't take away the fact that ultimately we're not in complete control and it would be a fallacy to pretend otherwise.

Expectation / Outcome model of Happiness

One way[239] to look at happiness is as the difference between Outcome and Expectations, i.e.

$$\text{Happiness} = \text{Outcome} - \text{Expectations}$$

If the Outcome exceeds what we were expecting, then we end up becoming happy, and unhappy if it drops below expectations.

As Outcome is not under our control, anyone following this game plan for happiness, is gambling with their happiness, and has effectively turned their happiness over to others to determine.

---

9   Later in the chapter I'll be looking at other ways of defining happiness

Another trap is that Expectations tend not to be fixed, and are a bit like climbing a hill, where once we've reached the summit of one hill – we find another yet taller hill in the horizon, with the process itself being never ending. Therefore even if we meet expectations, our happiness would only last a short period until we've adapted to what we have and are on the lookout for the next high.

For someone following this model of happiness, the only sure way of achieving continuous happiness is to keep expectations low, ideally zero, that way no matter what the outcome does, one would always be in positive happiness territory and we avoid the scenario of expectation inflation.

In his poem "If", Rudyard Kipling[10] advises:

> "If you can meet with Triumph and Disaster
> And treat those two imposters just the same.
>
> ...
>
> Yours is the Earth and everything that's in it,
> And – which is more – you'll be a Man, my son!"

Here Kipling is recognizing that Outcome is actually outside our control and we need to be careful not to be fooled into thinking we determined the outcome, the danger being success might go to our head or failure lead to depression.

The Bhagavad Gita, the book of Hindu scriptures advises "Karam karo fal ki chinta mat karo" which translates to undertake work / action without worrying about the fruits of your labour. In effect the Gita advise is to sever the link between the task and its outcome. Given that the outcome is not under our control, that's sound advise and a sure route to happiness as we've no longer linked the outcome to the task and see them both as separate loosely coupled but ultimately uncorrelated events[11].

30.6 Religion and Culture

Culture
Cultures vary greatly in their value systems, and norms for managing and organizing

---

10   Rudyard Kipling - If http://www.businessballs.com/ifpoemrudyardkipling.htm
11   As an example, at the time of writing I have no idea whether this book will sell a few hundred, a few thousand or tens of thousands, however I'll be perfectly content regardless of the actual sales.

interpersonal and family relationships. With love / belonging being one of the basic human needs identified by Maslow[12], this variation can have a large impact on the quality of life and happiness experienced by individuals.

For example, Suneel, a London based Indian friend of mine and his family share their house with his parents and grandparents, all four generations living together under the same roof. Contrast this with their neighbour whose parents live a hundred miles away and whose grandparent's are in an old people's home. With four generations living together at Suneel's house, there's a far richer social interaction taking place, and it would be regarded as sacrilege to suggest to Suneel his grandparents might be put in an old people's home.

Cultural values will also drive workplace norms and what's deemed as acceptable and reasonable behaviour and terms. It will also drive people's expectations of their civic and governmental institutions, and consequently their behaviour. Thus culture acts as an overarching layer that helps define a lot of other behaviours and norms that in turn impact on happiness.

Religion

By providing a structural and contextual framework for living, religion helps deal with life's ambiguities, replacing them with certainties and as a consequence religion has a range of benefits and disbenefits.

As mentioned earlier[13], religion provides a ready-made community and appeals to our need for relationship; helps manage stress; deal with uncertainties such as life after death and provides an illusion of control over what's ultimately uncontrollable.

However it also has disbenefits: consumes resource; creates divisions; fosters a sense of arrogance; may hold back social development; formalises prejudices; numerous cultural and religious practices[14] which adversely impact on people's lives and levels of happiness.

Some specific examples may help further illustrate:

> Christianity offers the opportunity to confess one's sins and receive absolution, effectively helping leave the past behind and move forward.

---

12 Section 30.4
13 See Section 28.1 for a full discussion of the benefits and disbenefits.
14 Discussed in Section 29

Hinduism, with its belief in reincarnation, provides people with the rationalisation that their condition in this life is related to their behaviour in their previous life; effectively redirecting and channelling their frustration away from blaming others and back onto themselves and encouraging good behaviour to avoid a repetition in their next life.

The benefits and disbenefits created by religion have the potential to act upon us and impact our levels of happiness. Due to the broad reach of cultural and religious practices its effect will also touch people who themselves might be unbelievers.

30.7 Comparison with others

There are mixed views on the wisdom of comparing oneself with others. Some see it a recipe for unhappiness, and that we should strive to be content in ourselves as unique individuals. Others see it as something inevitable. It's worth exploring some of the issues involved.

Benchmarking

Organizations of all sorts benchmark themselves against others in their sector and use this as a gauge to determine effectiveness and potential for improvement. In the UK the government too has done this with school league tables, and comparison of hospital performance has led to clinical issues being uncovered. Investment management too uses benchmarking by classifying companies into sectors and comparison of their performance with sector norms.

Clearly benchmarking is an established and useful management tool. It seems odd therefore to try and deny its use for our own personal self-management.

Social Feedback Loop

By comparing ourselves with our peers / contemporaries we're able to establish a measure of how well we're doing and use the difference to act as a spur to incentivise us to put in extra effort. As mentioned earlier[15] nature itself employs a feedback loop to drive the evolution process. So in a sense, feedback loops and comparisons are a natural way of self-management, and from that perspective comparison with others can be seen as a vital part of a social feedback loop.

---

15   Section 23.2: Continuous Innovation emulates Natural Evolution

It would be equally valid to compare ourselves against a pre-determined life plan or goals as well, and in reality we'd probably do both.

Illogicality of making comparisons on specific outcomes

As discussed earlier[16], we don't have complete control over outcome. Therefore strictly speaking, it's not logical to make comparisons on any particular or narrow outcome as we're comparing something that's not really under our control or directly attributable to only us.

However over a time period it might be expected that external factors may balance each other out i.e. we won't have a series of bad luck or good luck. Hence in making comparisons it would be wiser to take a more holistic approach and consider accumulated performance over a period of time and across a number of factors, rather than performance in any specific area or project.

Choice of whom to compare against and avoiding self-fulfilling prophecies

If we choose individuals against whom to compare ourselves, then we immediately run into the difficulty of whom to choose to compare against. Left entirely to us, there's the danger that we'll simply choose people to validate and confirm our predetermined convictions about our performance, making it a self-fulfilling prophecy i.e. if we think we're doing better than others we might choose people whom we know are worse off and vice-versa.

To avoid the danger of it becoming a self-fulfilling prophecy and validating our pre-held belief, it would be wiser to compare against the average of a broad group rather than any particular individual.

Clustering around the mean

One of the problems with comparison with others is the risk we end up grouping around the average. People who perceive themselves as performing less well than the average would be motivated to try and boost their performance and therefore approach the mean. However people achieving more than the mean run the risk of being tempted to rest on their laurels with the consequence of remaining close to the mean and reducing the spread above the mean.

To escape the gravitational pull of the average, it's important for high achievers to avoid comparison with the mean and instead look to compare themselves against their own potential for achievement.

Comparison summation

As discussed above, provided we do the comparison taking a number of factors into account and looking over a period of time, and comparing ourselves against the average of a group or our potential rather than self selecting individuals, then comparison can act as useful feedback helping incentivise us to maximise our potential.

30.8   Government

Impact on hierarchy of needs grouping

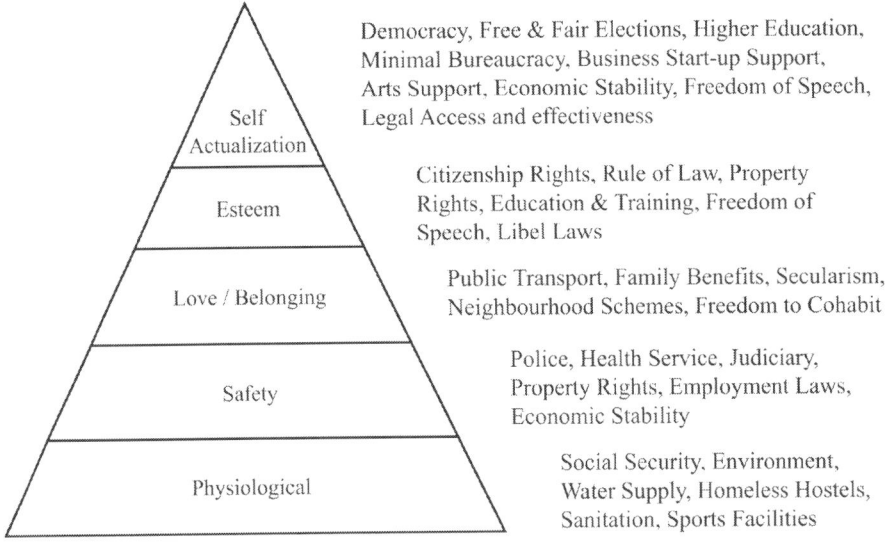

Figure 15: Influence of Government on the Needs Hierarchy

By providing the contextual framework within which we live our lives, Government has a huge influence on our potential happiness. The Hierarch of Needs diagram discussed earlier captures the main groups of needs in our lives, and as shown in Figure 15, Government has a key role to play and has a large influence[17] on each of the need groups.

17   For brevity, I have not included the rationale for the linkage between influence factors and the need groups in Figure 15, however for the main, they should be straightforward to deduce and relate.

Therefore Governments and their behaviour are a major determinant of our levels of happiness, with the most important attributes for self-actualisation, and therefore happiness, being democracy and free and fair elections and their absence would question the legitimacy of the government[18].

When asked whether government's prime objective should be "greatest happiness" or "greatest wealth" an overwhelming 81% wanted happiness as the goal with only 13% wanting greater wealth[19].

Minimum enforceable global standards of Governance
As Government has such a major impact on the levels of happiness achievable by its citizens, as a world community it's something of a disgrace that we have allowed poor governance to flourish under the cover of "sovereignty".

We need to lay down minimum global standards of governmental behaviour and put in enforceable systems that can override sovereignty and ensure adherence to these minimum standards, as well as look to export best practise through expanding the scope of country unions, both of these discussed in earlier sections[20].

Gross National Happiness
In 1972 Bhutan's fourth King, Jigme Singye Wangchuck, coined the term Gross National Happiness (GNH) to describe the more holistic approach towards development being followed by Bhutan. The central idea is that happiness is not achieved by exclusively focusing on economic development and promoting GDP, instead one has to consider the broader aspects and impact of any new proposed development on the wider environment and society.

The four pillars of GNH are:

Promotion of Sustainable Development
Preservation and promotion of Cultural values
Conservation of the Natural environment
Establishment of Good Governance

18   As also discussed earlier in Section 2.9
19   Britain's happiness in decline
     http://news.bbc.co.uk/1/hi/programmes/happiness_formula/4771908.stm
20   Chapter 2 (Section 2.5), and Chapter 4

The assessment of proposed policies in Bhutan includes looking at their impact on GNH[21] which has been made a formal part of the decision making process.

There is a risk that by saying one's focus is "happiness" rather than economic development, it may become a crutch to explain away and provide cover for poor economic performance, quietly overlooking that a strong economy can allow the country to buy a lot of services such as health, leisure, education etc that in turn can boost happiness.

Despite its long focus on happiness, Bhutan has been placed at number 132 out of the 182 countries ranked[22] in the Human Development Report 2009, and I fail to see what there is to be happy about a 17 year shorter life expectancy compared to other people[23] in the same part of the world.

The Centre for Bhutan Studies has drawn up a range of indices to determine GNH values, set benchmarks and track performance[24].

Should others adopt the Gross National Happiness approach?

With happiness seemingly a higher order objective than wealth, it's surprising that in the four decades since GNH was launched, more countries have not taken it up.

Looking more closely, although laudable, the four pillars of GNH are truisms that ought to be followed by any rational government. Furthermore the assessment of proposed new policies for their impact on GNH is somewhat similar to the Environmental Impact Statement required under US law, or equally to the Planning System in the UK which in its enquiries sets out to balance and decide on the best course of action taking into account views of all stakeholders.

Although the indices drawn up to measure GNH appear helpful, ultimately the truest index is that delivered by voters in a general election in a vibrant democracy with universal suffrage[25] and free and fair elections; in the private of an election booth people will take a call on how happy they are with the incumbent party and vote accordingly.

---

21   Gross National Happiness   http://en.wikipedia.org/wiki/Gross_national_happiness
22   Bhutan, Human Development Index
      http://hdrstats.undp.org/en/countries/country_fact_sheets/cty_fs_BTN.html
23   Bhutan has a 65.7 year life expectancy compared to Japan's 82.7 years or Republic of Korea's 79.2 years.
24   Centre for Bhutan Studies   http://www.grossnationalhappiness.com/gnhIndex/intruductionGNH.aspx
25   Incidentally, Bhutan has not got universal suffrage, as "religious" people are presumed to be above political considerations and denied suffrage.

Therefore in a functioning democracy, the general election result is the ultimate implementation of a GNH index with the electorate booting out people they are unhappy with and parties vying to present policies to make the maximum number of people happy.

One may be tempted to write off GNH as a catchy label for things being done implicitly in a democracy, however due to the prominence of anything to do with the economy, it's helpful to have the GNH label to emphasize that economic development is not an end in itself and overall happiness is a far more important goal, provided it's not used to excuse poor economic performance.

Annual Happiness Performance Statistics

It's fairly straightforward to measure and track economic progress as we have money as the unit of measure. However lacking a happiness currency, the measurement and tracking of happiness is far harder and risks being overlooked. A happiness reality check once every few years at a general election is too coarse and infrequent for efficiency.

If something is not being directly measured and reported upon, there's a tendency for it to recede into the background and get overlooked. It's worth remembering the words (box, figure 16) of guidance from William Thomson (Lord Kelvin).

> "I often say that when you can measure what you are speaking about, and express it in numbers, you know something about it; but when you cannot measure it, when you cannot express it in numbers, your knowledge is of a meagre and unsatisfactory kind; it may be the beginning of knowledge, but you have scarcely in your thoughts advanced to the state of Science, whatever the matter may be."
>
> *from 'Electrical Units of Measurement' lecture delivered at the Institution of Civil Engineers, London (3 May 1883)*

Figure 16: William Thomson (Lord Kelvin)

Currently when the government does something to change people's lives but which doesn't have a direct impact on the economy, the change tends to be relatively transparent compared to changes that affect the economy. Anything that affects the economy gets incorporated and its impact seen in the overall quarterly economic figures, however there's no similar numeric or focal point for non-economic factors and hard to get an overall view. Therefore non-economic change (improvement or deterioration) only comes to the general public's attention if it makes the national papers, and thus the media acts as a kind of report card on government performance, helping explain most government's obsession with the media.

Media reporting is fine and should continue, but it would be good to have something in parallel that's more carefully measured, auditable and provides an overall picture. It would be good feedback for governments to receive annual happiness figures in the same way as annual economic performance figures. The annual happiness figures would help increase the visibility of the outcome of non-financial initiatives[26] and the increased attention and focus allowing timely corrective action to be taken when required.

People could be mandated to fill in an annual Happiness Return along with their annual tax returns providing feedback on their happiness looking at key aspects of governance as well as performance on the factors driving happiness. The scores of the annual Happiness Returns would provide trackable performance data on key aspects of governance allowing trends to be exposed and better overall management.

The Happiness Return is ultimately a survey, but due to our familiarity with monetary units of measure and their ease of use, I'd propose using the "Satisfaction Pounds" concept suggested earlier[27] in the discussion on measuring public sector performance.

The maximum satisfaction pounds allocatable for each of the different aspects of governance would be proportional to their relative priority and importance, thereby increasing the relevance of the overall Satisfaction Pounds score.

30.9   Living Standards

No long-term impact on happines

"Wow! I just turn this handle and water comes out..." or "Look at this! I press this switch and the whole room is bathed in daylight, isn't that cool...?" Were someone to say either of these statements, you would be justified to be puzzled and surprised to have something that basic being pointed out. Yet at moments in the past these

---

26   i.e. initiatives that don't have any direct impact on the economy e.g. dealing with hooliganism
27   Section 24.7

changes to our personal lives were regarded as huge advances and the talking points of their day.

Advances in living standards clearly must make us happy at the time as they make life more pleasant. However as time passes, we increasingly become accustomed to the changes and as we adapt to them they lose their novelty and gradually shift from the foreground into becoming part of the background until eventually they become part of the environment without raising a second thought or glance.

Accompanying that shift, the initial increase in happiness decays over time and in some sense behaves as a radioactive source reducing its radioactivity by half in every half-life time period. As it reduces by half in every half-life the radioactivity never disappears but decays to a very low level, in a similar fashion the happiness caused by any particular improvement in our standard of living decays over time.

Therefore we arrive at the somewhat counter intuitive conclusion that one would not expect increases in living standards to have any long-term lasting impact on our levels of happiness.

Alternative derivation of no long-term impact on happiness

The same conclusion may be arrived at following a different line of reasoning. As a basic emotion, our ancestor's way back in time too would have experienced feelings of happiness. However our current standards of living are many orders of magnitude higher than those few thousand years ago. Therefore if standard of living were to have any lasting long-term impact on happiness levels, then by now we would have overdosed many times over on happiness.

Importance to overall progress

The hypothesis that our happiness from any specific improvement subsides over time, with our levels of happiness returning to some average level has had an important side effect. Had the happiness impact lasted into the long term, we might have been tempted to rest on our laurels and enjoy the good life. However as the impact and happiness levels subside, our desire to retain the momentum and keep our happiness at high levels motivates us to continually seek new developments and further improvements in living standards.

The same happiness half-life decay behaviour, which stops us from deriving long-term satisfaction, also keeps us motivated to seek continual improvements, and is one of the reasons for our success and huge progress as a race.

A paradox – Better off but not as happy

The lack of a long term relationship between happiness and living standards leads to an interesting paradox, one can be a lot better off but yet not as happy as someone living in an earlier time period who had a far lower standard of living.

Lets say N is the norm for living standards now, and some time in the past when standards of living were lower the norm was P (figure 17). If things don't work out for someone in the current time frame and they achieve a standard of living of N*, lower than the average N, then being aware that they haven't met the average expectations, they may feel some disappointment leading to unhappiness.

Now lets take a person in the past, who's been very successful and achieved a standard of living of P*, considerably higher than P, the norm for the time. Sensing that they've done rather well for themselves and surpassed expectations, they're likely to feel pleased with themselves and happy.

We therefore arrive at the somewhat paradoxical situation that a person with a higher standard of living (N*) is less happy than a person in the past with a lower standard of living (P*).

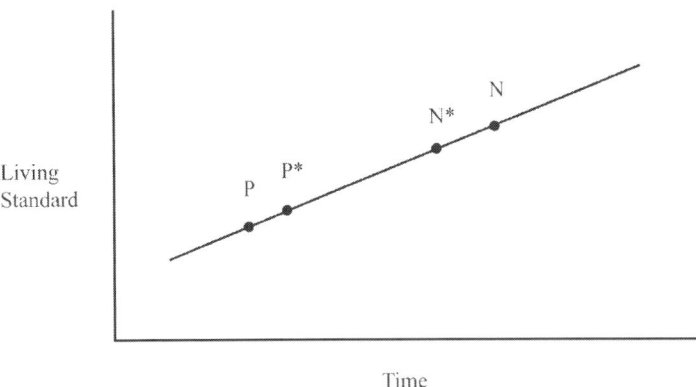

Figure 17: Over achiever at P* is happier than under achiever at N*

Over time as our living standards rise, our expectations rise in tandem and the bar to being happy gets continually raised.

Adapting to a decline in living standards

As noted earlier in the discussion on countries[28], political mismanagement can lead to the country suffering a sharp decline in living standards. In that situation the same processes and feedback loops discussed earlier come into play.

Whilst there would be an initial drop in happiness as people come to terms with declining overall standards, they would recover and become used to the new status quo, at which point there would be a drop in expectations and a corresponding lowering of the bar to being happy.

With the lowered bar, and the decline in standards fading from people's memories as they become accustomed to living under the new regime, happiness levels would recover to their norm and long term average.

Being able to adapt in this way allows us to stay happy and avoid melancholy and its associated ill health issues, and our adaptability in this way and ability to keep cheerful along with its health benefits is a key part of our survival instincts as a race.

Corollary – happiness trends only of value in the short term

As happiness tends to gravitate towards its long term mean, there is not much value in making comparisons of happiness over the long term, as over the long term one would expect little difference in happiness levels.

Therefore when seeking feedback on policy, it's the changes in happiness occurring in the short term, taking place before expectations have had time to change, that are of relevance.

30.10 Happiness – Continuum or State?

In our quest for happiness, something that's often overlooked is appreciating the nature of happiness and whether it's a continuum or a state. The distinction is not academic and should have bearing on our actions.

Continuum Behaviour

In a continuum model, happiness would behave like a bank account and as we

---

28   Section 2.5 and 2.6

undertook more of the activities likely to make us happy it would continually increase the credit in our happiness "bank account", that presumably we could "draw down" on to buy our way out of any future unhappiness.

State Behaviour

In the state model of happiness we define a few discrete states e.g. not happy, slightly happy, moderately happy, happy, very happy and our happiness measure would fall into one of these categories.

Once we're in the very happy state, as there is no further state to move on to, we'll remain in the same state even if we continue to carry out the actions that had moved us into this state.

This may be visualised as a glass of water where each time we perform actions leading to happiness it's analogous to putting a bit of water into the glass raising its level. The happiness level rises however once the glass is full then even if we continue pouring in more water, the level remains constant.

Likely nature of happiness

Being a sensation or emotion, happiness is biologically based, with magnetic resonance scans of the brain having shown changes within our brain patterns and blood flows when we are happy[29].

If happiness were a continuum then the changes in pattern and flows in our brain would have to keep on increasing in intensity as we became happier and there would need to be some form of fairly sophisticated calculations going on evaluating and keeping track of our amount of happiness and then switching on the appropriate number of "happy" cells. That form of sophistication although trivial for a computer system, seems overly complex for a biologically based system.

Anything based on physical patterns and flows would be expected to have a natural limit or saturation point, after which the patterns and flows occupy a steady state due to biological limitations and the physics involved.

Another clue to the nature of happiness comes from the fact that one moment we can be very happy, but on receiving some bad news e.g. the death of a close relative, we can be catapulted into a state of unhappiness.

---

29   Happiness and Brain Activity
     http://news.bbc.co.uk/player/nol/newsid_4810000/newsid_4812500/4812550.stm?bw=bb&mp=
     wm&news=1&bbcws=1

Therefore happiness is more likely to be a state rather than a continuum.

Consequences of happiness being a state

A common feature of most human systems is a tendency to overshoot the target. The reason being our assumption the future will behave in the same way as the past; an example being the volatility of stock markets which regularly over and under shoot.

As we go through life and take actions leading to an increase in happiness, there's the risk that we implicitly view happiness as a continuum and even after we've entered a state of happiness we continue performing the same actions thinking that as in the past, they will lead to further increases in happiness.

However using the thesis that happiness is a state, once we've reached the top happiness state then further actions won't really result in any increased happiness and are similar to pouring water into an already full glass.

The concern is the superfluous activities consume valuable resources of time and effort and can distract us, reducing our overall enjoyment of life, a point appreciated by some[30] who've taken corrective action to reprioritise their lives.

30.11 Subjectivity

Most will be familiar with the cliché "Is the glass half full or half empty" which encapsulates the idea that the same external fact may be interpreted entirely differently by two individuals, one seeing it as a cause for melancholy and the other for rejoicing.

Being an emotion or sensation, happiness is subjective and depends upon our interpretation of the external facts. This may be visualised as an interpretive and processing layer between the external world and us as shown in figure 18.

---

30   But will it make you happy?
      http://www.nytimes.com/2010/08/08/business/08consume.html?_r=2&pagewanted
      =1&ref=general&src=me

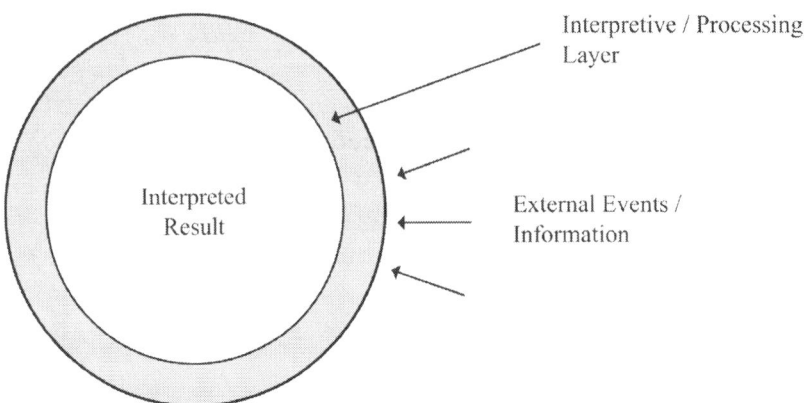

Figure 18: Interpretive / processing layer leading to subjectivity

The interpretive layer handles incoming information and processes it using a mixture of conscious and sub-conscious input, delivering an interpreted result in a split second. The interpretive layer is a function of our upbringing, culture, religion, education, values, personality and experience.

Altering the interpretive layer to boost happiness

A cost effective way of increasing happiness is to alter people's interpretive / processing layer in such a way as to lead to increased happiness. Psychologists feel that there may be a 10 to 15 % uplift, relief from depression and increased well being[31,32]. Ideally this could be delivered as a training and educational program sponsored by government.

At first this may seem a bit like smoke and mirrors or sleight of hand, as nothing appears to have changed in the real world and is this ducking real responsibility or manipulating the results. Another objection might be is this some form of brain washing and infringing civil liberties.

Is the change real?

The question of whether the education / training leads to real changes is best answered via an analogy. If we have a computer system and decide to have new

31   The Science of Happiness http://news.bbc.co.uk/1/hi/programmes/happiness_formula/4783836.stm
32   Staying happier for longer http://news.bbc.co.uk/1/hi/programmes/happiness_formula/4903464.stm

software written to upgrade a particular functionality, after the software has been installed no one would have qualms that we've made real changes and altered the physical world.

The education and training courses that people would go through to alter their interpretive / processing layer is in effect installing new "biological software" into their brains and just as the computer software lead to new functionality, so too the new biological software would lead to changed patterns of thought and evaluation of events.

Is it brain washing or an infringement of civil liberties?

I see the education and training not as "telling" people what to think, but as helping them gain an appreciation of how to interpret events taking a more balanced and holistic view of life. In a way it's building up a tool box of life skills allowing them to deal with the ups and downs of life in a more informed and relaxed way rather than being taken by surprise and feeling they're on a roller coaster with no idea of what's around the next bend.

As it's purely educational and imparting new skills and processes, with people free to make up their own minds, any fears of brain washing or infringement of civil liberties would be unfounded.

Implementing an educational training programme

Because of the scale of the programme it's best sponsored by government and delivered by established further education providers. The programme would have almost universal relevance; therefore delivery via distance learning would be a key priority using providers such as the Open University in the UK and their counterparts in other countries.

Given its potential for enhancing lives and its cost effectiveness, a programme such as this needs to be a key priority in the portfolio of any government seriously interested in improving its peoples well being.

30.12 Money

The greatest wealth is to live content with little.

~ Plato

Frederick Herzberg's motivation and hygiene factors

Frederick Herzberg, the clinical psychologist and pioneer of job enrichment classified Money as a Hygiene Factor[33], his term for something that was not motivational in itself but whose lack would lead to dissatisfaction. Put another way, if you had a shortage of money you would be dissatisfied, but on receiving a pay rise its impact would only last a short term.

Herzberg was concerned with motivation, however there appears a close relationship between happiness and motivation, and using happiness as a proxy for motivation, transforms Herzberg's theory into the corollary that money should not by itself lead to happiness, however its lack would lead to unhappiness. Therefore we need a certain amount of money to satisfy our low level basic needs for security, healthcare, food and shelter and if our income is unable to meet these basic needs then we'll be unhappy. However as our income rises above a threshold level required to satisfy these low level needs, then further increases in income lose their effectiveness and follow a law of diminishing returns.

Wealth is not a vaccine against life

Looking over the years, I've been surprised by the number of people who've committed suicide despite being in line to inherit large fortunes and a position in high society.

We all have a lot to live for, but for these people – born with a silver spoon, this was especially true. Yet their wealth and position failed to inoculate them against life's dramas and ultimately lead to them becoming that unhappy and desolate that they tragically chose to end their lives.

Not wishing to make points out of anyone's grief, but it serves as a stark reminder that wealth and money are not ends in themselves and other factors such as relationships are more important and in the final analysis trump wealth.

Average National Income

Over the last four decades there has been considerable debate amongst economists over the nature of the relationship between average income and happiness. A theory known as the Easterlin Paradox[34] suggested there was no link between the level of

---

33   Frederick Herzberg motivational theory   http://www.businessballs.com/herzberg.htm
34   Does Economic Growth improve the human lot? Some Emperical Evidence.
     http://graphics8.nytimes.com/images/2008/04/16/business/Easterlin1974.pdf

a country's economic development and its average happiness level, the reason given that as incomes grew so too did expectations, offsetting any positive effects of the higher income on well being.

With the availability of additional data, other economists[35] [36] have reassessed the Easterlin Paradox and found a positive correlation between economic development and happiness, raising an ongoing debate as to the exact behaviour.

The initial reports used Real GNP with no mention made of any Purchasing Power Parity adjustments, however money is somewhat abstract and people experience it through the lens of the basket of goods it purchases them. Hence a low income in a less developed country with a lower cost of living may feel similar to a higher income in a more developed country. The later reports adjusted figures for purchase power parity, which may have made a slight difference and help tease out a correlation.

It's now generally accepted that as countries develop their happiness rises with income until average income reaches around £10,000 when it hits a law of diminishing returns and tends to level out reaching a plateau[37,38]. With access to higher income, governments have more flexibility to undertake actions and programmes helping to raise happiness levels.

The levelling out of happiness after £10,000 fits in well with earlier discussions on Hierarchy of Needs[39] and money acting as a Hygiene factor and is consistent with the behaviour predicted in the section on Living Standards[40]. It is borne out by the US and UK experience, where happiness doesn't appear to have reacted to rising average income levels over the long term.

Over the past thirty years the median income in the US has risen however this has not been accompanied by any increased happiness[41]. In the UK research[42] done for

35   Economic Growth and Subjective Well-Being: Reassessing the Easterlin Paradox
      http://bpp.wharton.upenn.edu/betseys/papers/Happiness.pdf
36   Wealth and Happiness Revisited http://www2.eur.nl/fsw/research/veenhoven/Pub2000s/2003e-full.pdf
37   The Science of Happiness   http://news.bbc.co.uk/1/hi/programmes/happiness_formula/4783836.stm
38   The Good Life fails to make Britain Happy
      http://www.timesonline.co.uk/tol/news/uk/article786284.ece?token=null&offset=0&page=1
39   Section 30.4, once basic needs are met then people focus on self-actualisation
40   Section 30.9 Living Standards
41   Does Economic Growth improve the human lot? Some Emperical Evidence.
      http://graphics8.nytimes.com/images/2008/04/16/business/Easterlin1974.pdf
42   Britain's happiness in decline http://news.bbc.co.uk/1/hi/programmes/happiness_formula/4771908.stm

the BBC found that despite being three times richer, Britain was less happy in 2005 than in the 1950's. Post World War II Japan had a seven-fold rise in income, which still failed to translate into an increase in happiness[268].

The World Values Survey project asked people to rate how happy they were and mapped this against GNP per capita[269]. This showed there were many countries with low incomes, which had the same happiness levels as countries with many times their income level e.g. Venezuela with a third of the income of the US had a similar happiness level as the US.

A graph of Life Satisfaction versus Real GDP per capita adjusted for purchasing power shows a correlation[270], however the graph also shows that there are a large number of countries with hugely different income levels sharing the same Life Satisfaction level. For example[271], Turkey with its GDP of $8000 has the same life satisfaction level as Zambia that has a GDP of $1000.

The fact that countries can have such widely varying income levels and yet experience similar levels of happiness, suggests that the non-monetary factors of family, relationships, religion, government and cultural outlook have an equal if not greater impact on happiness.

30.13 Happiness is a Decision – Not an Outcome

Most people are about as happy as they make up their minds to be.
~ *Abraham Lincoln*

Case study – Josh's Roller Coaster Fortnight

Tight lipped and with a deep frown hanging over his forehead, Josh slowly walked out of the office with his boss's words still ringing in his ears - he was to be made redundant with immediate effect...

---

43   Maybe Money does buy Happiness after all.
      http://www.nytimes.com/2008/04/16/business/16leonhardt.html?_r=2
44   A Plateau of Happiness
      http://www.nytimes.com/imagepages/2005/10/03/science/20051004_HAPP_GRAPHIC.html
45   Measuring Satisfaction, New York Times
      http://www.nytimes.com/imagepages/2008/04/16/business/20080416_LEONHARDT_GRAPHIC.html
46   This is just one example, each life satisfaction level has many countries across a wide income range.

On his way home, Josh went over the situation realising that with his wife expecting their third child, the last thing he wanted was to default on the payments on their new home. Despite the bright July sunshine, he walked indoors with a heavy gloom overhanging. On hearing the news his wife Jenny tried to be optimistic but both knew with the current recession, he'd be very lucky to get another job soon and people in their previous neighbourhood had been unemployed for over a year. Soon the pretence at optimism disappeared, replaced by a dread of the forthcoming economic hardship.

That evening Josh felt a sudden stab of pain in his side, and as it was still sore the following morning, decided to see his doctor. On examination, Dr Jones suggested it probably was stress related but he should go to the local hospital that afternoon and have some tests done.

Couple of day's later, Josh's perusal of the job ads was interrupted by a call from the Doctor's surgery asking to see Josh and Jenny. On the way in they wondered if it was related to the new baby as the Doctor had asked for Jenny to be there. On arrival at the surgery, a sombre faced Dr Jones got them seated and explained the tests had shown Josh was in an advanced stage of cancer with at best six months to live.

Stunned and in disbelief, the couple went home and the rest of the week went by in a daze. The kids were left with their grandparents whilst Josh and Jenny tried to come to terms with the news and putting a brave face on it whilst going to pieces inside.

Early the following week, the couple were surprised to receive a home visit from Dr Jones. The doctor appeared agitated and brushing aside pleasantries, requested they move to the living room as he had some important news. Once they were seated, the doctor explained the laboratory had made a one in a million mistake and mixed up Josh's specimen with that of another patient, and that Josh's own tests showed him to be perfectly healthy with nothing wrong with him.

Josh and Jenny were both ecstatic on hearing the news and their joy knew no bounds. Calling their parents to tell them the good news they decided to go out that evening to a local restaurant and celebrate. After meal that evening while they savoured their coffee, the earlier difficulties over Josh's job now seemed trivial and had fallen away, and both were positive about the future and in a jubilant mood as they headed for the dance floor.

The Case Study on Josh's fortnight illustrates how a situation causing a considerable amount of unhappiness and despondency, when viewed from a different perspective can appear trivial and unimportant.

Therefore if we can find a way of altering our perspective and viewpoint, we should be able to reduce unhappiness and rise above incidents that might otherwise pull us down.

Changing our Attention

Altering our perspective and viewpoint will benefit from an attempt to understand which thoughts get focus and priority within our attention span and which get relegated to the long grass of our mind.

Our brains appear hardwired to give a higher priority to changes taking place in the current timeframe. There's sound evolutionary logic for that, if we were in a jungle the slight stirring of grass in a far corner could signal the presence of a predator or of prey and demands our immediate attention for survival.

We have to cope with a lot of information, and clearly it would be inefficient and poor design to store it all. What appears to happen is that if a set of memories is not accessed that frequently then it'll get increasingly compressed, losing detail on each compression cycle. If however it gets accessed, then that marks it as important and it gets spared some of the scavenging.

Memory datasets[47] that are relatively static are not going to attract our attention due to the lack of change and hence are much more likely to gradually whither away from our memory and attention span.

The result of our selective attention span is that when it come to being happy, if we're not careful we're likely to give undue attention to what's happening in the here and now and overlook the more static memory datasets that might have had bearing on our overall mood.

A Balanced View

At any point in time, most people will be able to list at least fifty reasons why they should be thankful for their current situation, each reason a cause for celebration and happiness. At the same time they would also have been able to list fifty reasons how things might have been better, each item a potential cause for melancholy.

Although challenging at the time, the here and now state is really just one of those

---

47   By a memory dataset I mean a set of memories about a particular topic or concept

hundred reasons and needs to be treated as such to avoid it usurping a greater priority than it deserves and skewing our decision on happiness.

So how are we to decide which of these two sets of reasons is the more compelling? Due to their diverse nature, it's difficult to compare the impacts of different reasons and in no way can it be an exact science and so we end up with a set of good reasons to be happy and equally good reasons to be unhappy, each set with roughly equal significance.

Effectively therefore we're free to follow whatever our emotional predilection happens to be and once we've made the decision, whichever way we choose, we'll have the reasons to bolster and reaffirm our choice.

Ultimately therefore, the slightly surprising result is that being happy boils down to making a personal choice and a decision to be happy.[48]

> *Each morning when I open my eyes I say to myself: I, not events, have the power to make me happy or unhappy today. I can choose which it shall be. Yesterday is dead, tomorrow hasn't arrived yet. I have just one day, today, and I'm going to be happy in it.*
> ~ *Groucho Marx*

---

48   Excluding people suffering from clinical depression, which as a medical condition is outside the scope of their personal choice

31. Work–Life Balance

While all aspects of our life are important, without a balance, you
become addicted and like all addictions you lose.

~ Catherine Pulsifer, Balance of Life

When people were asked to choose their two most important sources of happiness, half chose relationships and a quarter chose health, with less than 10% choosing work fulfilment. On asked to state in their own words what happiness meant to them, surprisingly the second largest group of responses were related to contentment and inner peace[1].

Relationships need time to develop and nurture, as does the self-actualisation discussed earlier[2], however many people find they're busy all week with work and then spend the weekend on chores and catching up along with some rest and recuperation to get ready for the next week. Therefore even though work fulfilment is only a small contributor to our happiness, it can easily crowd out other aspects.

31.1   Lump of time vs. Lump of Work approach

If we imagine a group of people get shipwrecked and end up on an uninhabited island. They could define their situation in two ways, either as either having a lump of time within which to do things, or as having a lump of work that needed doing.

Going with the lump of time approach they would decide on fixed working hours for each day, say eight, and over time as they became more efficient and productive their overall output would continuously grow and their island community become wealthier however they would only have a small amount of leisure time.

If however they went with the lump of work approach, once they had finished their

---

1   Britain's happiness in decline http://news.bbc.co.uk/1/hi/programmes/happiness_formula/4771908.stm
2   Section 30.4, Hierarchy of Needs

days work they would be free to follow their own pursuits. Over time as they became more efficient and productive, they would get the work done in ever shorter time periods and their leisure time would continually increase.

31.2   Breaking the Productivity Consumption Spiral

As a society we've followed a lump of time strategy, and any time saved from gains in productivity gets reinvested into producing other items, resulting in an increase in output, consumption and living standards.

The increase in living standards has had a profound impact on our quality of life, with advances in medical standards and improved living environments leading to an increase in life span. However as discussed earlier[3], it hasn't lead to an increase in happiness levels.

I feel the next major step change in our happiness levels will come via adjusting our work life balance and instead of reinvesting time saved from productivity gains back into yet more production and consumption, we need to put the time saved towards an increase in our leisure time.

This redirection of time savings is made more pressing by the impact our addiction to a high production / consumption lifestyle is having on the planets eco-systems with Global Warming[1] emerging as a real threat.

31.3   Benefits from Reducing the Working Week

It seems somewhat lopsided to spend the majority of our time on something that most of us don't see as their main sources of happiness. Reducing the working week would correct this imbalance and allow us to spend time on things more likely to make us happy.

For example, a shorter working week would allow us the time and space to develop and strengthen relationships and for maximising our potential through self-actualisation, both of which should lead to increased happiness.

3   Section 30.9 Living Standards

This increase in happiness combined with a less hectic lifestyle will help lower stress levels, which in turn should lead to improved physical and mental health[2].

The shorter working week is also likely to give a boost to employment levels, which fits well with the fact that people are healthier and living longer, and able and wanting to work till an older age.

Due to the amount of time spent working, we tend to define ourselves in terms of our job. This causes difficulties when people get made redundant or retire as they feel they're not just losing a job but also their sense of identity. Reducing the working week would allow us to rediscover ourselves through developing new interests and aspects of our personality, leading to a more diverse identity and greater resilience.

Finally, although it's a side effect and not the main objective[3], a shorter working week can be viewed as laying fallow part of our productive capacity (our labour) and act as a safety valve relieving some of the pressure on the environment from global warming.

31.4   Changing the Work Mindset

Case study – Stuart's Commute

It was a Tuesday morning, and Stuart dozed in the train to work, reliving the weekend's events. It had been a fun packed weekend and they'd spent all four days in the Lake District hiking.

Thinking he'd been completely out of touch with the news, Stuart pulled out the paper and his eye caught a headline saying that a Treasury Minister had floated the idea of increasing the working week from three days to five as a measure to boost economic output. The headline immediately dispelled any vestiges of drowsiness and wide-awake Stuart scanned the report in complete disbelief.

After going over some of the benefits, the article dwelt on the problems acknowledging that the concept was probably a non-starter as people just wouldn't accept giving up so much of their life and would see it as a form of modern day slavery.

Reassured, shaking his head at the naivety of some in government, Stuart mused that it was probably someone trying to grab headlines and get noticed rather than a serious attempt, after all no one would really be that daft...

As the case study on "Stuart's Commute" illustrates, people get used to their way of life and often simply can't contemplate any change. However there's nothing magical about having a two day weekend and it's not a law of nature.

Further resistance may come from the point noted earlier that people often get their sense of identity from their job and reducing time at work may be perceived as losing part of their identity.

However at the end of the day no one last thoughts are "I wish I had spent more time in the office" and we need to bear that in mind when thinking what an appropriate working week might be. As there are benefits to be had by reducing the working week and society has reached a level of productivity where we can afford to do so, we owe it to ourselves to seriously consider it.

A quick fix would be to increase employee rights to flexible working arrangements, however the longer term more strategic solution would be to reduce the working week progressively from five days to four days and further on possibly to three days.

31.5   Legally Binding Flexible Working Rights

When it comes to flexible working arrangements, the final call is generally left with the employer to decide on what suits them with the onus to consider requests "seriously". In the absence of legally binding employee rights, it's easy for an employer to procrastinate and eventually turn down requests.

It would be a sign of social maturity to allow employees legally binding rights to flexible working hours and arrangements. They could for example choose to convert a full time job into a three or four day per week job, with pay being adjusted pro-rata. These rights would ideally be enshrined as part of our fundamental human rights.

Having these rights would allow people to trim their working week to ensure a better fit with their lifestyle and circumstances, leading to increased happiness and contentment.

Employers too would need some protection, with employees needing to give a suitable advance notice, allowing the employer sufficient time to make alternate arrangements to ensure that any gaps gets covered and the new work schedule can be met without adverse impact.

31.6 Moving to a Shorter Working Week

Human nature being what it is, any cut in income would be seen as a retrograde step. In addition, most people are used to an established pattern of income and expenditure, hence the idea of taking a pay cut to move to a shorter working week would go down like a lead balloon.

Therefore the move to a shorter working week needs to be done without any perceived impact on income. Assuming an average working week of 37.5 hours[4] if we reduce our working week by 45 minutes each year, then over ten years we'd have reduced our working week by one day, and be on a four-day week. Each year, firms would be expected to improve productivity on aggregate so that they can produce the same quantity of goods and services even though their labour input is reducing annually.

Reduction per Annum:	45	minutes / week
	0.75	hours/week
Standard Day:	7.5	hours/day

Year	Hours	Minutes	Days	Productivity Increase	Cumulative Productivity Increase
0	37.5	2250	5	0	0
1	36.75	2205	4.9	2.00%	2%
2	36	2160	4.8	2.04%	4%
3	35.25	2115	4.7	2.08%	6%
4	34.5	2070	4.6	2.13%	8%
5	33.75	2025	4.5	2.17%	10%
6	33	1980	4.4	2.22%	12%
7	32.25	1935	4.3	2.27%	14%
8	31.5	1890	4.2	2.33%	16%
9	30.75	1845	4.1	2.38%	18%
10	30	1800	4	2.44%	20%

Figure 19: Reducing working week from 5 days to 4 days

4   Section 26: Global Warming

The analysis in figure 19 shows that provided firms increase their productivity by 2.0% to 2.4% annually, they could absorb the annual reduction in working week whilst still producing the same quantity of goods and services.

In effect the rise in hourly labour costs is being compensated for by the corresponding rise in average productivity, and rather than reinvesting the time saving into fresh production, it's being released into leisure time.

The movement towards a shorter working week needs to be made on a multilateral basis with all the major industrial countries moving in lock step towards the shorter week. Were a single country to make the move unilaterally, then due to the rise in its relative labour costs it would face a steady migration of industry and lose out on new investment opportunities. However if all countries moved together towards the new standard then relative industrial status quo and employment levels would be maintained.

It may prove difficult to get all industrial countries to agree on reducing the working week, and although against tariffs as being inherently distorting, this may be an instance where with WTO approval there would need to be a tariff imposed on exports from countries staying out of the reduced working week scheme. The tariff would ensure countries adopting the scheme were not adversely affected.

Sectors of the economy that were unable to improve productivity could see the rise in labour costs as potentially inflationary and there may need to be some form of structural grants or special fiscal treatment of particular sectors to avoid the labour rate rise becoming inflationary in those sectors.

Once the ten years are up and we're at a four-day week, then making further reductions becomes harder and so for phase two I'd see a more gradual reduction of 30 minutes per year, so that in a further 15 years we'd have brought the working week down to 3 days per week.

Reduction per Annum:	30	minutes / week
	0.50	hours/week
Standard Day:	7.5	hours/day

Year	Hours/ Week	Minutes / Week	Days	Productivity Increase	Cumulative Productivity Increase
10	30	1800	4	0	0
11	29.5	1770	3.93	1.67%	2%
12	29.0	1740	3.87	1.69%	3%
13	28.5	1710	3.80	1.72%	5%
14	28.0	1680	3.73	1.75%	7%
15	27.5	1650	3.67	1.79%	8%
16	27.0	1620	3.60	1.82%	10%
17	26.5	1590	3.53	1.85%	12%
18	26.0	1560	3.47	1.89%	13%
19	25.5	1530	3.40	1.92%	15%
20	25.0	1500	3.33	1.96%	17%
21	24.5	1470	3.27	2.00%	18%
22	24.0	1440	3.20	2.04%	20%
23	23.5	1410	3.13	2.08%	22%
24	23.0	1380	3.07	2.13%	23%
25	22.5	1350	3.00	2.17%	25%

Figure 20: Reducing the working week from 4 days to 3 days

The analysis in figure 20 shows that we'd need productivity increases of between 1.7% and 2.1% per annum over each of the fifteen years to achieve the drop in working week to three days in a non inflationary manner whilst keeping weekly salary levels constant.

It would be up to employers and employees to work out the ideal working arrangements taking into account the sector requirements as well as their preferences and working to an annualised hours contract. Thus some people may extend the weekend to four days and work throughout the year whilst others would prefer to work five-day weeks and then take five months of the year off to attend to their own interests.

There would need to be exceptions made for particular situations such as people undergoing training e.g. junior hospital doctors, who would be allowed to work longer hours to ensure training didn't get too elongated. Other professions such as long distance lorry drivers would also get exemptions as there would be no point having their weekend start if they're four days drive away from home and so they would take longer time off between assignments.

Moving to a 3-day week requires a 40% increase in productivity. Whist hard to achieve overnight, improving at 2% annually should be feasible when one factors in technical and process innovations and low current productivity levels. A recent report on public sector productivity found local authority junior staff productive only 32% of the time during working hours compared to an average of 44% in the private sector[5].

There's also an element of Parkinson's Law of work expanding to fill the time available and the new working arrangement would require management to become more capable and imaginative and manage people by output rather than time present on the job.

A triumvirate of the UN, WTO and the IPCC[6] would ideally drive the programme, which would deliver a three-day working week within 25 years. The rational for the triumvirate being the UN are needed due to it being a multilateral programme, the WTO because of the impact on trade and the possible need for special tariffs for non-participants and the IPCC as a catalyst because of their interest in the potential easing of pressure on the global environment.

Once the triumvirate had put together the programme, a detailed proposal would need to be ratified by the countries involved. This would involve informing their publics in each country on the details of the programme, how it would work and its likely impact on their lives over the forthcoming decades, followed by a public referendum to ratify taking part in the programme.

5   Council workers 'unproductive' for most of the day, research finds
    http://www.peoplemanagement.co.uk/pm/articles/2010/08/council-workers-unproductive-for-most-of-
    the-day-research-finds.htm
6   United Nations, World Trade Organization and Intergovernmental Panel on Climate Change

Appendix A: Monies owed due to Excessive Greenhouse Gas[1] Emissions and use of other countries' atmosphere

Country	Population	CO_2 Per Capita	Total CO_2	Excess CO_2 Per Capita	Excess Cost Bn $	Excess Cost Per Capita $
USA	308,792,000	23.5	7,256,612,000	17.90	331.7	1074
Russia	141,927,297	13.7	1,944,403,969	8.10	69.0	486
Japan	127,430,000	10.5	1,338,015,000	4.90	37.5	294
Canada	34,020,000	22.6	768,852,000	17.00	34.7	1020
Germany	81,757,600	11.9	972,915,440	6.30	30.9	378
Australia	22,173,000	26.9	596,453,700	21.30	28.3	1276
United Kingdom	62,041,708	10.6	657,642,105	5.00	18.6	300
South Korea	49,773,145	11.4	567,413,853	5.80	17.3	348
Saudi Arabia	25,721,000	16.2	416,680,200	10.60	16.4	638
Italy	60,275,846	9.7	584,675,706	4.10	14.8	246
France	65,447,374	9	589,026,366	3.40	13.4	205
Ukraine	45,982,936	10.3	473,624,241	4.70	13.0	283
Spain	45,989,016	10.1	464,489,062	4.50	12.4	270
Iran	74,196,000	8.2	608,407,200	2.60	11.6	156
South Africa	49,320,500	9	443,884,500	3.40	10.1	205
Poland	38,163,895	9.8	374,006,171	4.20	9.6	252
United Arab Emirates	4,599,000	38.8	178,441,200	33.20	9.2	2000
Taiwan	23,119,772	11.8	272,813,310	6.20	8.6	372
Netherlands	16,593,900	13.8	228,995,820	8.20	8.2	494
Venezuela	28,683,000	10	286,830,000	4.40	7.6	265
Kazakhstan	15,776,492	12.7	200,361,448	7.10	6.7	425
Argentina	40,134,425	8.2	329,102,285	2.60	6.3	157
Kuwait	2,985,000	35	104,475,000	29.40	5.3	1776
Czech Republic	10,512,397	13.7	144,019,839	8.10	5.1	485
Belgium	10,827,519	13.2	142,923,251	7.60	4.9	453
Qatar	1,409,000	55.5	78,199,500	49.90	4.2	2981
Turkmenistan	5,110,000	18.9	96,579,000	13.30	4.1	802
Greece	11,306,183	11.5	130,021,105	5.90	4.0	354
New Zealand	4,358,700	18.8	81,943,560	13.20	3.5	803
Mexico	107,550,697	6.1	656,059,252	0.50	3.2	30
Ireland	4,459,300	16.7	74,470,310	11.10	3.0	673
Austria	8,372,930	11.5	96,288,695	5.90	3.0	358
Israel	7,509,000	11.5	86,353,500	5.90	2.7	360
Finland	5,356,700	13	69,637,100	7.40	2.4	448
Uzbekistan	27,488,000	6.9	189,667,200	1.30	2.1	76
Denmark	5,534,738	11.5	63,649,487	5.90	2.0	361
Singapore	4,987,600	11.3	56,359,880	5.70	1.7	341
Belarus	9,489,000	8.5	80,656,500	2.90	1.7	179
Hungary	10,013,628	8.3	83,113,112	2.70	1.6	160
Norway	4,860,900	11.2	54,442,080	5.60	1.6	329
Portugal	10,636,888	7.9	84,031,415	2.30	1.5	141

1   CO_2 in Tonnes of CO_2e without land-use change, Year 2005

Country	Population	CO_2 Per Capita	Total CO_2	Excess CO_2 Per Capita	Excess Cost Bn $	Excess Cost Per Capita $
Bulgaria	7,576,751	8.6	65,160,059	3.00	1.4	185
Uruguay	3,361,000	12.7	42,684,700	7.10	1.4	417
Slovakia	5,421,937	9.3	50,424,014	3.70	1.2	221
Oman	2,845,000	12	34,140,000	6.40	1.1	387
Trinidad & Tobago	1,339,000	19.6	26,244,400	14.00	1.1	822
Mongolia	2,671,000	11.9	31,784,900	6.30	1.0	374
Libya	6,420,000	8.3	53,286,000	2.70	1.0	156
Sweden	9,340,682	7.4	69,121,047	1.80	1.0	107
Bahrain	791,000	25.4	20,091,400	19.80	0.9	1138
Bolivia	9,879,000	6.9	68,165,100	1.30	0.8	81
Switzerland	7,779,200	7.3	56,788,160	1.70	0.8	103
Estonia	1,340,021	14.4	19,296,302	8.80	0.7	522
Luxembourg	502,207	27.5	13,810,693	21.90	0.7	1394
Slovenia	2,054,030	10.1	20,745,703	4.50	0.6	292
Romania	21,466,174	6.1	130,943,661	0.50	0.6	28
Croatia	4,435,056	6.9	30,601,886	1.30	0.3	68
Malaysia	28,306,700	5.7	161,348,190	0.10	0.2	7
Brunei	400,000	13.9	5,560,000	8.30	0.2	500
Cyprus	801,851	10.5	8,419,436	4.90	0.2	249
Iceland	317,593	11.1	3,525,282	5.50	0.1	315

Appendix B: Compensation Due for use of their atmosphere for absorbing other Countries Greenhouse Gases[1]

Country	Population	CO$_2$ Per Capita	Total CO$_2$	Excess CO$_2$ Per Capita	Compensation Due Bn $	Compensation Due Per Capita $
India	1,177,761,000	1.7	2,002,193,700	-3.90	275.4	234
Bangladesh	162,221,000	0.9	145,998,900	-4.70	45.7	282
Pakistan	168,874,500	1.5	253,311,750	-4.10	41.5	246
Indonesia	231,369,500	2.7	624,697,650	-2.90	40.2	174
Nigeria	154,729,000	2.1	324,930,900	-3.50	32.5	210
Ethiopia	79,221,000	1	79,221,000	-4.60	21.8	275
Philippines	92,226,600	1.7	156,785,220	-3.90	21.6	234
Vietnam	85,789,573	2.1	180,158,103	-3.50	18	210
Congo, Dem. Rep.	66,020,000	1.6	105,632,000	-4.00	15.8	239
Tanzania	43,739,000	0.1	4,373,900	-5.50	14.4	329
Kenya	39,802,000	0.3	11,940,600	-5.30	12.6	317
Sudan	39,154,490	0.3	11,746,347	-5.30	12.4	317
Egypt	77,932,000	3	233,796,000	-2.60	12.1	155
Myanmar	50,020,000	2.2	110,044,000	-3.40	10.2	204
Afghanistan	28,150,000	0	0	-5.60	9.5	337
Uganda	32,710,000	1.1	35,981,000	-4.50	8.8	269
China	1,336,150,000	5.5	7,348,825,000	-0.10	7.8	6
Morocco	31,740,000	1.6	50,784,000	-4.00	7.6	239
Ghana	23,837,000	0.4	9,534,800	-5.20	7.4	310
Nepal	29,331,000	1.5	43,996,500	-4.10	7.2	245
Mozambique	20,226,296	0.1	2,022,630	-5.50	6.7	331
Yemen	23,580,000	0.9	21,222,000	-4.70	6.6	280
Côte d'Ivoire	21,075,000	0.4	8,430,000	-5.20	6.6	313
Madagascar	19,625,000	0.2	3,925,000	-5.40	6.4	326
Cameroon	19,522,000	0.4	7,808,800	-5.20	6.1	312
Sri Lanka	20,238,000	0.7	14,166,600	-4.90	5.9	292
Burkina Faso	15,757,000	0.1	1,575,700	-5.50	5.2	330
Niger	15,290,000	0.1	1,529,000	-5.50	5	327
Malawi	15,263,000	0.1	1,526,300	-5.50	5	328
Mali	14,517,176	0	0	-5.60	4.9	338
Peru	29,132,013	2.8	81,569,636	-2.80	4.9	168
Angola	18,498,000	1.3	24,047,400	-4.30	4.8	259
Colombia	45,333,000	3.9	176,798,700	-1.70	4.6	101
Zambia	12,935,000	0.2	2,587,000	-5.40	4.2	325
Guatemala	14,027,000	0.9	12,624,300	-4.70	4	285
Chad	11,274,106	0	0	-5.60	3.8	337
Syria	21,906,000	2.7	59,146,200	-2.90	3.8	173
Cambodia	14,805,000	1.6	23,688,000	-4.00	3.6	243
Zimbabwe	12,523,000	0.8	10,018,400	-4.80	3.6	287
Rwanda	9,998,000	0.1	999,800	-5.50	3.3	330
Guinea	10,069,000	0.2	2,013,800	-5.40	3.3	328
Haiti	10,033,000	0.2	2,006,600	-5.40	3.2	319

1   CO$_2$ in Tonnes of CO$_2$e without land-use change, Year 2005

Country	Population	CO₂ Per Capita	Total CO₂	Excess CO₂ Per Capita	Compensation Due Bn $	Compensation Due Per Capita $
Senegal	12,534,000	1.8	22,561,200	-3.80	2.9	231
Algeria	34,895,000	4.2	146,559,000	-1.40	2.9	83
Benin	8,935,000	0.3	2,680,500	-5.30	2.8	313
Burundi	8,303,000	0	0	-5.60	2.8	337
Brazil	192,559,000	5.4	1,039,818,600	-0.20	2.3	12
Cuba	11,204,000	2.2	24,648,800	-3.40	2.3	205
Dominican Republic	10,090,000	1.9	19,171,000	-3.70	2.2	218
Tunisia	10,432,500	2.3	23,994,750	-3.30	2.1	201
Tajikistan	6,952,000	0.5	3,476,000	-5.10	2.1	302
Togo	6,619,000	0.2	1,323,800	-5.40	2.1	317
Papua New Guinea	6,732,000	0.7	4,712,400	-4.90	2	297
Honduras	7,466,000	1.1	8,212,600	-4.50	2	268
Paraguay	6,349,000	0.6	3,809,400	-5.00	1.9	299
Ecuador	14,138,000	3.3	46,655,400	-2.30	1.9	134
Iraq	30,747,000	4.6	141,436,200	-1.00	1.8	59
Sierra Leone	5,696,000	0.2	1,139,200	-5.40	1.8	316
El Salvador	6,163,000	1	6,163,000	-4.60	1.7	276
Nicaragua	5,743,000	0.8	4,594,400	-4.80	1.7	296
Eritrea	5,073,000	0.1	507,300	-5.50	1.7	335
Central African Republic	4,422,000	0.1	442,200	-5.50	1.5	339
Kyrgyzstan	5,482,000	1.9	10,415,800	-3.70	1.2	219
Costa Rica	4,579,000	1.5	6,868,500	-4.10	1.1	240
Liberia	3,476,608	0.1	347,661	-5.50	1.1	316
Mauritania	3,291,000	0.6	1,974,600	-5.00	1	304
Georgia	4,385,400	2	8,770,800	-3.60	0.9	205
Congo, Rep.	3,683,000	1.4	5,156,200	-4.20	0.9	244
Laos	6,320,000	3.1	19,592,000	-2.50	0.9	142
North Korea	24,051,706	5	120,258,530	-0.60	0.9	37
Panama	3,454,000	1.9	6,562,600	-3.70	0.8	232
Lesotho	2,067,000	0.1	206,700	-5.50	0.7	339
Gambia	1,705,000	0.2	341,000	-5.40	0.6	352
Armenia	3,230,100	2.5	8,075,250	-3.10	0.6	186
Albania	3,170,000	2.9	9,193,000	-2.70	0.5	158
Guinea-Bissau	1,611,000	0.2	322,200	-5.40	0.5	310
Moldova	3,567,500	3.2	11,416,000	-2.40	0.5	140
Jordan	6,316,000	4.2	26,527,200	-1.40	0.5	79
Chile	17,040,000	5.1	86,904,000	-0.50	0.5	29
Namibia	2,171,000	1.4	3,039,400	-4.20	0.5	230
Botswana	1,950,000	2.3	4,485,000	-3.30	0.4	205
Turkey	72,561,312	5.5	399,087,216	-0.10	0.4	6
Jamaica	2,719,000	3.8	10,332,200	-1.80	0.3	110
Swaziland	1,185,000	0.8	948,000	-4.80	0.3	253
Djibouti	864,000	0.5	432,000	-5.10	0.3	347
Lebanon	4,224,000	4.4	18,585,600	-1.20	0.3	71
Bosnia & Herzegovina	3,767,000	4.3	16,198,100	-1.30	0.3	80
Fiji	849,000	2	1,698,000	-3.60	0.2	236
Gabon	1,475,000	3.7	5,457,500	-1.90	0.2	136
Solomon Islands	523,000	0.4	209,200	-5.20	0.2	382
Guyana	762,000	2	1,524,000	-3.60	0.2	262
Bhutan	697,000	0.6	418,200	-5.00	0.2	287
Comoros	676,000	0.1	67,600	-5.50	0.2	296
Cape Verde	506,000	0.6	303,600	-5.00	0.2	395

Country	Population	CO$_2$ Per Capita	Total CO$_2$	Excess CO$_2$ Per Capita	Compensation Due Bn $	Compensation Due Per Capita $
Mauritius	1,288,000	2.7	3,477,600	-2.90	0.2	155
Belize	322,100	2.8	901,880	-2.80	0.1	310
Maldives	309,000	2.4	741,600	-3.20	0.1	324
Vanuatu	240,000	0.4	96,000	-5.20	0.1	417
Samoa	179,000	0.8	143,200	-4.80	0.1	559
Latvia	2,248,400	4.6	10,342,640	-1.00	0.1	44

310 *Appendix C*

Country	Population	CO$_2$ Per Capita	Total CO$_2$	Excess CO$_2$ Per Capita	Excess Cost Bn $	Compensation Due Bn $	Own CO$_2$ Cost Bn $	Total Owed Bn $	Total Owed Per Capita $
China	1,336,150,000	5.5	7,348,825,000	-0.10	0	7.8	440.9	433.1	324
India	1,177,761,000	1.7	2,002,193,700	-3.90	0	275.4	120.1	-155.3	-132
USA	308,792,000	23.5	7,256,612,000	17.90	331.7	0	435.4	767.1	2484
Indonesia	231,369,500	2.7	624,697,650	-2.90	0	40.2	37.5	-2.7	-12
Brazil	192,559,000	5.4	1,039,818,600	-0.20	0	2.3	62.4	60.1	312
Pakistan	168,874,500	1.5	253,311,750	-4.10	0	41.5	15.2	-26.3	-156
Bangladesh	162,221,000	0.9	145,998,900	-4.70	0	45.7	8.8	-36.9	-228
Nigeria	154,729,000	2.1	324,930,900	-3.50	0	32.5	19.5	-13.0	-84
Russia	141,927,297	13.7	1,944,403,969	8.10	69.0	0	116.7	185.7	1308
Japan	127,430,000	10.5	1,338,015,000	4.90	37.5	0	80.3	117.8	924
Mexico	107,550,697	6.1	656,059,252	0.50	3.2	0	39.4	42.6	396
Philippines	92,226,600	1.7	156,785,220	-3.90	0	21.6	9.4	-12.2	-132
Vietnam	85,789,573	2.1	180,158,103	-3.50	0	18.0	10.8	-7.2	-84
Germany	81,757,600	11.9	972,915,440	6.30	30.9	0	58.4	89.3	1092
Ethiopia	79,221,000	1	79,221,000	-4.60	0	21.8	4.8	-17.0	-215
Egypt	77,932,000	3	233,796,000	-2.60	0	12.1	14.0	1.9	25
Iran	74,196,000	8.2	608,407,200	2.60	11.6	0	36.5	48.1	648
Turkey	72,561,312	5.5	399,087,216	-0.10	0	0.4	23.9	23.5	324
Congo, Dem. Rep.	66,020,000	1.6	105,632,000	-4.00	0	15.8	6.3	-9.5	-143
France	65,447,374	9	589,026,366	3.40	13.4	0	35.3	48.7	745
Thailand	63,389,730	5.6	354,982,488	0.00	0.0	0.0	21.3	21.3	336
United Kingdom	62,041,708	10.6	657,642,105	5.00	18.6	0	39.5	58.1	936
Italy	60,275,846	9.7	584,675,706	4.10	14.8	0	35.1	49.9	828
Myanmar	50,020,000	2.2	110,044,000	-3.40	0	10.2	6.6	-3.6	-72
South Korea	49,773,145	11.4	567,413,853	5.80	17.3	0	34.0	51.3	1032
South Africa	49,320,500	9	443,884,500	3.40	10.1	0	26.6	36.7	745

Appendix C: Total Cost of Greenhouse Gases[279] by Country

1   CO$_2$ in Tonnes of CO$_2$e without land-use change, Year 2005

Country									
Spain	45,989,016	10.1	464,489,062	4.50	12.4	0	27.9	40.3	876
Ukraine	45,982,936	10.3	473,624,241	4.70	13.0	0	28.4	41.4	901
Colombia	45,333,000	3.9	176,798,700	-1.70	0	4.6	10.6	6.0	133
Tanzania	43,739,000	0.1	4,373,900	-5.50	6.3	14.4	0.3	-14.1	-323
Argentina	40,134,425	8.2	329,102,285	2.60	0	0	19.7	26.0	649
Kenya	39,802,000	0.3	11,940,600	-5.30	0	12.6	0.7	-11.9	-299
Sudan	39,154,490	0.3	11,746,347	-5.30	0	12.4	0.7	-11.7	-299
Poland	38,163,895	9.8	374,006,171	4.20	9.6	0	22.4	32.0	840
Algeria	34,895,000	4.2	146,559,000	-1.40	0	2.9	8.8	5.9	169
Canada	34,020,000	22.6	768,852,000	17.00	34.7	0	46.1	80.8	2376
Uganda	32,710,000	1.1	35,981,000	-4.50	0	8.8	2.2	-6.6	-203
Morocco	31,740,000	1.6	50,784,000	-4.00	0	7.6	3.0	-4.6	-143
Iraq	30,747,000	4.6	141,436,200	-1.00	0	1.8	8.5	6.7	217
Nepal	29,331,000	1.5	43,996,500	-4.10	0	7.2	2.6	-4.6	-155
Peru	29,132,013	2.8	81,569,636	-2.80	0	4.9	4.9	0.0	0
Venezuela	28,683,000	10	286,830,000	4.40	7.6	0	17.2	24.8	865
Malaysia	28,306,700	5.7	161,348,190	0.10	0.2	0	9.7	9.9	349
Afghanistan	28,150,000	0	0	-5.60	0	9.5	0.0	-9.5	-337
Uzbekistan	27,488,000	6.9	189,667,200	1.30	2.1	0	11.4	13.5	490
Saudi Arabia	25,721,000	16.2	416,680,200	10.60	16.4	0	25.0	41.4	1610
North Korea	24,051,706	5	120,258,530	-0.60	0	0.9	7.2	6.3	263
Ghana	23,837,000	0.4	9,534,800	-5.20	0	7.4	0.6	-6.8	-286
Yemen	23,580,000	0.9	21,222,000	-4.70	0	6.6	1.3	-5.3	-226
Taiwan	23,119,772	11.8	272,813,310	6.20	8.6	0	16.4	25.0	1080
Australia	22,173,000	26.9	596,453,700	21.30	28.3	0	35.8	64.1	2890
Syria	21,906,000	2.7	59,146,200	-2.90	0	3.8	3.5	-0.3	-11
Romania	21,466,174	6.1	130,943,661	0.50	0.6	0	7.9	8.5	394
Côte d'Ivoire	21,075,000	0.4	8,430,000	-5.20	0	6.6	0.5	-6.1	-289
Sri Lanka	20,238,000	0.7	14,166,600	-4.90	0	5.9	0.8	-5.1	-250
Mozambique	20,226,296	0.1	2,022,630	-5.50	0	6.7	0.1	-6.6	-325
Madagascar	19,625,000	0.2	3,925,000	-5.40	0	6.4	0.2	-6.2	-314
Cameroon	19,522,000	0.4	7,808,800	-5.20	0	6.1	0.5	-5.6	-288
Angola	18,498,000	1.3	24,047,400	-4.30	0	4.8	1.4	-3.4	-181
Chile	17,040,000	5.1	86,904,000	-0.50	0	0.5	5.2	4.7	277

Country	Population	CO$_2$ Per Capita	Total CO$_2$	Excess CO$_2$ Per Capita	Excess Cost Bn $	Compensation Due Bn $	Own CO$_2$ Cost Bn $	Total Owed Bn $	Total Owed Per Capita $
Netherlands	16,593,900	13.8	228,995,820	8.20	8.2	0	13.7	21.9	1322
Kazakhstan	15,776,492	12.7	200,361,448	7.10	6.7	0	12.0	18.7	1187
Burkina Faso	15,757,000	0.1	1,575,700	-5.50	0	5.2	0.1	-5.1	-324
Niger	15,290,000	0.1	1,526,300	-5.50	0	5.0	0.1	-4.9	-321
Malawi	15,263,000	0.1	1,526,300	-5.50	0	5.0	0.1	-4.9	-322
Cambodia	14,805,000	1.6	23,688,000	-4.00	0	3.6	1.4	-2.2	-147
Mali	14,517,176	0	0	-5.60	0	4.9	0.0	-4.9	-338
Ecuador	14,138,000	3.3	46,655,400	-2.30	0	1.9	2.8	0.9	64
Guatemala	14,027,000	0.9	12,624,300	-4.70	0	4.0	0.8	-3.2	-231
Zambia	12,935,000	0.2	2,587,000	-5.40	0	4.2	0.2	-4.0	-313
Senegal	12,534,000	1.8	22,561,200	-3.80	0	2.9	1.4	-1.5	-123
Zimbabwe	12,523,000	0.8	10,018,400	-4.80	0	3.6	0.6	-3.0	-239
Greece	11,306,183	11.5	130,021,105	5.90	4.0	0	7.8	11.8	1044
Chad	11,274,106	0	0	-5.60	0	3.8	0.0	-3.8	-337
Cuba	11,204,000	2.2	24,648,800	-3.40	0	2.3	1.5	-0.8	-73
Belgium	10,827,519	13.2	142,923,251	7.60	4.9	0	8.6	13.5	1245
Portugal	10,636,888	7.9	84,031,415	2.30	1.5	0	5.0	6.5	615
Czech Republic	10,512,397	13.7	144,019,839	8.10	5.1	0	8.6	13.7	1307
Tunisia	10,432,500	2.3	23,994,750	-3.30	0	2.1	1.4	-0.7	-63
Dominican Republic	10,090,000	1.9	19,171,000	-3.70	0	2.2	1.2	-1.0	-104
Guinea	10,069,000	0.2	2,013,800	-5.40	0	3.3	0.1	-3.2	-316
Haiti	10,033,000	0.2	2,006,600	-5.40	0	3.2	0.1	-3.1	-307
Hungary	10,013,628	8.3	83,113,112	2.70	1.6	0	5.0	6.6	658
Rwanda	9,998,000	0.1	999,800	-5.50	0	3.3	0.1	-3.2	-324
Bolivia	9,879,000	6.9	68,165,100	1.30	0.8	0	4.1	4.9	495
Belarus	9,489,000	8.5	80,656,500	2.90	1.7	0	4.8	6.5	689
Sweden	9,340,682	7.4	69,121,047	1.80	1.0	0	4.1	5.1	551
Benin	8,935,000	0.3	2,680,500	-5.30	0	2.8	0.2	-2.6	-295
Azerbaijan	8,922,300	5.6	49,964,880	0.00	0	0.0	3.0	3.0	336
Austria	8,372,930	11.5	96,288,695	5.90	3.0	0	5.8	8.8	1048
Burundi	8,303,000	0	0	-5.60	0	2.8	0.0	-2.8	-337
Switzerland	7,779,200	7.3	56,788,160	1.70	0.8	0	3.4	4.2	541
Bulgaria	7,576,751	8.6	65,160,059	3.00	1.4	0	3.9	5.3	701
Israel	7,509,000	11.5	86,353,500	5.90	2.7	0	5.2	7.9	1050

Honduras	7,466,000	1.1	-4.50	0	2.0	0.5	-1.5	-202
Tajikistan	6,952,000	0.5	-5.10	0	2.1	0.2	-1.9	-272
Papua New Guinea	6,732,000	0.7	-4.90	0	2.0	0.3	-1.7	-255
Togo	6,619,000	0.2	-5.40	0	2.1	0.1	-2.0	-305
Libya	6,420,000	8.3	2.70	1.0	0	3.2	4.2	654
Paraguay	6,349,000	0.6	-5.00	0	1.9	0.2	-1.7	-263
Laos	6,320,000	3.1	-2.50	0	0.9	1.2	0.3	44
Jordan	6,316,000	4.2	-1.40	0	0.5	1.6	1.1	173
El Salvador	6,163,000	1	-4.60	0	1.7	0.4	-1.3	-216
Nicaragua	5,743,000	0.8	-4.80	0	1.7	0.3	-1.4	-248
Sierra Leone	5,696,000	0.2	-5.40	0	1.8	0.1	-1.7	-304
Denmark	5,534,738	11.5	5.90	2.0	0	3.8	5.8	1051
Kyrgyzstan	5,482,000	1.9	-3.70	0	1.2	0.6	-0.6	-105
Slovakia	5,421,937	9.3	3.70	1.2	0	3.0	4.2	779
Finland	5,356,700	13	7.40	2.4	0	4.2	6.6	1228
Turkmenistan	5,110,000	18.9	13.30	4.1	0	5.8	9.9	1936
Eritrea	5,073,000	0.1	-5.50	0	1.7	0.0	-1.7	-329
Singapore	4,987,600	11.3	5.70	1.7	0	3.4	5.1	1019
Norway	4,860,900	11.2	5.60	1.6	0	3.3	4.9	1001
United Arab Emirates	4,599,000	38.8	33.20	9.2	0	10.7	19.9	4328
Costa Rica	4,579,000	1.5	-4.10	0	1.1	0.4	-0.7	-150
Ireland	4,459,300	16.7	11.10	3.0	0	4.5	7.5	1675
Croatia	4,435,056	6.9	1.30	0.3	0	1.8	2.1	482
Central African Republic	4,422,200	0.1	-5.50	0	1.5	0.0	-1.5	-333
Georgia	4,385,400	2	-3.60	0	0.9	0.5	-0.4	-85
New Zealand	4,358,700	18.8	13.20	3.5	0	4.9	8.4	1931
Lebanon	4,224,000	4.4	-1.20	0	0.3	1.1	0.8	193
Bosnia & Herzegovina	3,767,000	4.3	-1.30	0	0.3	1.0	0.7	178
Congo, Rep.	3,683,000	1.4	-4.20	0	0.9	0.3	-0.6	-160
Moldova	3,567,500	3.2	-2.40	0	0.5	0.7	0.2	52
Liberia	3,476,608	0.1	-5.50	0	1.1	0.0	-1.1	-310
Panama	3,454,000	1.9	-3.70	0	0.8	0.4	-0.4	-118
Uruguay	3,361,000	12.7	7.10	1.4	0	2.6	4.0	1179
Lithuania	3,329,227	5.7	0.10	0	0.0	1.1	1.1	342

Country	Population	CO₂ Per Capita	Total CO₂	Excess CO₂ Per Capita	Excess Cost Bn $	Compensation Due Bn $	Own CO₂ Cost Bn $	Total Owed Bn $	Total Owed Per Capita $
Mauritania	3,291,000	0.6	1,974,600	-5.00	0	1.0	0.1	-0.9	-268
Armenia	3,230,100	2.5	8,075,250	-3.10	0	0.6	0.5	-0.1	-36
Albania	3,170,000	2.9	9,193,000	-2.70	0	0.5	0.6	0.1	16
Kuwait	2,985,000	35	104,475,000	29.40	5.3	0	6.3	11.6	3876
Oman	2,845,000	12	34,140,000	6.40	1.1	0	2.0	3.1	1107
Jamaica	2,719,000	3.8	10,332,200	-1.80	0	0.3	0.6	0.3	118
Mongolia	2,671,000	11.9	31,784,900	6.30	1.0	0	1.9	2.9	1088
Latvia	2,248,400	4.6	10,342,640	-1.00	0	0.1	0.6	0.5	232
Namibia	2,171,000	1.4	3,039,400	-4.20	0	0.5	0.2	-0.3	-146
Lesotho	2,067,000	0.1	206,700	-5.50	0	0.7	0.0	-0.7	-333
Slovenia	2,054,030	10.1	20,745,703	4.50	0.6	0	1.2	1.8	898
Macedonia	2,048,620	5.2	10,652,824	-0.40	0	0.0	0.6	0.6	312
Botswana	1,950,000	2.3	4,485,000	-3.30	0	0.4	0.3	-0.1	-67
Gambia	1,705,000	0.2	341,000	-5.40	0	0.6	0.0	-0.6	-340
Guinea-Bissau	1,611,000	0.2	322,200	-5.40	0	0.5	0.0	-0.5	-298
Gabon	1,475,000	3.7	5,457,500	-1.90	0	0.2	0.3	0.1	86
Qatar	1,409,000	55.5	78,199,500	49.90	4.2	0	4.7	8.9	6311
Estonia	1,340,021	14.4	19,296,302	8.80	0.7	0	1.2	1.9	1386
Trinidad & Tobago	1,339,000	19.6	26,244,400	14.00	1.1	0	1.6	2.7	1998
Mauritius	1,288,000	2.7	3,477,600	-2.90	0	0.2	0.2	0.0	7
Swaziland	1,185,000	0.8	948,000	-4.80	0	0.3	0.1	-0.2	-205
Djibouti	864,000	0.5	432,000	-5.10	0	0.3	0.0	-0.3	-317
Fiji	849,000	2	1,698,000	-3.60	0	0.2	0.1	-0.1	-116
Cyprus	801,851	10.5	8,419,436	4.90	0.2	0	0.5	0.7	879
Bahrain	791,000	25.4	20,091,400	19.80	0.9	0	1.2	2.1	2662
Guyana	762,000	2	1,524,000	-3.60	0	0.2	0.1	-0.1	-142
Bhutan	697,000	0.6	418,200	-5.00	0	0.2	0.0	-0.2	-251
Equatorial Guinea	676,000	6.7	4,529,200	1.10	0	0.0	0.3	0.3	402
Comoros	676,000	0.1	67,600	-5.50	0	0.2	0.0	-0.2	-290
Solomon Islands	523,000	0.4	209,200	-5.20	0	0.2	0.0	-0.2	-358
Suriname	520,000	5.3	2,756,000	-0.30	0	0.0	0.2	0.2	318
Cape Verde	506,000	0.6	303,600	-5.00	0	0.2	0.0	-0.2	-359
Luxembourg	502,207	27.5	13,810,693	21.90	0.7	0	0.8	1.5	3044
Malta	416,333	6.5	2,706,165	0.90	0	0.0	0.2	0.2	390

	Population	CO$_2$ Per Capita	Total CO$_2$	Excess CO$_2$ Per Capita	Excess Cost Bn $	Compensation Due Bn $	Own CO$_2$ Cost Bn $	Total Owed Bn $	Total Owed Per Capita $
Brunei	400,000	13.9	5,560,000	8.30	0.2	0	0.3	0.5	1334
Bahamas	342,000	6.5	2,223,000	0.90	0	0.0	0.1	0.1	390
Belize	322,100	2.8	901,880	-2.80	0	0.1	0.1	0.0	-142
Iceland	317,593	11.1	3,525,282	5.50	0.1	0	0.2	0.3	981
Maldives	309,000	2.4	741,600	-3.20	0.0	0.1	0.0	-0.1	-180
Barbados	256,000	4.5	1,152,000	-1.10	0	0.0	0.1	0.1	270
Vanuatu	240,000	0.4	96,000	-5.20	0	0.1	0.0	-0.1	-393
Samoa	179,000	0.8	143,200	-4.80	0	0.1	0.0	-0.1	-511
St Lucia	172,000	2.2	378,400	-3.40	0	0.0	0.0	0.0	132
São Tomé and Principe	163,000	0.7	114,100	-4.90	0	0.0	0.0	0.0	42
St Vincent & Grenadines	109,000	1.6	174,400	-4.00	0	0.0	0.0	0.0	96
Grenada	104,000	2.2	228,800	-3.40	0	0.0	0.0	0.0	132
Tonga	104,000	1.2	124,800	-4.40	0	0.0	0.0	0.0	72
Kiribati	98,000	0.3	29,400	-5.30	0	0.0	0.0	0.0	18
Antigua & Barbuda	88,000	5.1	448,800	-0.50	0	0.0	0.0	0.0	306
Seychelles	84,000	7	588,000	1.40	0	0.0	0.0	0.0	420
Dominica	67,000	1.6	107,200	-4.00	0	0.0	0.0	0.0	96
St Kitts & Nevis	52,000	2.8	145,600	-2.80	0	0.0	0.0	0.0	168
Palau	20,000	5.7	114,000	0.10	0	0.0	0.0	0.0	342
Cook Islands	20,000	2.9	58,000	-2.70	0	0.0	0.0	0.0	174
Nauru	10,000	11	110,000	5.40	0	0.0	0.0	0.0	660
Niue	1,500	1.7	2,550	-3.90	0	0.0	0.0	0.0	102
Global[1]	**6,751,128,878**	**5.60**	**37,784,227,057**	**-**	**788.8**	**788.6**	**2267.1**	**2267.3**	**336**

Made in the USA
Charleston, SC
28 November 2010